Don Berry

Don Berry (1932-2001) considered himself a native Oregonian, despite the fact that he was born in Minnesota, with a lineage from Fox Indians. After attending Reed College, where his housemates included poet Gary Snyder, who shared his interest in Eastern metaphysics, Berry began a lifetime of pursuing his many passions: playing down-home blues and composing synthesizer music, sumi drawing and painting, sculpting in bronze, exploring theoretical mathematics, and writing for prize-winning films.

In addition to his three novels about the Oregon Territory (*Trask, Moontrap,* and *To Build a Ship*), published in the early 1960s, Berry wrote *A Majority of Scoundrels*, a history of the Rocky Mountain fur trade. An early Internet pioneer, he also created a remarkable body of literature that exists now only in cyberspace.

To Build a Ship

by

Don Berry

introduction by Jeff Baker

Oregon State University Press
Corvallis

A NORTHWEST REPRINTS BOOK

The paper in this book meets the guidelines for permanence and durability of the Committee on Production Guidelines for Book Longevity of the Council on Library Resources and the minimum requirements of the American National Standard for Permanence of Paper for Printed Library Materials Z39.48-1984.

Library of Congress Cataloging-in-Publication Data
Berry, Don.
  To build a ship / by Don Berry ; introduction by Jeff Baker.-- 1st OSU Press ed.
     p. cm.
  ISBN 0-87071-040-0 (alk. paper)
  1. Oregon--Fiction. 2. Shipbuilding--Fiction. 3. Frontier and pioneer life--Fiction. I. Title.
   PS3552.E7463T6 2004
   813'.54--dc22

                                    2004007873

Oregon State University Press
101 Waldo Hall
Corvallis OR 97331-6407
541-737-3166 • fax 541-737-3170
http://oregonstate.edu/dept/press

OREGON STATE
UNIVERSITY

Introduction

by Jeff Baker

A few years ago, I was standing on the bank of the Clackamas River with Robin Cody, author of *Ricochet River*, a novel set on the same river we were skipping rocks across. We were talking about other novels set in Oregon and how there are only a few really good ones.

H. L. Davis' *Honey in the Horn* is the only novel by an Oregonian to win the Pulitzer Prize, and that was in 1936. Bernard Malamud wrote *A New Life* in Corvallis and based it on a fictionalized Oregon State University, then moved to Vermont before the locals figured out they were being teased.

Cody said he thought the Great Oregon Novel was *Sometimes a Great Notion* by Ken Kesey. No doubt about it, Cody said—*Sometimes a Great Notion* is big, it's raw, it's stylistically inventive, it gets right what it's like to live in this rugged, beautiful land.

True enough, I said. I love that book, and I think it shows Kesey's brilliance way more than *One Flew Over the Cuckoo's Nest*. There's one novel that's better, though, one that has more to do with who we are as Oregonians and how we came so far in such a short time and lost so much along the way. It's *Trask* by Don Berry, and it changed my life when I read it as a teenager.

Cody's next rock whizzed suspiciously close to my ear. He liked *Trask* just fine but thought *Notion* was more ambitious and more successful on more levels. Kesey was aiming higher, he said, and he pulled it off. He wrote about a family, a town, an industry, a way of life. Nobody's come close to getting so much about Oregon into one book and doing it in such an intense, exciting way.

I still like *Trask* better, I said. We agreed to disagree and went back to skipping rocks over the green surface of the river. Three years later, Berry and Kesey were dead. They were Oregon's best fiction writers of the post-World War II generation and, despite obvious differences in temperament and style, had much in common. Both were born elsewhere but considered Oregon their home. Both did their best work before they were thirty in marathon sessions of intense creative concentration they were unable or unwilling to repeat in later years. Both turned away from writing novels in favor of other, more personal artistic pursuits that included living their lives as art, and both spent their last years experimenting with technology that didn't exist when they were ambitious young writers.

There's a statue of Kesey in downtown Eugene. His life is celebrated by his many friends and his novels have never been out of print. His influence on twentieth-century American culture is immense—as a link between the Beat Generation of the 1950s and the counterculture of the 1960s, as a proponent of drug use to expand consciousness, and as a rebel who took every opportunity to cheerfully challenge authority.

Berry's life and accomplishments are less well-known but no less interesting. He was a key figure—along with Gary Snyder, Philip Whalen, and Lew Welch—in the small group of writers who attended Reed College in the late 1940s. A self-taught researcher who never took a history class, he wrote an influential history of the Rocky Mountain fur trade called *A Majority of Scoundrels*. A musician, a painter and sculptor, a filmmaker, a poet, an essayist, and a spiritual seeker, toward the end of his life he put his restless energies into an amazing Web site (www.donberry.com) and became one of the first writers to fully explore the possibilities of the Internet.

His most important artistic achievement is the three novels (*Trask*, *Moontrap*, and *To Build a Ship*) published between 1960 and 1963 and written in a spasm of sustained creativity unequaled in Oregon literature. All three are set in the Oregon Territory in the decade before statehood and form a loose trilogy that tells the story of our state's origins better than any history book. They are set firmly on Oregon soil and mix historical figures such as Elbridge Trask, Joe Meek, John McLoughlin, and the Tillamook chief Kilchis with fictional characters. Berry believed fiction could tell larger truths as effectively as history and shared the opinion of Ben Thaler, the narrator of *To Build a Ship*, who thought "literal truth is not the important consideration … history tells us only what we have already made our minds up to believe."

More than forty years after they were first published, Berry's novels speak for themselves and need no detailed explication. (It is interesting but not necessary, for example, to know that unlike Berry's childless Trask, the real Elbridge Trask—after whom the Trask River is named— and his wife Hannah had eight children before leaving the Clatsop Plains for Tillamook Bay.) A brief examination of who Berry was, how he wrote these remarkable books, and what he did with the rest of his life can provide a more complete context in which to appreciate a true Northwest treasure.

Berry was born January 23, 1932, in Redwood Falls, Minnesota. His parents were touring musicians; his father played the banjo and guitar, his mother was a singer. His father left the family when Berry was two and did not see his son again until Berry was eighteen, although they enjoyed a friendly relationship in later years. His mother moved frequently around the Midwest and Berry said he attended six schools in five states one year. Berry was small for his age and extremely intelligent, the kind of kid who had to get adults to check out books for him from the library. In grade school, he was given the nickname "China" for his interest in the far east.

By the time he was fifteen, Berry and his mother were living in Vanport, the city that was destroyed by a flood of the Columbia River in 1948. Berry took the newspaper notice of his death in the flood as an opportunity to leave home and disappear. He attended high school in Portland and was offered scholarships in mathematics by both Harvard and Reed.

In 1949, Berry was attending Reed, working in the bookstore and sleeping on top of a boiler he tended on campus. He was invited to live in a house on Southeast Lambert Street with several other students, including Snyder, already a serious student of Eastern philosophy and on the way to becoming one of the finest American poets of the twentieth century; Whalen, a Portland native who became a prominent Beat poet and later a Buddhist monk; and Welch, another poet whose *Ring of Bone: Collected Poems 1950-71* is one of the best books from the Beat era. The young men formed what they called the Adelaide Crapsey-Oswald Spengler Mutual Admiration Poetasters Society and drank wine, wrote poetry, and goofed off for the better part of two years.

"It was probably the birth canal for the Beat Generation," said Berry, who was more interested in painting than poetry at the time. "It was classic post-war Bohemianism, and also one of the richest experiences of my life. The quality of minds involved was extraordinary, and it was also hugely funny."

As a freshman, Berry was one of the editors of the Reed literary magazine. "I once rejected a poem as being too derivative of Lew Welch," he remembered. "Lew gave me hell later, because he had written it."

Berry, Snyder, and Whalen studied with the legendary calligrapher Lloyd Reynolds, an inspiration to generations of Reedies. Reynolds would tell his students, "You've got a million bad letters in your fist, and the only way to get rid of them is to write them down."

"Lloyd was one of the four great teachers of my life," Berry said. "Not necessarily in any specific detail, but in the sense that he was the first teacher who ignited me, as a candle is ignited from a flame already burning. He showed the most astonishing confidence in my ability. When I was a freshman, Lloyd had me deliver the lectures on Chinese art to his art history classes. Those were the only lectures they received on the subject, and Lloyd seemed content. At the time, it seemed perfectly reasonable to me … The clichés of a young artist. Lordy, lordy."

Berry left Reed in 1951 to earn a living. He had met his future wife by this time and was beginning to write science fiction, a genre that appealed to him because he could sell stories, learn to write, and let his imagination wander freely. His goal was to write a short story every week and he sold about a dozen between 1956 and 1958. But he wanted to write something different, a commercial novel set in the present day on the Oregon coast, and wanted, he said, "to include some folk stories, or Indian legends, or something to give some local depth and flavor."

Wyn Berry brought home a study by Reed historian Dorothy Johansen of coastal Indian cultures around 1850. Berry's reaction to it, as described in a 1997 email, deserves to be quoted at some length:

> This was not academic history, it was a complilation of very personal anecdotes and records of ordinary people—not "history-makers."

At one point Dorothy Jo was describing a trip made by Elbridge Trask from the northern coast down to Tillamook Bay (where he later settled) to scout out land. She commented that nobody ever could figure out why he made some particular decision.

Well, I knew why, because it was exactly the decision I would have made under the circumstances. And at that instant, I had a small epiphany about the nature of history. History was actually made by people. People like me, even. This had never occurred to me before, as I had no sense of history myself, and no particular interest in it.

That night I climbed up on the roof of the Red House and sat on the peak to watch the sunset over the fields and the Willamette River. I had demonstrated that I could write commercial magazine fiction. But I increasingly felt that if I wanted this career to last for twenty or thirty years I would have to write something that was deeper, that used more of me than commercial writing, or I would eventually become bored. I have always preferred doing things I don't know how to do.

Watching that sunset, I decided to change direction completely. I decided to write a serious novel of history, and Elbridge Trask's exploratory trip to Tillamook Bay would be the story, and Trask the main character. The next morning I drove down to the Oregon coast, and eventually found the Tillamook County Historical Museum.

The museum was a treasure trove for Berry, who said that the material he found there served as the basis for all three novels. He spent several weeks reading and copying everything in sight, then moved on to the Oregon Historical Society in Portland. He said he wrote *Trask* at the same time he was doing his research, "and by the time I had finished the research, I had also finished the novel."

Maybe so, but there is much that it is in the novel that can't be found in a museum. A bare-bones summary of the plot doesn't begin to do it justice: In 1848, Elbridge Trask, once a trapper and mountain man, has settled on the Clatsop Plains but feels restless. He decides to take a trip to Tillamook Bay and is accompanied by Wakila, a young Clatsop Indian, and Charley Kehwa, a *tamanawis* man or spiritual leader of the tribe, who acts as a guide. The party travels from present-day Gearhart south along the coast across Tillamook Head, Cape Falcon, and Neahkanie Mountain. After a shocking, unexpected tragedy, they reach the bay and are greeted by Kilchis, the chief of the Killamook tribe (Berry notes in *A Majority of Scoundrels* that Tillamook was usually spelled with a "k" sound until 1852). As a result of a power struggle within the tribe and to prove his worthiness, Trask volunteers to go on a vision quest called the Searching, a purification ritual involving fasting and prayer. He survives it, at great cost, and is free.

What is initially most striking about *Trask* is its clear, sure sense of place. Glen Love, professor emeritus of English at the University of Oregon and a great champion of Berry's work, wrote in a short study of his novels that "a regional work of literature may be defined as one in which landscape is character, perhaps the central character, so much so that a change in setting would completely alter and destroy the essential quality of the work."

By that standard, *Trask* is a regional work. With love and precision, Berry describes everything from Short Sands Beach ("the white lines of breakers were tiny as they marched slowly in, and along their humped green backs ran the quicksilver reflections of the sun") to a rainstorm in the Coast Range ("The rain came like whiplashes, driven out of the low clouds with a startling viciousness. It drummed and whacked against the waxy leaves of the salal with such force it seemed certain to tear them from their stems.")

Everyone in *Trask* is unsettled and unsure of where they fit. Trask has traveled the world as a sailor and a mountain man before settling on the Clatsop Plains but now is itching to strike out for somewhere new. Wakila has come of age in a tribe that has been decimated by smallpox and is now succumbing to gambling and alcohol. Charley Kehwa is a spiritual leader who has lived among whites and knows the inevitability of their push for land and power. He sees in Trask a rare white man who respects Indian culture and perhaps can prevent what happened to the Clatsop from happening to the Killamooks.

Trask's restlessness is much more than a mountain man's independence and love of freedom. In an unsure, inarticulate way, he is on a quest to find a deeper meaning to his life long before he goes on the Searching. He explicitly rejects Christianity and Western society but is unsettled by Charley's dreams and premonitions. He looks to nature and looks within himself in a way that reflects a traditional Eastern path toward enlightenment without ever explicitly stating it.

That this takes place in a novel set in the Oregon Territory in 1848, within the context of an adventure story about first contact between white settlers and Indians, is remarkable. It's as if Berry gutted a Louis L'Amour novel and replaced it with Somerset Maugham's *The Razor's Edge*. The Searching scenes are the soul of the novel and the final chapter (added, according to Wyn Berry, when the novel was in galleys) is stunningly powerful, a coda that gives fresh meaning to all that has come before.

"All his senses shared the same bright clarity; the intensity of any simple act of perception was almost unbearable," Berry writes. "The sheer brilliance of color was blinding; the sweet, clear tone of every sound came to him almost as a physical shock, making him catch his breath. The swinging glide of a gull came to have an almost-grasped significance that kept his mind hovering on the edge of joy."

Trask had a troubled publishing history. Berry said his first agent told him "there was no possible way he could submit such a book to publishers, and thought it better if we parted ways. Which we did." A different agent sold the book to Doubleday, where it was turned over to an editor who Berry thought "confused himself with an author." Unwilling to make the requested changes, Berry returned his advance and withdrew the book at Christmas of 1958. Viking Press eventually bought it and published it in 1960, to strong reviews. (The *Saturday Review* called it great. The *Northwest Review* said it was the best first novel by an Oregonian since *Honey in the Horn*.)

Berry already had moved on. *A Majority of Scoundrels: An Informal History of the Rocky Mountain Fur Company* was published in 1961. It is an amazing work, a combination of scholarship and narrative that proves true the cliché about history coming alive and shows why many of those closest to Berry considered him a genius. He did much of his research through microfilms from the Missouri Historical Society and was able to go where some of the finest western historians of the century—men such as Hiram M. Chittenden, Dale Morgan, and Bernard DeVoto—had gone before and break new ground.

Moontrap (1962) and *To Build a Ship* (1963) were mostly written while Berry was traveling, first in France and then around the world. He carried copies of some of the material he had found in the Tillamook museum with him, including a typed copy of pioneer Warren Vaughn's diary that is the backbone of *To Build a Ship*. Wyn Berry, who read and edited all of her husband's manuscripts, said there was something in what the pioneers did and thought that moved Berry.

"He identified with their values," she said. "He thought the kind of quiet, everyday heroism they had was undervalued in the present day, and he felt many of the agriculture people had sold their birthright. The mountain men, the guys who had to adjust to society—he loved them the most."

There are references to Elbridge Trask in both *Moontrap* and *To Build a Ship* and the books make sense when read in succession. There are plenty of discrepancies and departures from the historical record, all of them falling under the large umbrella of artistic license. Berry said 90 percent of *To Build a Ship* comes from Vaughn's diary but the novel is narrated by Thaler, not Vaughn, and has a sensibility that is wholly Berry's.

Like *Trask*, *Moontrap* has a lead character who is a mountain man struggling to find a place in settled society. In this case, the setting is Oregon City in 1850 and the character is Johnson Monday, a trapper who wants to make a home with his Indian wife but has "never really been willing to accept this new world he was living in. He had never committed himself fully, and now he had to pay for it."

Monday pays for his independence early and often, and so do others who live outside the boundaries drawn by the newcomers. Monday's old trapper friend, an unrepentant, uncivilized mountain man named Webster T. Webster, is the comic relief, the moral center, and the scene-stealer of *Moontrap*. Monday wrestles with his dilemmas; Webb curses at his and clings hard to the life he loves. Webb is Berry's most memorable character, one the author said jumped up during the novel's creation and demanded a larger role.

A brilliantly rendered centerpiece of the novel is the trial and hanging of a group of Cayuse Indians for the Whitman massacre six months earlier. The Indians who were hanged almost certainly were not directly involved in the massacre at the Walla Walla mission, a fact that didn't give pause to those who executed them.

After the hanging, Monday and Webb visit John McLoughlin. Berry's sketch of the eagle in his roost at Oregon City, retired from the Hudson's Bay Company and fighting futilely against the Americans who were biting the hand that had so generously fed them, is a poignant snapshot of McLoughlin's final years:

> "I heard there was some trouble about the land," Monday said, embarrassed. The trouble was simply that the Americans, Thurston most prominently, were methodically stripping McLoughlin of all his holdings in the Oregon country, their only legal weapon a campaign of hate against the "damned Jesuitical rascal of a Hudson's Bay man."
>
> "Yes, yes, quite. But it has all been turned over to intermediaries for settlement now, and I am a bit hopeful. I am expecting them momentarily with the papers. But now—" McLoughlin suddenly swept his arms up in a great despairing gesture to heaven. "*Now*, Mr. Monday."

When civilization comes crashing down on Monday, it is Webb who takes frontier revenge for his friend and flees to Saddle Mountain, where he holds off the pursuing mob and builds a moontrap, a more explicitly Eastern practice than anything in *Trask*. Berry said that despite his immersion in Chinese literature and friendship with Snyder and Whalen, he did not study Zen Buddhism until a good ten years after he wrote his novels.

To Build a Ship is different in tone and style than the novels that preceded it. It is narrated in the first person, by someone who is not a skilled mountain man and not a fair-minded friend to the Indians.

History tells us that the kind of me-first moral relativism that consumes Thaler was more typical of the white settlers to the Oregon Territory than the open-minded, live-and-let-live attitude of Trask and Monday. Indians in Oregon were wiped out by disease, killed by settlers or local militia, and moved to reservations, in a very short time after first contact.

"The cumulative death rate for Oregon Indians is estimated by 1850 to have ranged between 50 and 90 percent in some originally heavily populated areas," notes the *Atlas of Oregon*. "… What disease began, warfare completed."

It is to Berry's credit that he wrote honestly and sympathetically about Indians during a time (the late 1950s and early '60s) when attitudes toward them had not noticeably begun to change. Thaler, a rationalist who puts the construction of the ship above anything his conscience might be trying to tell him, is still sensitive enough to recognize that he "has never known a more intelligent man of any color" than Kilchis. When Kilchis asks Thaler why Trask did not come back and tells him Thaler must keep the peace in Tillamook Bay, he knows he is asking the impossible from someone not capable of giving it. The settlers came, and the Indians soon disappeared.

So did Berry. After four books in four years, a National Book Award nomination (for *Moontrap*) and a stack of great reviews, nothing. He wrote a children's book called *The Mountain Men* in 1966, but published no more novels for the rest of his life. Why?

When I made contact with Berry in 1997, via email, that was the first question I asked him. This is his reply:

> At different times I've been interested in different explorations. Some of these explorations involved writing (my primary medium), but many did not. Writing is not my "career." I have no idea what a "career" is. Basically, I have wandered the world physically and mentally, most of the time fascinated and astounded by what I discover, and sometimes putting that astonishment into words, or music, or film, or bronze, or design, or teaching, or philosophy.
>
> The trilogy of Oregon novels and historical works were all done before I was thirty. *Moontrap* and *To Build a Ship*

were written in France while I was travelling around the world with a packsack, a guitar and a typewriter.

I am also hopelessly inept at the business side of art, and don't have the patience to deal with it. I am not a dependable source of a predictable product. The vast majority of my life work—in all forms of art and thought—doesn't fit into market categories. And I don't think a marketing committee ought to determine whether what I write gets read or not.

Berry did not make much money from his novels. Wyn Berry estimated he never made more than about a thousand dollars per year from his writing, excluding movie options, and Berry guessed he averaged about a hundred dollars per year in royalties for twenty years. (There was some movie interest—Jack Nicholson briefly held the rights to *Moontrap* just before he won the Oscar for *Cuckoo's Nest*.) Berry was frustrated that he made money more easily from science fiction than historical novels. At that time, he thought of himself more as a painter than a writer, he wanted to travel and follow his interests wherever they led, so why spend all that time writing novels?

"He never valued his own work very highly until much later in his life," said Wyn Berry, who always was the primary supporter of the family. "He didn't expect great things, but he was annoyed that he wasn't making a living."

However, there was more writing that never got published. Wyn Berry said her husband wrote a sequel to *Trask* that he burned because he felt it didn't work as a story and put another finished novel called *Eye of the Bear* "into the fire." Love writes that Berry destroyed these books "because he realized he had not been changed by the experience of writing [them]." Wyn Berry said he was "a very accurate critic, but fierce in all ways."

Berry did have a regular job for a while, as a writer on the film unit at KGW in Portland. There he met a gifted producer and director named Laszlo Pal and began a collaboration that lasted more than thirty years. Berry worked as a writer on many of Pal's award-winning documentaries and on industrial and institutional films, which he enjoyed because he could immerse himself in a subject and learn all about it. Pal accepted Berry's wandering ways and Berry said that "if I disappear for five or six years, he accepts that, and when I return we can resume work together again as though no time has passed."

Berry wrote some commissioned books, such as *The Eddie Bauer Guide to Flyfishing* and *Understanding Your Finances*, and taught creative writing at the University of Washington and other colleges. He built a bronze foundry on Vashon Island for his sculpture and played in a band called Vashimba that performed the music of the Shona tribe of Zimbabwe. He spent several years living in a boat in Eagle Harbor, off Bainbridge Island.

And he discovered the World Wide Web. His Web site, Berryworks, contains a historical novel set in the goddess culture of Minoan Crete called "Sketches from the Palace at Knossos," eight different short stories, a children's book, some essays (including "On the Submissiveness of Women in Tango" and the beautiful "Snapshots of My Daughter, Turning"), twenty-one chapters about living on Eagle Harbor called "Magic Harbor," a large amount of poetry, art, and philosophy. Some of the writing is excellent and all of it is original and wholly Berry.

He was passionate about the possibilities of the Internet and a strong believer in it as a creative medium. "Long before I set up my studio in cyberspace, I had been exploring in a different literary form—a mosiac of individual pieces, rather than linear narrative," he said. "Each individual piece … can be read separately, in any order. In Berryworks, you can move from any place to any other place, with a single hyperlink. Everything is available simultaneously."

Everything is available simultaneously, and for nothing.

"I am invariably asked why someone who has been nominated for the National Book Award would simply give their work away," he said. "But I have never been part of that world. It has always been my dream to write exactly what I want to write and give it away to anybody who wants it. Cyberspace makes that possible. And I didn't get paid for probably 90 percent of the other work I've done, so it's not all that different. Economically I'm marginal and always have been, even when the books were new."

Berry was cautious but curious when I contacted him in 1997. He wanted to have Berryworks reviewed as a whole, the way a book is reviewed, and wanted to do everything by email. Six months of electronic exchanges led to phone calls and finally a meeting in a coffee shop on Vashon Island. Berry suffered from chronic pulmonary obstructive disease, the result, he said, of "forty-five years of rolling cigarettes out of pipe tobacco." He needed oxygen for any exertion and carried a portable tank when he left his house. He spent up to ten hours every day on-line but did confess to a weakness for "Xena, the Warrior Princess."

Berry died in Seattle on February 20, 2001. At the end of his life, he knew he would be remembered for *Trask* and *Moontrap* and *To Build a Ship* and *A Majority of Scoundrels* and was pleased and proud that people still read them.

"When I wrote *Trask* I didn't even have any idea anyone would read it," he said. "As to the durability of these works, it is much like watching your children grow up. After twenty years or so you think 'good lord, how did that ever happen?'

"A writer can plan to make a book entertaining, or plan to make a book interesting, and many other things. But a writer cannot plan to make a book last. That is not in our hands."

To Build a Ship

There is a pleasure sure
In being mad which none but madmen know.
    —Dryden

Chapter One

The first thing I heard about the Bay was that there was a man down there who lived in a tree. It bothered me, perhaps unreasonably. It wasn't the first time I had ever heard of men living in trees, of course. There were whole tribes of them in Africa, families and everything, a kind of half-monkey, half-man that lived in trees and swung around from branch to branch. But that was different; mainly it was thousands and thousands of miles away, so it didn't worry me. But *this* man was right here in the Oregon Territory of the United States of America. Not a hundred miles away, where I could go and see for myself. It didn't seem—decent. I was in my early twenties at the time and had a lot of illusions about the human race I have since lost.

"Well—what kind of man *is* he?" I asked.

Willy Cooper, who was having his wheat ground at the same time as I, said, "Just a man, Ben. You know, like you and me."

"A white man."

"So."

"Well, what the hell's he *eat*, Willy? I mean, like pine cones and roots and things?"

"Hell, Ben, I don't know." Willy shrugged, because he didn't really care. It made me slightly embarrassed that *I* should care so much. The first image I'd gotten in my head was of this fellow hanging upside down by his knees from a branch, looking all around. I think that was what was so hard.

In one last attempt to get some information that would make this thing clear in my head I asked him, "What kind of a tree?"

"Cedar, I hear. Lots of cedar down there, you know, Ben. On the coast I mean."

I turned it over in my mind. It didn't help. Didn't matter *how* I looked at it, cedar, pine, or fir, no white man had a right to be hanging by his

knees in a tree in the Year of Our Lord eighteen hundred and fifty-one.
It wasn't right.

So it was this idle conversation in the Oregon City Mill that started
me thinking serious about the Bay, decided me to go down there. I had
only been in the Oregon Country for about a year, had not taken out a
land claim as yet, and was still working harvest for other fellows to see
me through the next winter. No woman, no relatives. Free as a bird
and twice as lonely.

I didn't go immediately, of course, as I hadn't made up enough reasons.
No sane man goes roaring down to a new and wild country from
civilization just because he hears there's a man living in a tree. Or rather,
no sane man admits it right out, even to himself. But I've found that
you generally make up your mind to go someplace and then start
inventing all the good reasons for it. In the case of the Bay it wasn't too
hard, as there was not much information about it. If you wanted to know
you *had* to go see. During the winter of '51-'52 I stewed and fretted
around and picked up enough justification that by spring I was jumpy
as a cricket to get down there and see it with my own personal eyes.

From the bits of information I could pick up, it seemed to be a sort
of Terrestrial Paradise. A lovely little bay, the entrance sheltered by a
sandbar so the water never got too rough, even during the coastal
storms. Walled in by mountains on all sides. The only way in was by
Indian trail across the Coast Range from the Willamette Valley, or the
beach running south from Astoria. The richest land in the whole of
the Oregon Territory—you could plant flies and harvest eagles—and
so forth. No families as yet, perhaps a dozen men batching it, like
myself. In time families would come down, but the women were always
reluctant to take their children to a place where there wasn't any school.
And you know how it is with reluctant women. But in the meantime
the first-rate land was there, open for Donation Land Claims like the
rest of the Territory. All you had to do was tell the government *which*
320 acres of Eden suited you, and it was yours.

In short, a nice private place where a man could build up a future
for himself in grand style. The enormous isolation I regarded as an
assurance of privacy, as I was looking for advantages. In any case it
would pose no serious problems, as I heard the tiny settlement had

connections with a firm of Boston merchants. Each year they sent in ships, loaded with everything a man might need, and took off the Bay's produce at high prices. It seemed logical, considering what a marvelous port it was, particularly for the rough and stormy Oregon coast. And it stood to reason that there must be *someplace* on the face of the earth where a man was given a fair shake; it was just a question of finding it.

The more I thought about it, the more it seemed inevitable that the Bay would be the future New York of the Pacific Coast. Oregon City and Portland, inland on the Willamette, were too far from the sea. Astoria meant crossing the terrible Columbia bar and fronting the vicious river mouth itself; the litter of broken ships scattered up and down the coast testified to that. It was clear to me that the site of the future great metropolis of the Oregon Territory had not yet been discovered.

This was my own personal chance to get in at the beginning of something really big. It was obvious that in a few years time every acre of that country would be worth a small fortune. And you may be sure that I was well decided to ask more than twenty-four dollars in beads for *my* share. As with most Americans who have studied history, one of my deepest regrets is that I did not own Manhattan when the time came that those Dutchmen wanted to buy it. And here was the New Manhattan, the Western Manhattan, free for the taking.

By the spring of '52, then, I was terrified that the Others would get there first. When somebody mentioned the Bay in conversation I stiffened, and shut my mouth, saying nothing and appearing uninterested. When somebody *didn't* mention it, it scared me worse, as it was clear they were plotting to go down there in secret. It was, in retrospect, a fairly futile way to pass the winter, working myself up into a terrible state of nerves like that. But Oregon winters are such that there is not a great deal else to do. So I built imaginary Manhattans at considerable length, went over every foot of the journey in my mind a hundred times or better, prepared my pack and unprepared it, counted my single frying pan a dozen times, just to be sure. It always came out One.

In the last part of April, 1852, I started out, heading south down the Willamette Valley in order to divert suspicion, looking for the trail

that was reported to lead across the Coast Range from the territory of
the Kalapuya Indians. Feeling very spunky, I can tell you, and singing
a little song of my own devising:

> *With my pack upon my back*
> *And my frying pan in my hand*
> *I am bound for the Tillamook land.*

Intending to profit fully from this unparalleled opportunity to own
the New Manhattan. And intending to see the man that lived in a tree.

2

The Indians had several methods of marking a trail, all of which were
useless. The most common was to make two perpendicular cuts in the
bark of a tree, about an inch apart. Then a horizontal cut at the top,
and the strip of bark, sometimes a foot long, was peeled downward and
left hanging. It was very clearly not the work of nature. It seemed
unnatural to the elk, too. The bulls, either enraged or curious about
this phenomenon, immediately scraped it off with their antlers, leaving
an irregular patch of rubbed bark no different from any of the others,
which were numerous.

The second method was to insert a stick in a slit of bark, pointing in
the direction of the trail. This served very well, one time. The next
Indian that came along the trail had a tendency to pull the stick out of
the bark and examine it carefully to make sure it was indeed an artificial
sign. Then he threw it off into the brush and went on. It is no wonder
one often came upon Indians wandering around aimlessly. It was not
due to lack of industry, as the Methodists claimed. They were simply
following Indian trails, which is to say, they were lost. It is their privilege,
as they were here first.

Thus, the fact that I lost my own way on my trip to Tillamook is
neither surprising nor my fault. The plain fact is that most of us were
lost most of the time while traveling overland. You simply blundered
along in the general direction intended, looking hopefully around from
high points and asking directions of anyone you happened across.

My own "guide" I met on the third day out, a Kalapuya with a little boy behind him on his horse. I was by that time in the Coast Range, but still wandering around on the eastern slope, well before the divide.

We exchanged the usual Jargon greeting, *klahowya*, and he dismounted. I gave him a bit of tobacco and asked him where the ocean was.

"*Nika nanitch salt chuck. Ka salt chuck?*"

He pointed west. As the sun was low in the afternoon sky, it told me little I did not already know.

"*Nika ticky nanitch Tillamook illahee.*"

It was perfectly all right with him if I wanted to see the Tillamook country. He puffed contentedly on his pipe and pointed into the setting sun again. After a bit more conversation of this sort, I found he was heading toward the ocean himself. He was taking his little boy, who was, I would guess, about seven years old, to see it. The Kalapuya were an inland tribe, but with that vast expanse of water so near, it was normal that they should want to see it at least once.

My new friend and guide, whose name I never learned, agreed to let me come along with him for two dollars. While selected quite at random, the price was reasonable, and I accepted. I did not have two dollars, but the agreement was more important than the sum and I was confident something could be worked out on reaching our destination.

As it was too late for much more traveling that day, we made camp where we had met, in a small prairie. The Kalapuya had no provisions with him except for several blankets he was taking down to trade with the coastal people, which would pay for his son's ocean-view treat. We ate well, however, as I had bacon and flour in sufficient quantity. When the night came there was a sudden chill in the air, and we sat close around our little fire. The light was sucked into the darkness all around, and the night was clear. I believe the climate has changed, as I remember nights more clear than they are now, and the stars brighter. The Milky Way spread luminous over our heads and the black silhouettes of the hills and ridges around us were like a frame for its glow. Our little fire was clearly the center of the universe, a bright warmth in the midst of the cold and silent night.

We let the flame go down to red coals, and the tiny circle of light drew in and in until there was only the glow among the ashes. Somewhere in the infinite blackness the Kalapuya's horse rustled his picket rope. At last, without a word, the Indian wrapped himself and his son together in their blanket and lay down beside the fire. I watched the shifting blacks over the surface of the coals for a few moments more, and then took my own blanket out of the pack. The cold was severe now, with the fire's warmth gone, and I shivered.

I rolled myself in. On the opposite side of the coals I could see two glinting red reflections, the dying fire repeated in the eyes of the Kalapuya as he watched me.

"*Cultus pasisi*," he grunted.

Mine was, in fact, a worthless blanket, but I did not think it his place to say so. I answered rather shortly that it would serve, and he was silent again for several minutes.

"*Mika mitlite—inapoos?*" he asked finally.

I told him I had no fleas that I knew of. He unwrapped himself from his blanket and went to his little stack of merchandise. He brought back a fine Hudson's Bay three-point blanket, warm enough for a battalion.

"You take," he said in the Jargon. "More warm. But—you leave no *inapoos*. *Good* blanket, *kloshe* pasisi."

He went back to his own, where his son waited silently, watching us both with great dark eyes in the night.

"Sell good blanket, me. No *inapoos*," he said reflectively. "Warm." He wrapped himself and the boy up again and lay on his back, looking quietly up at the stars scattered across the depth of the sky like the phosphorescent wake of a great night-traveling ship.

We were together for three more days. Each night the Kalapuya repeated the ritual he had established. Either he enjoyed it so much he felt it worth doing again, or he forgot having done it before. I gave more guarantees of my flealessness in those four nights than in all the rest of my life together. Each morning he examined his blanket meticulously, inch by inch, and folded it neatly with the rest. He explained to me that it was not the simple presence of *inapoos* that made a blanket undesirable, but the presence of foreign *inapoos*. The people liked to provide their own, and it is quite true that there is a certain security in familiarity.

All these interrogations were in some measure humiliating to me, but as the nights remained very cold I found I was not as humiliated as I was warm, and raised no objections.

During these days the boy did not speak once. It is possible that being so young he spoke only his own language, and was not familiar with the universal Chinook Jargon. Or he may simply have had nothing to say. An Indian will often remain silent when he has nothing to say, which gives them the reputation of being taciturn.

It was toward the middle of the morning on the last day that we reached a ridge from which we could see the ocean. A small bay was directly ahead of us, and I could not repress a sudden excitement at this first glimpse of the Garden of the World, as it seemed to me. The Kalapuya contented himself with pointing at the vast expanse of gray that stretched out to the horizon, saying simply, *"Salt chuck."* The boy studied it carefully, intently, storing it away in his memory. After this brief period we set off again, moving somewhat faster now for the excitement.

The sun came out of the overcast around noon and I was sorry we had come down off the high ridge, as I would like to have seen it sparkling on the sea. But I told myself I would have many years to contemplate that spectacle; for the moment the problem was to reach the Bay itself. After struggling through a series of small but very steep ridges, thickly grown with brush beneath the firs, we came out at the water's edge around four o'clock. Against all hope, I had been scanning the countryside with great care as we moved, on the chance I might catch a quick glimpse of the man that lived in the tree. In this I was disappointed, and shortly after discovered why.

My Kalapuya made contact with the Indians who inhabited this region, living in a small concentration of plank houses at the mouth of a tiny river. His son went scuttling off to the beach, squatting there on his haunches and staring fascinated as the great lines of breakers rolled in and thundered into foam.

From the Kalapuya's conversation it soon developed that we were not in the Tillamook country at all. This small bay was some fifty miles south of the Bay for which I was headed. There has been a confusion somewhere, which everyone regretted. On a journey of some hundred miles we had made an error of fifty, which was not encouraging. However, the way was now plain, as I had only to follow the beach north and sooner or later I would reach 'home.'

According to the Indians here the going would not be very difficult. There were small groups near almost every river I had to cross, so I could get someone to ferry me across.

In spite of his inefficiency I had found my Kalapuya an excellent traveling companion, and I took leave of him with some regret. He was regretful, too, but in his case I believe it was because I refused to pay him the two dollars for misleading me so royally.

Before leaving, I asked how I would be certain of the Bay I sought, where the Tillamooks lived. I was told there would be no difficulty, as it was unique on all the coast. The headman, the *tyee*, of the Tillamooks was black, black as charred wood, from their demonstration.

And there was a white man there who lived in a tree.

3

The remainder of the trip, another four days, was uneventful. It was vastly more difficult than it had been represented, of course, but I already knew it was impossible to get reliable information from Indians. There are only two degrees of difficulty recognized in their scheme of things; very, very easy and impossible. "Impossible" means nobody has ever tried it, as often as not through simple lack of interest. "Easy" means that it has been accomplished within the memory of living man.

At the whim of tide and terrain I was often obliged to double inland, forcing my way through the unbelievably dense brush of the coast forest, in which I was lucky to make a hundred yards an hour. This, combined with a series of headlands, points, ridges, humps, and downright mountains, served to lower my spirits considerably.

It also began to rain around noon of the first day, and continued for the remainder of my trip. At first I sought shelter under the roof of thickly twined branches, but these soon became soaked and the steady, dripping cascades from above were worse than the rain in the open. After a few hours it appeared that there were no dry places left in the world, so I reluctantly shouldered my pack again and made off. I was to be drowned in any case, and decided I might as well cover a few more miles in the process.

By the second day my pack was fully ten pounds heavier. My flour had turned to paste, congealing in a disgusting clot that had to be scraped off the bacon. My coffee had turned to coffee, and seeped steadily through the bottom of the pack, staining the rear of my jeans, my legs, and leaving a brown trail behind me that quickly disappeared into the dark wet sand of the beach.

The nights were the same, but colder. I deeply regretted the fine blanket of my Kalapuya friend, and I thought about it a good deal. I had used it sufficiently that it seemed like my property anyway, and I rather resented being deprived of it. I would have bought it, but it was a three-point blanket. On the traditional system of "a point's a plew," it was thus worth three prime beaver skins in trade, or a cash value of near fifteen dollars. I had not seen cash money in the value of fifteen dollars since I came to Oregon. And considering my state, it was obvious that I had nothing else to offer. One frying pan, beginning to rust; one pair boots, turning to mush; one pair jeans, blue forward, wet amidships, and brown aft. And one brain, moldy, to judge from my mood, condition not guaranteed.

It occurred to me that I had probably less to offer than any other creature in the world. This in itself was a sort of distinction, though it did not much cheer me. I resolved that on my next trip to Paradise I would search out the dry season. At that moment I would have preferred Hell by far, as I understood it was warmer and dryer than I had been recently.

This will roughly sketch my mood and condition when I first saw the Bay I had dreamed of, it seemed, all my life. Any pleasure I might have found in reaching the end of my road was water-logged and soggy. Achievement is always so, I've found. By the time you succeed it is either too late, or you are tired, cold, and wet. The sharp joy you might have felt—that you in fact anticipated eagerly at the beginning—has foundered in the process of attaining your goal.

So I gazed stupidly at the Promised Land, wondering vaguely what I was going to do now, as Eden appeared to be as wet as the rest of the world. There was a cluster of five or six Indian houses near the outlet of a river, and I made for this village, fascinated by the prospect of a roof as a moth by a candle flame.

The rain beat down so heavily that the outlines of the lodges were obscured by a fog of bursting droplets, but I could see that the construction was typical of these coast peoples. Split cedar planks two or three inches thick and up to thirty feet long formed the roof and low outside walls. The interior would be dug out some feet below the surface of the ground, a sort of pit, which made these lodges more spacious than they appeared from outside. There was a small oval opening in the end wall, covered by a flap of elkskin which, at the moment, was cascading water from its dangling bottom edge.

I approached the first lodge, and for want of anything better, rapped loudly on the wall beside the door. After a few moments the flap was lifted, and the wrinkled face of an ancient Indian woman appeared around the edge. She looked at me.

"*Klahowya,*" I said.

She continued to stare, then blinked suddenly and disappeared, dropping the flap behind her. I looked around at the other lodges. Where I was standing there was a steady near-torrent running from the roof peak, and I didn't know what to do. A moment later the flap lifted again, and the face of a man appeared, equally old.

"*Klahowya,*" I said.

He scratched his cheek absently and disappeared.

This interested scrutiny occurred twice more, in descending order of age. We had worked down to a young man of about twenty. This one emerged completely from the door and stood facing me. He was wholly naked, and carried no weapons. He looked me up and down, then suddenly lifted the elkskin flap and motioned me through.

I stooped through the door and almost stumbled down the three steps carved in the earth itself. The long dark room was full of the steady clattering roar of the rain. There were three fires and a place for a fourth, one near each corner. A sort of continuous step had been carved in the earth along each wall, about three feet above the level of the floor. On this sleeping bench a ragtag collection of Indians lounged or sat in various attitudes of repose. They were silent briefly when I came in, but quickly returned to their chattering conversations. The area around each fire appeared to be occupied by a family, as each area had its share of all ages, from the ancient crones to pudgy naked babies.

The young man who had finally permitted me to enter motioned me to the fire at the right-hand side of the door, which was apparently that of his family. I recognized the old woman and man who had first examined me at the door.

"*Klahowya,*" I said again, feeling very foolish.

The old man nodded and moved over a bit to make room for me on the bench. My eyes were smarting from the smoke that filled the lodge. One of the roof planks had been raised and supported with a long pole to serve as a smoke vent, but there was still a good deal in the air. Below this vent, of course, there was a long wet streak on the white sand that covered the earthen floor. Ventilation was obviously a question of inadequate compromise, as are most adjustments with the world. The more smoke you let out, the more rain you let in. While I did not understand their language, I gathered from the pointing and gesticulating that one family was ill-temperedly debating this very question.

Looking back, I believe I would have been frightened, had I not been so thoroughly miserable. After all, I did not know these people, and the Tillamooks, or Killamooks, had a rather bad reputation. They spoke a language related to the Nez Percé far to the east, rather than the Chinook dialect which was common among the other coastal tribes. This tended to keep them slightly apart from the other tribes, which in itself would have been sufficient to give them a nasty reputation, of course. In any case, I was not frightened, because there was certainly nothing they could do to me that would have made me any more miserable than I already was. Here was the fire, beginning to warm my clammy carcass, and here was my clammy carcass, beginning to be warmed. If they chose to eat me later, so much the worse. I could not have cared less.

'My' Tillamook family was discussing me in their language when two young men pushed the flap aside and came in. They wore flat, conical hats like those of the Chinamen, and short capes that reached to their hips. Hat and cape alike were made of a finely woven grass or reed of some sort. Whether this rain equipment was effective or not, I had no way of knowing. But as they, too, were entirely naked underneath, I knew they would be warm and dry before I was.

The young man of my family called them over, pointed to me, and chattered at them. They regarded me solemnly. One of them muttered something that sounded uncomplimentary and went off to the vacant corner. Borrowing a burning faggot from the neighboring fire, he began to kindle his own. The second was apparently more interested in the problem I posed, and squatted by the fire, stripping off his rain-cape and hat and putting them in a neat stack beside him. He and my young man then discussed me in a series of wholly incomprehensible guttural noises and grunts.

At last my young man turned to me. Leaning forward intently he said, "*Mika klatawa.* You go." He pointed to the door, but his eyes remained on me. At least he spoke the Jargon, which was a beginning.

I was highly reluctant to leave the first warmth I had seen in so many days, and tried to put him off by smiling.

"*Kah klatawa?*" I said. "Go where?" All the time smiling faintly as though it were a little joke between the two of us. I wasn't going anyplace unless they dragged me.

"*Tenasam. Tenasam.*"

It was a word I did not know. I tried to equivocate, being very friendly and ambiguous, but it was difficult. While I spoke the Jargon, I did not speak it fluently, nor did he. And in any case it is not a language it is possible to speak fluently. I found it more than a little difficult, moreover, to compose a convincing argument against going *tenasam* when I didn't grasp the subject of the conversation. In the end it was all quite useless, as my friend was insistent that I go.

Further, it seemed that the newcomer was to take me. He put on his broad coolie hat, though he left the cape behind. Regretfully I left the lovely fire with its warm, choking aura of smoke. We set off again in the rain, which was now being whipped about viciously by a spasmodic wind from the sea.

Ahead of me my guide marched firmly, stark naked in a tube of rain that poured down from the brim of his broad hat. It was more than absurd, the parasol-like canopy above the brown body with its buttocks jogging up and down as he walked. I didn't know which was the more ridiculous, he with his hat or myself, dragging behind with the vivacity and spirit of a drowned slug, faithfully lugging my pack of flour-paste and weak coffee. But that was how it was when the Tillamook and I went *tenasam*.

4

The Indian set a good two-forty pace, and it was about half an hour later that we rounded a small point of the Bay. The Indian stopped and pointed ahead. Some distance off, and obscured by whipping veils of rain, there was a squarish stack of weathered lumber. It perched on a tiny bluff just at the Bay's edge, as close to the water as it could get without being taken out by the tide.

"*Tenasam*," the Tillamook said, pointing. "*Tenasam.*" He turned abruptly and started back the way we had come.

I peered through the rain at the pile, grayish against the dark of the forest behind. Suddenly I saw a window in the middle of it, and realized it was not, after all, a random stack of boards left out to weather, but a shanty of sorts.

In fact, as I approached, my opinion wavered back and forth several times between woodpile and cabin. Finally I was certain it was a more or less conscious construction of man's intelligence; a woodpile would have been more sturdy. In the gusts of wind that whipped off the Bay the little structure seemed to shake itself like a wet dog. It shuddered alarmingly, and I wondered if I had arrived just at the critical moment when it would collapse into the sea and be washed out in the tide.

It stood, however, and continued to stand in defiance of what we laughingly call the laws of nature. I approached the window. As I leaned forward to look inside I was suddenly confronted by a ghostly visage hanging just a few inches from my own, on the other side of the salt-frosted glass. I had just time to observe a shock of blond hair, a startled expression, and a face that seemed drawn from a fairy tale, something about gnomes and elves. Then the apparition darted suddenly out of sight, leaving me with my heart thudding ponderously from the shock.

After a moment I walked around the back; the front was perched so close to the edge of the little bluff I was afraid of falling off. However, there was neither door nor window in any of the other walls. Through a crack between two boards an eye watched my tour. It was not a comforting sensation.

In perfect frankness, I was getting angry. I had been traveling for nine days. I had been inspected for fleas, soaked by rain, frozen and hungry, examined by disembodied heads for god knows what serious defects, surveyed by naked savages in smoke-filled lodges and finally dragged out into the howling tempest by a walking nudity of a parasol man. I am not demanding by nature, but I sincerely felt I deserved something better of the world.

I was circling the cabin immersed in thoughts of this general nature, and I believe I was working myself up to the point of unreasonable violence, such as kicking the whole damned contraption into the sea and going home. But on the opposite side from the window there was a stick-and-mud-plastered chimney, and from the chimney there emerged a faint vapor of blue smoke that was quickly whipped off into nothingness by the wind. That changed everything. There was a fire in that cabin. If it was dry enough for a fire to burn, it was certainly dry enough for me.

I went to the front and knocked very politely on the door, as I had at the Indian lodge. A gust of wind knocked at the same moment, and the little structure wavered badly. I didn't care. Let it fall, I thought illogically, just as long as I get inside.

The door opened a bit, and the gnomelike pale face appeared again like a frightened shrew at its hole.

"Hello there," I said my friendliest way. "My name's Ben Thaler. I'm from the Valley and I've been traveling nine days and I'm soaked clear through to the other side and I wonder if I could come in for a bit and get dry. I don't want to bother you or any—"

The door opened a little wider, perhaps inadvertently. I made for it, getting my shoulders inside and catching a glimpse of the warm and cheery light of the fire.

The little man backed away apprehensively and said, "Yus," very softly.

I stripped off my pack and squatted in front of the fire, smiling my most ingratiating smile at my reluctant host. He cleared his throat.

"Yes?" I encouraged.

"Uh—uh, the pack. Maybe you could—"

I looked at the pack, and saw what he meant. The bottom was a gooey mess of flour-paste and coffee stain, and was oozing all over the floor like an open wound. I jumped up quickly and stuck the pack outside. "Sorry," I said, hurrying back to the fire.

He cleared his throat again. "You're wet, man," he said.

"Noticed that myself," I said cheerily. I suddenly thought I was going to cry, I was so damned wet and cold and miserable.

"Well, uh—take off them clothes, you'll—you'll catch your death." He stripped a blanket off the bed and handed it to me. I got rid of my soggy clothes and huddled up in the blanket.

"I'm sorry I—pushed in like that," I said. "But I really had to get dry. I thought I was going to die or something if I didn't get dry. I was scared you weren't going to let me in."

He frowned worriedly down at the floor. "Yus," he said finally. "You—you had a awful kind of a look out there." He blinked uncertainly at me and returned his attention to the floor.

I wasn't surprised any, but the warmth of the fire soothed me and the utterly miraculous dryness of the blanket was like the touch of an angel's wing on my skin. I had the greatest luxury known to man, a dry blanket when you're wet and cold. It didn't seem important that I also had an awful kind of a look.

"Uh—name's Sam Howard," he said. "Sam. People call me Little Sam. I don't mind much."

This was the solution, then. He was *tenasam*, or rather, Tenas Sam, Little Sam in the Jargon.

"Well, Sam," I told him. "I don't care what people call me, long as they call me for supper." I was beginning to cheer up.

"You want some supper?" he said, a little bewildered since it was still the middle of the afternoon.

I didn't know whether I was more disappointed that he didn't appreciate my wit, or pleased at the prospect of food. I settled for the food. It was getting to be a habit. For nine days I had methodically sacrificed my self-esteem for the welfare of my body, putting up with all sorts of humiliations for a little comfort. In thinking it over I could not say I regretted it, and it is a policy I have scrupulously followed ever since.

Physically, Little Sam Howard was not so abnormal as my first startled glimpse had led me to believe. At least not quite. He was very small and his head—with a huge halo of blond hair and tiny pointed chin—seemed large out of all proportion to his body, as though there had been a mistake made in assembling him. But that was nearly all, and surely no more than a reasonable departure from the image of God.

However, I discovered in the next few hours that he was the most monstrously shy human being I had ever met. As I ate, I tried to make conversation, so as not to give the impression of an exaggerated eagerness. It was virtually impossible. Little Sam sat staring worriedly into the fire with his hands clasped tightly between his knees.

"Looks like we may get a late spring," I said, between bites of the good elk steak he had nervously prepared for me.

He bobbed his head, horribly embarrassed by the lateness of the spring.

"Probably mean a nice fall, though," I added.

Sam ducked, as though I had thrown something. You could tell he hoped he would not be held responsible for the character of the fall, good or bad. His timidity was almost overwhelming, and I became embarrassed and tongue-tied myself, out of sympathy. I soon learned to avoid direct questions, as they posed for Sam an almost unsolvable problem. Someone had deliberately made a demand on him; would he be able to satisfy it? did he want to? and—if he were *wrong?*

The expenditure of energy in all this was enormous. He clenched his fists between his knees, he bit his lower lip, a vein on his forehead throbbed, had it been a little warmer he would have been drowned in nervous sweat.

This timidity was in part a result of the fact that Sam Howard was more sensible to the presence of other human beings than anyone I have ever known. The simple presence of people in the same room drained energy from him like wringing a sponge. It was impossible *not* to make demands on him, for being there was already a demand.

I later learned that before coming to live solitary at the Bay, Sam had been a builder, a shipwright. It was not only his trade, it was his life, but he had been forced to abandon it. As a shipwright he probably had few equals in the world. His skill was, by normal human terms, virtually without limit, as I was to discover. But for Sam—it was never enough. Imperfection tortured him, haunted him, made his life a constant long penitence. And a man who is wounded by imperfection will spend much of his time hurting, as there is a good deal of it about.

A piece of lumber with a tiny crack in one end was, for Sam, a source of anguish, and I speak perfectly literally when I say he would pass a haunted, sleepless night over it. A peg not driven perfectly flush was an agony; a crooked timber a direct accusation.

In short, the world in Sam's eyes was intended to be perfect, and he himself could never live up to the image. His responsibility was universal, and he shouldered the burden of all the mistakes in this world. He was guiltier than anybody, for he was guilty of it all.

Humanity was the sole error for which Sam did not entirely accept the blame. But that was Somebody Else's doing, and he once told me in perfect seriousness that he believed the human race had been invented to annoy him.

Thus, in spite of his skill and love, shipbuilding had become intolerable for him, a mistress of whom he was unworthy. There was not only the demanded perfection of his trade, but the constant presence of humanity, which he could neither accept nor control.

This description is the result of the reflection of years, many of them. I have had much cause to reflect on the character of Little Sam Howard. Like all descriptions of a man, it misrepresents him, because it is so simple. He was, after all, a man, and one dealt with him as a man like any other, so far as it was possible. He ate, slept, worked like the rest of us, and it is likely that another might simply find that he was unusually hard to talk to. I had no idea at the time how much Little Sam's peculiarities would affect my life, nor that in time I would come to share some of his guilt. I just shrugged to myself and thought, hell, we're all a little bit peculiar if it comes to that.

I was too young to be concerned about such things, and found Sam's shyness a hindrance, no more, as it made it more difficult to get information out of him. And information was what I desperately wanted. I have always had an enormous hunger for information, which is quite inexplicable since more often than not I do not even use the information I already have.

In any event, after some desultory conversation, during which I became more and more embarrassed, I finally blurted out the thing that was uppermost in my mind.

"Sam—listen, Sam," I said. "Is it true there's a fellow down here as lives in a tree?"

He looked up from the fire in astonishment, meeting my eyes briefly. He chewed at his lip, and turned quickly back to the fire, squeezing his hands between his knees.

He closed his eyes tightly before he answered, screwing up his courage. "Yus," he admitted, so softly I leaned forward to hear. "Name of Joe Champion, him."

He was so miserable in admitting it that I sympathized deeply with him. It was obviously the first time he'd realized he was guilty that Joe Champion had decided to live in a tree.

Chapter Two

1

My first night at the Bay was thus spent curled up on the floor of Sam Howard's rickety, shivery cabin, while the coastal storm roared and prowled around the walls, poking in wet claws of wind. Sometime in the early morning, before false dawn, I was wakened by the dying of the storm and lay drowsily listening to silence, as attentively as though it were sound.

The next week I spent aimlessly tramping the Bay, picking out the 320-acre claim the future would know as "Ben Thaler's place." I was deeply conscious of my responsibility. Misty, unborn generations of Thalers hiked with me, peering critically over my shoulder every time I paused to survey a hillock or valley that appealed to me. The first few days I tried to see it all through their eyes, but I plainly couldn't. After a while I got very annoyed and resentful and had practically made up my mind never to marry, so there wouldn't *be* any future generations of Thalers to criticize a choice I was making as best I could. It was just spitefulness on my part, of course.

Under the sun the Bay was not nearly so desolate as my first, rain-soaked glimpse, and I was quickly able to restack some of my illusions. The first morning was exceptionally beautiful. The thick bed of ferns that blanketed the whole half-moon of land was still wet from the storm, and the sun rising over the knobby peaks of the coast range picked out individual droplets like some unimaginable dew fall. The forest was lush and fresh, as though it had been born in a rush of green brilliance under the rain. The sensation of richness and fertility and growth was overwhelming. Out at sea the rollers remained huge for several days, swinging in long stately lines to thunder down across the sandbar, seeming to shake the ground under my feet. The purity of their whiteness in the sun was awesome, and I thought this was probably the most perfect meeting of land and sea God had ever created.

For my land claim I finally chose a tract some distance back from the sea, hoping to avoid the violence and misery of the rainstorms, which were fresh in my mind. The river-bottom land with its rich dark soil was attractive at first, but I avoided it, as it is a source of disease. My land was prairie land, grazing land—or would be, after the near-solid ranks of timber had been cleared off. As in all the coastal forests a dense mat of ferns and brush smothered the soil, but with my future-pointing eyes I could see it all cleared, with vast herds grazing the emerald-green pastures.

The impression of richness and fertility in the Bay was strongly tinged with loneliness, and the sense of isolation was sharp. The flat and fertile plain ran back perhaps six or seven miles from the sea. It raised itself in a line of gentle undulations, as though preparing for the great effort, and suddenly swept up to form the knobby, twisted humps of the Coast Range itself. This single passage of hills was the sole transition. The mountain barrier isolated us from the interior as effectively as any prison wall. It was clear that any settlement here would live or die according to its communications with the Outside, and equally clear that this meant the sea. This impression was confirmed when I talked to some of the other men who had already taken up claims on the land.

Warren Vaughn was perhaps the easiest to talk to, a heavy-set Valley man who had come in the year before. He was sensible and stable, with no pronounced eccentricities. So much so that it made me vaguely unquiet at first. I'm afraid it is a fact that a perfectly normal man does not throw up goods and job to wander down into a deserted and isolated Bay to live with the Indians, cut off from the society of his kind, hacking out of the raw land a tiny clearing not half as big as what he left behind. The reasons they invent are always the same—good land, opportunity, etc., etc. But there are few indeed who can look you in the eye. It is a question of excusing acts already committed, and that is always embarrassing. In plain fact there is a deep unrest that churns in the belly of a man and makes him move. The rest is fantasy.

Being normal and sensible myself, I knew it was *possible*; but still . . . In any event, the only marked eccentricity I ever discovered in Vaughn was that he was always right. He didn't say so. But you knew it, down deep inside you. If Vaughn told you the sky was green, you realized for the first time what an ass you'd been all your life to think it was blue.

Vaughn was of my opinion regarding transportation. "The sea's our lifeline, Ben," he said. "Hell, lots of ways we're closer to China than we are to the Valley."

I thought about it. "Well, I expect some day there'll be a wagon road into the Valley. That'll make a lot of difference."

Vaughn laughed, throwing back his head. "Ben, my boy," he said tolerantly, "that's what *I* used to think, too. But just figure it over a minute. How wide you think you'd have to make a wagon road into the Valley?"

"Ten feet, maybe? Twelve? Wagon and team won't take no more'n that, surely."

"It ain't the wagons, friend, it's the *trees.* You got it in your mind wrong, Ben. Storms, deadfalls, stuff like that. Why, after a good storm you'd have five hundred firs lyin' across your road between here and the Yam Hill district. No, you'd have to cut yourself a road wide enough that falls wouldn't block her after every little wind. Now ain't that right, Ben? Admit I'm right, now."

"Yes, well—I guess, if it comes to that, I guess you're right, there."

"So," Vaughn continued, leaning forward slightly. "Them firs in the Coast Range, they run maybe a hundred and fifty feet, right?"

I looked at him, startled. "Vaughn—you ain't sayin' you'd have to build a road a hundred and fifty feet *wide?*"

"Oh, no. Oh, no."

I leaned back a little, relaxing. "Well, god, that's better. I mean, to make a road—"

He lunged forward, pinning me with his confident eyes. "*Three hundred feet*, Ben! *Three* hundred. Because, you see, them trees are liable to fall from *both* sides of the road."

He was clearly right, and I wondered why it had taken me so long to realize that a wagon road was a sort of figment in my head.

"No, Ben, you just get 'road' right out of your mind. There ain't *never* going to be a road going inland. This here's coast country, she's tied to the sea."

I was vaguely uneasy about it still, but Vaughn was such a sensible man and he'd thought it all out so carefully I felt like a fool to argue.

"Well," I said finally, "I guess it's a good thing you got connections."

"Connections? What connections?"

I looked at him, surprised again. I hoped he wasn't going to convince me there was no such thing as a ship. "Well, I heard you boys had connections with a big Boston sea-company."

Vaughn sighed, and pulled at his nose. "Yes, that's Means, Captain Means. But he ain't exactly a big company, Ben. He's got a couple of sloops up to Beverly, Maine. He comes out and sets up a cooperage on the beach once a year when the salmon start runnin' into the Bay. Buys fish from the Indians, stacks 'em in barrels, and then runs on home."

I frowned. "Take more'n a sloop to support a honest-to-god settlement."

"Hell, Ben," Vaughn said impatiently. "Nothing bigger'n a sloop can get acrost the bar out there." He pointed vaguely out across the Bay to the line of breakers thundering down on the bar. "Sometimes not even that," he added. "There's boats tried half a dozen times and couldn't make it. Means is the only one who's kept it up regular."

I mumbled something about having heard this was a perfect anchorage.

"They say, they say. God, Ben, you know people say anything. You know that, don't you? I mean, there's some people get a idea in their heads and then they don't pay no mind to how things really *are*."

That was right, when I thought about it, but it still started getting me depressed again. I thought I didn't want to hear any more about the way things really *were*; not if it was all so discouraging.

"Oh, we ain't got it so bad, after all," Vaughn said, taking pity on me. "Means is a good man, he breaks his neck to get in here, and I half suspect he's an honest man to boot, though he charges thirty dollars a ton for freight."

My expression must have been worthy of remark, as Vaughn started laughing again. "Oh, I ain't sayin' he's *cheap*."

"Thirty dollars a ton!"

"That's it. But we get good money, too, don't forget. Fifty cents a bushel for potatoes, forty cents a pound for butter, seventeen dollars a barrel for salmon. All we need is more cows and more people. Mostly cows. Then, Ben my boy, we're going to be rich, thirty dollars a ton or not."

"Long as Means keeps going."

"Long as Means keeps going. Right now he's keepin' us alive, and that's all there is to it. But like I said, he's dependable and he's honest. You got to pay, is all."

We talked a bit longer, and Vaughn said when I got ready to clear some on my claim, he and the boys would give me a hand.

"That'd be real kind of you," I said. "I'm short on tools, sort of."

"It'll go better. Got to help each other out a bit or we all go under."

He clapped me on the back when I left, and I felt pretty good again. Thirty dollars a ton freight . . . But hell, it was all on paper anyway, no real money ever changed hands because there wasn't any around. I don't suppose it'd matter if you wanted to call it thirty thousand, long as everything else was called thousands, too. One of my troubles is, I've never got out of the habit of thinking of money as being real. It isn't my most important trouble, but it's one of them, and I like to keep track.

2

There is an art to cutting down a tree. Unfortunately, it is an art none of us had. One can, of course, simply cut through the trunk, which is more or less the way I had it in my mind. In that case the tree will probably fall down. However, it may not be for another twenty years, if it should hang up in other trees, and it is virtually certain not to fall in any desirable direction. After a lifetime which it sometimes seems I devoted to cutting down trees, I am convinced that they were not meant to be cut down. God intended forests to stand eternally, and He so constructed them. Then He gave man a fixed image of cleared land as Good, just for the hell of it.

Near the exact center of the land I had chosen was a small rise, on which I decided to build my cabin. The top of this tiny mound was strangely clear of timber, and this undoubtedly had something to do with my choice. It was not much in the way of a clearing—certainly

too small for a cabin and garden. As though half a dozen trees had
been plucked out of the forest. Still, it was something slightly different,
a landmark of sorts, something that struck the eye. And as most major
decisions are made on no more than that, I don't know why I should
feel any need to justify my choice. I was still somewhat annoyed with
all those future generations of Thalers riding on my back, and figured
if they didn't like the spot they could damn well find land of their own.

Vaughn did come when the time arrived, bringing tools and help
and, above all, his knowledge of woodsmanship. Sam Howard came
with him, feeling responsible for me since he had seen me first, and
also a huge, blondish giant with a perpetual sheepish smile, whom I
had not yet met. The big man made me a little nervous at first. He said
nothing at all. And when he was not actively engaged in *doing* something
he had a disconcerting habit of putting his hands on top of his head
and staring vaguely up at the sky with his mouth half open, as though
waiting for something to fall. His elbows stuck out like great, angular
ears.

Looking upward from my minuscule clearing was intimidating. Even
above the tiny empty space the vast spreading limbs of surrounding
trees formed a twisted and tangled web that was almost solid. It is one
thing to see the forest as a mass, and quite another to consider it as
individual trees to be cut down one at a time. All around us was a
perfect infinity of darkly massed trunks stretching upward into the sky.
You could see no more than twenty feet into the wall; after that, it was
a solid substance several thousand miles thick. Rank after rank of deep
gloomy firs that extended unbroken to the edge of the bay, and in the
other direction to the edge of the world, as nearly as I could tell.

The vastness, the incredible complexity of number and density that
was the forest, was terrifying. It was like contemplating the number of
stars, or the grains of sand on the beach.

I think we all felt the same thing as we looked around us in silence,
the same awe, tinged with desperation. It was like a nightmare of
helplessness. There was a vast disproportion somewhere; the endless
packed ranks of the forest, silent and eternal, being faced by—us. Four
tiny men with three axes and a crosscut saw.

The mood deepened into a conviction that there was no question of doing this thing. When I was finally faced with it, I didn't think it was possible to begin, there was simply no place to start. And once started, it would never finish. You could go on and on cutting trees in this country, and raise your children and your grandchildren and your descendants to the twentieth generation to devote their lives to cutting trees and it would never end. To learn humility, a man must stand in the midst of the Oregon forest. I was caught in a kind of awful paralysis, brought on by the simple contemplation of this infinity and my relation to it.

It was Vaughn who finally broke the silence.

"Let's take this one," he said. "It's small."

I think, very frankly, that Vaughn was profiting from this magnificent opportunity to perfect his lumbering technique, or at least his theory of it. We worked hard, all of us, and by noon had felled half a dozen trees. Our control had not been up to the required standard. The fallen trunks were tangled in a hideous mess of intertwining branches, resembling nothing so much as a pile of jackstraws. Getting them disentangled and limbed and dragged to a safe place for burning was going to be—difficult. Still, they had been standing straight and eternal, and now they were lying on the ground, which was already saying much.

Vaughn had showed us how to notch the tree on the side we wished it to fall. This we did with the axes. Then we cut through from the other side with the big falling saw and, in theory, the tree tipped into the notch and fell directly on a line with it. As we worked at the notch, Vaughn would occasionally step up with his ax and thrust the head in crossways. The tree would fall, he told us, in the direction indicated by the handle. It was both an impressive and a reasonable demonstration, and we believed it.

In practice—I don't know exactly what went wrong. We were lucky to guess within 180 degrees where the damned thing was going to go. However, as none of them had actually fallen over backward, we still felt we were ahead of the game. It seems a little strange in retrospect, but in all this we never questioned Vaughn's skill; our own crude physical performance was simply not up to that level. Understand, Vaughn himself made no effort to shift the responsibility, or even to pretend to a competence he didn't have. He was as puzzled by it as we were. But it was clear to everyone that when something went wrong the fault was elsewhere. It simply never occurred to any of us that *he* might be doing something wrong. It was just a part of his personality, that no one ever doubted him.

In the early afternoon we reached a tricky problem. A fir that was visibly inclined in the wrong direction and, to boot, had a pronounced bend in the trunk. Also in the wrong direction. It was a sick tree, an abnormal tree, and it was a tree that intended to fall in its own way, which was directly across the clearing.

"Well, now," Vaughn said cheerfully. He held his ax up, dangling it head down from his thumb and forefinger and gauging vertical from this handy plumb. He knew more things to do with axes than anybody I ever met. He squinted with one eye along the haft and came to the conclusion we all had: that the thing had a hell of a lean to it. However, it was now official.

"This here's going to be a wee bit harder, boys," Vaughn said.

There were other trees bunched around it, of course, thick as hair on the back of a dog. The likelihood of it hanging up seemed excellent, particularly with that nasty bend in the trunk. If that happened we'd be left with the job of cutting the tree on which it had caught. The combination of forces in the two trees was such that they might fall anywhere at all; there was no predicting what would happen. In discussing the problem Vaughn said the professional loggers called that kind of situation a "widowmaker," which had a rather discouraging ring. The longer I looked at that tree the more ominous it seemed to me. It was jammed from butt to tip with murderous possibilities.

"I'm going to leave that one," I said. "I like it."

"Nonsense," said Vaughn. "You can't leave it."

"Yes, I can. I like it. I'm going to look at it out my window. It has a variety to it, it isn't straight like all the rest."

"That's a sick tree, Ben."

"I'll take care of it."

Vaughn changed his tactic. "Where you say you were going to put the cabin?"

I showed him again, the place in the clearing. "See how nice that'll be?" I said. "I can see it right out the window there, it'll give me something interesting to look at."

Vaughn considered the cabin site silently. Then he considered the sick tree, looking it up and down and pulling at his nose. Finally he turned away with a sad shake of the head, and put his hand on my shoulder. "Well, it's up to you, Ben. It's your tree. It's been nice knowin' you, fellow. I'm sorry it had to end this way."

That threw me off balance right there. "End? What end?"

"You're a dead man, Ben," Vaughn said with infinite melancholy. "Just a matter of time. Look there for yourself. She wants to fall right down on your cabin."

I think there was something wrong about Vaughn when it came to trees falling down, I think it weighed on his mind or something. "Now listen, Vaughn," I started, "we can just—"

He wasn't listening, he was speaking thoughtfully and low. "You get your cabin built, Ben. It's warm and comfy, right? And the sun shines in your window, and you lean on your elbows and look at that tree. You get used to it. There you are, a month, two months. Pretty soon you take that tree for granted out there. 'My funny old tree,' you think to yourself. Maybe you wonder a little about it from time to time, but you tell yourself you're just imagining things. Then one night there's a storm. You got your fire up good, and you're warm and snug and happy, thinking how comfortable you are when there's all that terrible weather howlin' around outside. You're just snuggling down into your blankets. You hear a little 'crack,' but you say to yourself it's just the wind. You put your head down again. You're just dropping off, sleepy, sleepy, and—BANG!"

He slammed his hands together, making us jump, and destiny thundered through the roof of my cabin, crushing it into splinters and pinning the lifeless bloody corpse of me to the floor. It was a horrible way to go.

"Course, it's up to you, Ben," Vaughn said sincerely. "I mean, it's your tree, after all."

So, in spite of the fact that I have always been more frightened of the present than the future, we cut it down.

Vaughn looked triumphant as he sighted along his arm. "We'll lay her right down that little alley there. You're going to have to be careful with your notch on this'n, boys."

"That ain't where she wants to go," the blond giant said. I had not realized until this moment he could talk. He worked well, but the rest of the time, when Vaughn was explaining something, he just stood around with his hands on his head looking up at the sky. Now he felt he had said too much, and he blushed with embarrassment.

"That's where the *skill* comes in," Vaughn said. "Listen, I got a plan."

By his plan, we tied a line high up on the tree, and ran it out in the direction we wanted it to fall. We pegged it down, and cut our perfect notch. When she began to weaken, somebody jumped up on the line, tipping the tree in the right direction for a starter. After that she'd go right on her own. It seemed wholly unreasonable to me, but Vaughn said he'd seen professionals do it like that in difficult cases.

"Wait a minute," I said. "Then the tree falls right on the guy that's doing the pulling."

"He runs," Vaughn said. "Soon as he sees her coming, he runs. He's got plenty of time to get clear."

"Who's going to do it?" Little Sam said, obviously worried about the lack of precision in the whole operation.

"We'll worry about that later, first we got to get the line up there."

There was a stony silence from the crew. You could hear the breakers over the hill.

"Well, come on," Vaughn said impatiently. "I'm too heavy for climbing, I'd be better for pulling on the rope. Or—Sam, would you rather do the rope-pulling part?"

Sam shook his head miserably. "No, but I don't—"

"*Hup* we go, then," Vaughn said cheerfully. "Good boy, Sam." He had, with typical foresight, brought a coil of rope.

We tied one end of the rope to Sam's belt in the back. Then the big blond man and I hoisted him up on our shoulders, giving him enough height to reach the first branch. His foot was about six inches lower on my side, but there was no help for it.

He was shaking noticeably, Sam was, either from the uneven support or some inner disturbance. Finally he got a good grip on the first branch and hunched himself up to it. He turned around.

"Don't turn *around*, Sam," Vaughn encouraged him. "Climb!"

Sam climbed. He climbed very well and speedily, in fact, dragging the rope behind him and looking like a monkey on a string.

"Don't go around branches!" Vaughn called. "You get her tangled up."

"Well, I *got* to go around *some* of them," Sam hollered down. By this time he was about thirty feet up. After a moment he added, "Vaughn, I don't think you know what you're doing." I guessed that thirty feet must be the range of Vaughn's personality, and Sam had passed out of the magic circle.

"Don't grab the plow and look back!" Vaughn said. "Push on!" Turning to me he added confidentially, "Sam's got no confidence, is his trouble."

Finally Sam called, "I ain't goin' no higher, you guys." He was well up now, fifty feet or better.

"Ten more feet, Sam!"

"No."

Vaughn sighed and shrugged. "All right, tie her off, then."

Sam straddled a branch and began to untie the rope from the back of his belt, leaning his forehead against the trunk. He was very small, so high up, and we couldn't see what he was doing clearly. At last he finished, gave the line a couple of good yanks and called, "That's it."

For the first time he looked down at us. He poised that way for a long moment, straddling the limb, and suddenly grabbed the trunk with both arms.

"Sam," I called, "what's the matter?"

"Nothin'."

"Well, come on down, then," Vaughn said.

Sam didn't answer for a minute, and his voice sounded strangled when it filtered down to us. "I can't."

"Are you scared, Sam?" I asked him.

"No."

"COME ON DOWN, SAM!" the blond giant hollered in an enormous voice.

"I can't."

"He's froze," Vaughn said. "That's what they call it, froze. It's a kind of fear a guy gets up high. He's froze up there, he can't move."

"Well, that's all fine, what they call it," I said. "But what the hell are we going to *do?*"

Vaughn shrugged. "Nothin' *to* do. Case like that, you just wait till he thaws, is all. Have a bit of a smoke."

We hollered up to Sam that we were going to have a smoke and wait for him to thaw. We lit up and sat with our backs against trees, thinking it over. Sam perched over our heads like a ripe plum, which I suppose was how he felt. Once in a while somebody would call up, "How you feelin', Sam?" and he always said "All right," but he never started down.

"How long can he stay up there?" I asked. "I mean, when a man's froze like that, how long does it take to get un-froze?"

"Well," Vaughn said hesitantly, "that depends. But listen, I got a plan. *I* figure, only way to bust a scare like that is with a worse one."

It made me a little uneasy. "That don't sound right to me."

"Well, what have we got to lose?" Vaughn said reasonably.

"Little Sam," said the blond giant, almost under his breath.

"Now listen, Joe," Vaughn said. "Just you don't worry about a thing. Trust me, I got a plan."

"Joe?" I said, startled. I had not caught the big man's name before. "Are you Joe Champion?"

He seemed embarrassed, but nodded.

"God, I been *wanting* to meet you," I said. "Say, listen, do you—" I broke off sharply. Lord, I'd almost blurted out did he hang by his knees in his tree and look around, the way I had it in my mind.

"Do I what?"

"Do you, ah, do you like it around here?"

"Ben," Vaughn said impatiently, "what's the matter with your *mind?* You got a mind like a grasshopper."

"Yeah," Champion said thoughtfully. "I like it pretty well, I guess."

"I like it pretty well, too," I told him.

"Listen, you boys, I got a plan, and I'm going to give her a try, all right?"

Without waiting for an answer he picked up an ax and went to stand under the tree looking up at Sam.

"Sam!" he hollered. "I'm sorry, but we can't wait any more." He hefted back the ax and took a good swing. The bit thunked into the tree, making it quiver.

"VAUGHN!" Sam screamed.

"What?"

"DON'T CHOP ME DOWN!"

Vaughn took another swing, very well placed, and a little triangular chip came popping out of the cut.

"VAUGHN, JESUS, DON'T DO IT ANY MORE!" Sam's voice had a funny note in it, like he was crying.

Vaughn leaned over and picked up the chip, sniffing it appreciatively. He threw it over to us. "Smell that, boys, that's pretty." He looked up in the tree again. "Sam!" he hollered. "You better come down."

"I'M COMING!"

Unfortunately he didn't start fast enough to suit Vaughn, who swung the ax again determinedly.

"DON'T DO IT, I'M COMING! DON'T CHOP ME ANY MORE!"

And by God, Sam started down. We almost held our breath for him all the way. Vaughn walked back to Joe and myself and sat down, plunging the ax in the dirt. We were a little in awe, but Vaughn seemed to take it for granted that his plan would work; he was neither surprised nor particularly elated. He sighed contentedly and wriggled against a tree, scratching his back.

When Sam reached the ground he was pale and shaking. "Vaughn," he said, "Vaughn, you shouldn't of done that. God, you scared me so bad."

"Sam," Vaughn said patiently, "it was for your own good, now. You come down, didn't you? There's no telling how long you'd of been up there without that. I mean, maybe all night, even, you wouldn't want that. Cold, the rain comin' down. Gettin' hungry, holdin' on for dear life, just tryin' to keep your eyes open. Gettin' sleepier and sleepier, what with being so hungry and tired like that. And along about the middle of the night, you'd start drowsin' off. Just a little, maybe, you start drowsin' off and then—BANG!"

We jumped, Sam toppled off his branch and crashed down through the thick tangle of limbs, crushing his head on one, breaking an arm on another, until by the time he thumped into the ground with that terrible dull sound there was no more than a feeble spark of life to be extinguished. In the night small animals came to sniff the crumpled corpse.

You really had to hand it to Vaughn, the way he told you about things.

We cut the notch with special care, and when Vaughn's ax-trick showed it was going to fall in the right direction we ran the rope out and tied it to another tree just out of the line of fall.

I was not terribly surprised to find myself scheduled as line puller: Vaughn had, after all, only said he would be *better* at that than climbing. He hadn't actually said he'd *do* it. He and Joe Champion began hauling away at the big crosscut saw, gradually chewing their way into the opposite side.

"Now, wait a minute," I said. "Where'm I going to run?"

"Into the clearing, of course. You'll have lots of time. When she starts to come, you go, that's all. Ten yards and you're clear."

"Well, I'm going to practice once," I said.

"Go ahead and practice," Vaughn said, grunting over the saw.

"Well, dammit, let up on that *saw!* I don't want the thing falling on my head when I'm just *practicing.*"

Vaughn shrugged, but he was already a little tired, so they all gathered around and watched me practice. I stood under the line and made believe I saw the tree start coming. I took off toward the clearing, and when I reached the edge I dove as far as I could, crumpling up into a little inconspicuous, unhittable ball.

"That's good," Vaughn said. "That's very good. You got to get out of the way of the branches."

I picked my route carefully, removing small branches I might trip on, and whacking out the more troublesome clumps of brush with an ax. By the time I had practiced three or four times my belly was sort of scraped, but I felt safer. When I was really confident I could get out of there fast enough, they started again on the saw work.

"Jump up on that line a bit, Ben," Vaughn said.

I jumped up, letting my weight dangle from the taut rope. The tree didn't budge. This happened a couple more times, until I finally decided he was just getting me to do it when he wanted a little rest.

At last, when nobody expected it, there was a little cracking sound and the top of the tree wobbled.

"All right, boys," Vaughn said. "You get back in the clearing and watch. This might be dangerous here, cutting. Ben, where the hell you going? This is your tree."

I came back.

"Get up on that line, now."

"It ain't ready yet."

"Less'n you hold 'er the saw jams up."

I sighed and jumped up to dangle from the line like a hunk of drying meat. Vaughn went to work with a will. The saw scraped back and forth raspingly. I couldn't stop the tree from wobbling. The line on which I hung tightened and loosened as the trunk swayed, clamping down on the saw blade from time to time. It finally got a rhythm, and Vaughn could RASP RASP RASP before the cut closed down on the blade. It went that way for a while. *RASP RASP RASP* pause *RASP RASP RASP* pause. Champion and Little Sam were standing in the middle of the clearing, watching. Champion had his hands on top of his head, but he was watching the sawing instead of the sky, which was a sort of tribute.

"Listen," I hollered. "You guys get the hell out of my way, now. When I come I'm going to be movin' like a—"

CRACK!

Ponderously the treetop leaned. With a lovely smooth motion the rope slackened, lowering me to the ground as gently as a cloud.

"PULL!" Vaughn hollered.

I pulled with all my strength.

"Here she comes! Run, Ben, run!"

I waited, watching the top. It was clearly coming now, gathering speed. And just as clearly moving in the wrong direction. The tip swung in a wide circle, and the rope picked up from the ground and tightened again. With huge majesty the trunk headed straight for the clearing, where it had intended to fall from the very beginnings of time. I caught just a glimpse of the two bystanders, their mouths dropping open with astonishment and fear. Joe still had his hands on his head.

I started to run in the opposite direction, straight into the mass of brush toward the interior of the forest. I plowed into it like a cannonball, trying to get out of range of the branches. Finally I plunged face first into a big manzanita that sprang back like a mattress and stopped me flat. I prayed fast, and turned to see if I was dead.

The enormous trunk hesitated briefly as it reached the restraining limit of the rope. The line snapped like a thread. Vaughn had been watching the frantic scramble of the others as they thundered out of the clearing, rushing open-armed into the impenetrable brush. They penetrated it with amazing ease, just like diving into a lake.

For some reason this struck our lumberman so funny he started to laugh, and he was doubled over with glee when the trunk hit, shaking the clearing with the sound of thunder and earthquake. As the peak hit, the strains in the twisted trunk were discharged like an explosion. The trunk splintered like a gunshot and the base leaped off the stump as though it had been catapulted six feet in the air. The butt end swung over Vaughn's back and crushed into the earth on the other side of him, not a foot from his body.

He straightened up suddenly, all the glee gone and the color fading from his face, leaving it gray. He looked at the trunk on one side of him, the stump on the other, and then at the air over his head where a good ton of hurtling wood had passed a second before.

He blinked once, then sat on the stump, resting his back against the huge splinter of wood that remained standing vertically in the center. He pulled out his handkerchief and began to wipe his forehead. The rest of us emerged from our diverse prickly hideaways and ran over to him.

"It didn't hit you? You all right, Vaughn?"

He breathed heavily and he didn't answer, but he wasn't bleeding or anything. He wiped and wiped and wiped at his forehead with the handkerchief, as though there were a big indelible stain there. Gradually the color came back into his face, and his voice returned to him.

"By god," he said. "You boys were a sight, now. Just like a bunch of quail takin' to the brush. Never saw anything like it."

"Jesus, you almost killed us *all*, Vaughn. You damn near got every loving one of us."

"How come you run the wrong way, Ben?" he asked curiously. "You was supposed to run into the clearing."

"If I'd run there, I'd be *dead!*"

"Yeah, I know, but I just wondered. Because you was supposed to run there, the way the plan was."

He sighed deeply again and got up off the stump, taking long breaths. We were all sort of agitated, but Vaughn recovered first. He picked up the ax and wandered along the length of the fallen, split tree, poking casually at it with the ax blade from time to time. When he got out into the middle of the clearing he looked back around at the space where the tree had been.

"Well, hell," he said, looking at the ground again. "I expect this is as good a place to burn them logs as any."

He slung the ax one-handed at the trunk, burying the bit in the shattered wood with a lusty thunk.

"Boys," he said confidentially. "I don't mind telling you this is the toughest tree I *ever* cut down. It is, now. It was a real challenge to me."

Chapter Three

The cabin that was built that summer was the first home I had, the first thing I ever owned that I couldn't carry on my back. Sam Howard built it for me. After the remembrance of his own, I was at first reluctant, and I think I'd have refused if I had known how to do it. But I didn't know how, and when I saw what Little Sam could do with wood and tools I thanked God I didn't.

I never learned why his own cabin was in such utter contradiction to his skill and character. It must have been a perpetual agony for him to live in it, to live in the midst of one huge imperfection. Perhaps it was deliberate, I don't know. Some kind of terrible punishment he thought he deserved for being imperfect himself. When he built for me, everything was different. He made wood live; with his hands and a saw he gave life to what had been merely a hunk of tree lying on the ground. There was an uncanny feeling about Sam's work I have never been able to define. He understood about building as some men understand about women.

When my cabin was finished, it almost seemed a shame to inhabit it. It was a single room about ten feet by twelve, with a little window in the south wall opposite the fireplace. Reading that, I see it means nothing, it is merely a fact. I suppose the truth of the cabin is something that exists only in my own belly. Sometimes I used to sit outside when the sun bobbed down under the sea like a fishing float and watch the sky color shift into reds and golds that spilled down the walls of my home like flames. I felt so full inside, so soaked in the beauty of my cabin and my ownership that I didn't know what to do. I wanted to do more than just look at it, I wanted to eat it or something.

For the first time in my life I understood what it felt like to be rooted to one place, to be stable, and it was a strange feeling. The next year, or maybe the year after, I planned to replace the greased paper at the window with real glass. I probably spent hours debating it all in my mind, worrying that real glass might change it, might spoil the present perfection, for I could not understand on what that perfection was based. Having something you love is a dangerous thing, because change becomes your enemy. Loving something, a man is the natural prey of fear.

The summer of '52 was more like an explosion than a season. The dead and sullen skies gave way to the sun, as though God this year had decided to get along without any spring at all. The sun of June was like a razor, stripping off the crust of wet and dark we had lived with for endless months. Day after day it rolled up behind the Coast Range peaks, flooding them with fire, then pouring down across the half-moon bay like a tidal wave of heat and energy. The days were long and light, but went more quickly. There were suddenly ten thousand things a man wanted to do, and not enough time to begin any of them.

I think it must be a thing that happens only in a country like Oregon, where the winter crushes you into the ground and makes you something only half alive. The rush of summer makes you ten feet tall, and you can stand in the morning and feel the strength roll up out of your belly, drawn by the power of the sun. The ferns of the river-bottom land rustled in the soft breezes that came sliding off the bay and whispered *success success* to anyone who had the ears to hear. I was twenty-three years of age, I had my first home, and I was stepping across the threshold of a brand-new life, so big I could hardly believe it. There are not many moments like that in the life of a man.

I worked, I cleared, I planted seed potatoes, I plotted great things in the dusky sanctuary of my own cabin. It seemed unimportant that no man on the Bay had tasted bread or real coffee since January, that shoes were wearing out, that when a saw blade jammed and broke it was a catastrophe for all of us. There was a joy and a power in the air that made all these things seem minor.

In the fall of that first year I met our lifeline to the Outside, Captain Means. Means was a tall and genial Yankee, trying to pass the time between cradle and grave as pleasantly as possible, by his own statement. He had no grand ambitions of becoming rich on the backs of us settlers, in spite of the thirty dollars a ton freight charge he made. When I thought of some of his stories of doubling Cape Horn, thirty dollars seemed little enough. It was just the way it was; everything was expensive these days. The time was gone when a man went into a new country without money, without contacts, without anything. The world had changed, and in the middle of the Nineteenth Century after Our Lord contact with the civilized world was the most important thing there was.

Means brought in his freight every fall, and it was not enough, it was never enough. Others than myself had been caught up in the magic of the Bay, and settlers gradually came in from Outside to look it over. They always came in the summer, and of course there was not enough provision for the newcomers in the goods that had been ordered a full year before. We were short of everything. Our supplies were always a year behind our population. People drifted in, and by the middle of the winter the necessaries began giving out. Flour, coffee, sugar, clothing—one by one every item went in short supply and then became nonexistent. We faced every spring the same way, hopelessly behind and as primitive as the year before. And so there were many who drifted right on out again. Some stuck, and I was one of them.

Means did his best. He often brought more goods than had been ordered, but he was never able to predict how much would be needed. And there was a limit, certainly, to the degree he could personally finance the settlement of the Bay. Those who came in never had any cash money, no more than I had myself when I came. If they'd had money they'd have stayed home and spent it. Means knew it, but he did what he could, and there was no question in anyone's mind that our lives were dependent on the lone New Englander.

In point of importance, Means' trade was more with the Indians than with us. It was natural—they had a great deal more to offer, and the rate of exchange was better. He paid one pint of whisky for ten salmon, and the whisky was diluted by half with water. This was a harmonious combination of good will and good business on the part of the Captain. As he said, strong liquor was notoriously damaging to the Indians, and humanitarianism dictated moderation. Then too, water was cheaper than whisky and bought just as many fish. It was very practical and well thought out, and benefited all.

The winter of '52-'53 passed. I will say little about it. It was an Oregon winter. The summer of '53 was bad. There was a heavy frost on the third day of July, which made our celebration of the Glorious Fourth almost dismal, if such a thing was possible. But more worrying than dancing was done. All of us were thinking about our potatoes, and wondering if they would survive. There were two more frosts in the course of that vicious summer, and while the potatoes survived, they were extremely small. This was depressing, but as we had word that the rest of Oregon was even worse off we felt the Bay was good enough for us.

There was the faintest suggestion of a cloud on my own well-being, but I wasn't certain if I really resented it or not. The plain fact was that after two years I had still not been able to satisfy my curiosity about Joe Champion, the man who lived in a tree. My terrible craving to see this thing with my own eyes remained as strong as ever, but I was blocked at every turn. I became very sensitive and determined on the subject.

At first I had assumed it would all come about very naturally. But it never did, in spite of opportunities I skillfully created. For some reason I was quite ashamed of my enormous curiosity and didn't want anybody to know about it. They all seemed to take it for granted that Joe lived in a tree and I didn't want to appear any less worldly than Vaughn, say, who apparently never gave it a thought. I myself thought about it a lot. Again and again I went over the image in my mind, the image of him hanging upside down from his limb and looking around, until it was clearer to me than most of the things I had *really* seen in my life.

But from all appearances, Joe didn't receive in his tree, and a man certainly couldn't say "I want to see you up your tree, Joe." At least I couldn't. The practical aspects of life in a tree tormented me; *how* did a man live when he lived in a tree? Didn't he ever get dizzy? Didn't he ever fall? Did he feel a companionship with the birds?

The closest I ever got was by means of a sly question I had invented over long and brooding evenings. It was a question which would lead into conversation and explanation quite naturally, without my showing undue interest in how Joe lived. Very casually once, I asked him if he had a ladder, as though I wanted to borrow it or something. He said, "No."

No. That was all. He didn't have a ladder. He must shinny up the damned thing every night of his life. What if he was tired? What if he was drunk? I didn't know. Maybe I would **never** know. It preyed on my mind.

On the other hand, there is no denying that over the months Joe's tree became a cherished sort of thing for me. It gave me something to look forward to, for one thing. And above all—I suppose it will sound foolish, but it's true—it gave me a sense of mysterious purpose. I had the almost perpetual feeling that I was right on the edge of a discovery of enormous importance. The day I actually saw Joe up in his tree would be a day of huge significance. It would probably change the course of my life entirely, because I felt sure that I would *understand* things about the world I had not understood before. To touch this way of living, to cross the frontier of mysterious worlds, to be initiated into the secrets of the man who lived in a tree. No human being could remain unchanged by an experience like that. It was something I felt compelled to understand, to comprehend, and I knew that I would understand my own life the better because of it. If I could see it. If I could only **see** it. For better or worse, Joe's tree had become inextricably woven into my own sense of the meaning of the world. My life was unquestionably richer for it.

And I suppose this sense of hidden worlds to be unveiled became more precious to me as our lives became—not more comfortable, perhaps, but more conventional, more civilized. By the winter of '53-'54 there was an actual mail service from Astoria, and we felt less isolated, less cut off from the Outside. It was not official, of course, but it was just as good as if the government had organized it. Once a month an Indian boy would go off up the beach to the post office at Astoria, a round trip of about a hundred and forty miles. For this journey he charged only five dollars, which was certainly worth the price. News from Outside was more precious than gold. As the Indians held writing in a kind of superstitious awe there was never any difficulty with our postman. They were all greatly impressed with the "talking-paper," as they called it. We assured our messenger that if he got drunk or did anything wrong, the "talking-paper" would surely tell us, and this was sufficient to prevent any mishaps.

I myself never received any mail, as I had no one to write me. But I was in some obscure way as happy as the rest when the mail arrived; it was a kind of monthly holiday. For several days *everyone* was happy. I suppose it was simply the assurance that the Outside still existed. Living in the Bay, it was easy to doubt.

I was thus astonished when Vaughn came knocking at my door just after the April mail in '54. He was clutching a letter in his hand and looking as miserable as I have ever seen a man look. Nobody should look that way just after the mail has come, it wasn't normal.

"Vaughn, what's the—you look sick."

He pushed past me and sat at the table in the center of my little room. It was the first time I had ever seen him speechless. He stared at the fire and fingered his letter. Several times he started to say something, and couldn't get the words out. Finally he slid the letter along the table and returned his attention to the fire. "Read it, Ben," he told me. "Just read it, is all."

I picked it up and unfolded the sheet. On the outside it was addressed to MR. WARREN VAUGHN TILLAMOOK COUNTRY OREGON Hold at Astoria. The writing was beautiful and regular, written out by a real professional.

At first I couldn't understand why Vaughn was so upset. It was just a dunning letter, asking for rapid settlement of some debts. There were always half a dozen of them in every mail. There was nothing to do with them but bleach out the paper so we could use it for our own letters. This one wasn't even very nasty, as some such were. They were in considerable haste, they said, to "settle the estate." It was not until the very end that I realized what "estate" they were talking about— and what it meant to us.

Captain Means was dead.

2

Two nights later we got together at Vaughn's place, ten or fifteen of us. You would have thought we came for a burying, which was not too far from the truth.

In the two days I had had to think about it, it seemed inevitable that a burying there would be, the interment of the Bay and everything it meant. It changed things for me. Until then the potato coffee and the bark linings of my shoes, the lack of bread and flour and sugar half the year—it had all been a damned nuisance, but tolerable. Tolerable because it was temporary, tolerable as a price to pay for the life I was building myself at the Bay. But now—it was wasted. If the Bay collapsed as a settlement, the inconveniences of the last two years were suddenly unbearable. I had wasted twenty-four months of my life, thrown it away. At times like that a man tends to forget the joys. Joy is a present thing; it changes a man and then is gone. But the hardships were for the sake of the future, they were an investment suddenly stolen from us.

Vaughn's cabin had two rooms, which was why it was selected for the meeting. A mute line of men sat around the walls of the main room with the firelight flickering at their eyes and casting deep shadows at their cheeks. I think every man there was counting the cups of parched-potato coffee he had drunk in order to build something out of this Bay. For my own part, I had never had any sense of Having A Mission to make a community here—not until the dream suddenly collapsed and slipped out through my fingers as Means' life had slipped away from him so many thousands of miles away. Beverly, Maine. Where the hell was Beverly, Maine? Why should something that happened there mean the end of everything here?

The men in the cabin were those who had stuck. Through the rain and depression of the winters, the disastrous summer of '53, stuck through everything that had been thrown at them. They could not give up the Bay now, for in doing so they would admit they had been fools to stay as long as they had.

"Well, boys," Vaughn said. "What do we do now?" He was slumped at the table in the center, his hands in his pockets and his legs outstretched.

Eb Thomas cleared his throat. "Seems like the question is, where do we *go*, now."

"Hell, we can make it," I said. "What do we need Means for? We can pack stuff down from Astoria, we can make it somehow."

"Next time you go, Ben, bring me a hundred pounds of flour, two hundred of sugar and a cast-iron stove. If you got room in your pack."

"Eb's got horses."

"How many horses you figure it takes to make a shipload?"

The rest of the men looked hopefully at me while I was talking, then away.

"There's other captains than Means," somebody said.

"Yeah, but I'm damn scared they're all smarter than him, too," Vaughn said. "You know there's not one in a thousand'll risk his vessel on our bar. There's enough business on the Columbia that no man has to risk himself to take off *our* little bit of stuff. We hit it lucky with Means. Now we hit it unlucky, is all."

"Luck, hell," one of the men muttered. "This here Bay's cursed, nothin' *works* right. There ain't no way in, there ain't no way out. It's a goddam prison is what it is, a damn green prison."

"Get the hell out, then," another man snapped. "You don't want to ante up, get out of the game."

"All right, all right," Vaughn said. "*That* ain't doin' no good."

"He don't have to—"

"All right, all right."

In my mind there was no way to avoid seeing that the first man was right in a way. You could look at the Bay as a prison. But in my belly I was with the second; prison it might be, but it was *ours*, and all we had. Whatever the reality might be, we had our image and it was the image that made us jump.

"If we had a ship of our own—"

"We wouldn't of been payin' thirty dollars a ton to Means in the first place," Vaughn finished for him. "We *ain't* got one. Less'n one of you boys got eight or ten thousand dollars stacked away home."

"Jesus god, would a ship cost *that* much?"

"Tell you the truth," Vaughn admitted, "I don't know. But it'd cost what we ain't got, money. The figures don't make no mind."

"Hell," I said, trying to cheer things up a little. "I know where there's one we could have for free."

"Where's that?"

"Up the other side of Neahkahnie Mountain. Name of the *Shark*. She needs a little work, though."

It was good enough for a grin, at least. The *Shark* was a British man o' war that had run aground about ten years before up on the Columbia bar. She broke up and a part of her drifted clear down around

Neahkahnie. The people from Clatsop Plains had made off with the copper bolts that were left and burned the wood. There was still a lot of iron up there and the image of this rusty junk as the solution to our problems was absurd enough to cut some of the mean and evil feeling in the air.

"If *that's* what you want," Vaughn said, "there's a whole half a ship lyin' down at Netarts Bay, and *she* only busted up in '51."

"Can't call that seaworthy," I said.

"No," Vaughn admitted. "Right now she ain't much more'n pieces of rust tied together with imagination."

"Just stick a little wood in there between the rust and you'd never know the difference," I said negligently. "Not much."

"Wood we got," someone else said bitterly. "I damn near broke my back clearin' today. Listen, Ben, you couldn't give me a hand one of—"

He broke off, because Vaughn had suddenly lurched up from the table and was staring ahead of him as if he'd seen a dead man come to life. We all followed his eyes, but there was nothing to see but the wall.

"Listen," he said. "Listen, we'll do it."

"Do what, what the hell are you—"

"We'll build a ship. We'll build our own goddam ship!" He wheeled around, excited. "Listen, you said it. There's fittings lyin' around on the goddam *beach!* There's ships been breakin' up on this coast for a couple hundred years and half of 'em drift down here to get buried. Wood we got, you said that, you said it all, we got everything we need, we'll build our *own* damn ship!"

He was so excited he hopped. The rest of us were simply stunned. We'd been horseplaying, was all, to take our minds off the misery of having to leave the Bay. Now the joke had turned into something else, suddenly, and we didn't know what to make of it.

"Everything we got, except brains. What the hell do *I* know about building boats? I plow, is what *I* do."

"Sam!" Vaughn hollered, still hopping. "*Sam Sam Sam!* He knows all about it, it's his trade, he knows it all. We'll do it, we'll do it!"

I began to get excited, too. When Vaughn started jumping, everybody started jumping, it was his personality that did it. You could see it on their faces, you could see the idea igniting around the room like a chain of powder. The sullen-faced farmers looked at each other in astonishment and tried to figure it all out. We all started jabbering at once, and out of the boiling there came the question that really counted.

"But will Sam *do* it?"

"He'll do it," Vaughn said confidently. "He's no deserter, not Sam."

"Deserter, deserter? Hell, Vaughn, I can't follow you nine-tenths of the time. This ain't the *army* or nothing."

"By *god* it is!" Vaughn said, standing very straight at the table. "I hereby declare WAR!" He slammed his fist down on the table, WHAM, and it shook on its legs and we were almost deafened.

"Well, that's all fine, but war on *who?*"

"EVERYBODY! The whole damn *world!* They tried to stamp us down, they tried to run us out of the Bay, and I declare WAR on everybody but us!"

"Hooraw!" somebody hollered. "War on everybody!"

And that was how it was. It may even have been the most absurd war ever declared, which would be saying a good deal. A couple of dozen farmers isolated on the Oregon coast, declaring war. I think we were sensible men when we dragged into Vaughn's cabin that night. We knew we were beaten, we were accepting the inevitable, and we were reluctantly ready to give up to it. But we were no longer sensible when we roared out into the night, howling our defiance at the moon. We had gone mad, declaring war on the whole damned world and its stupid indifference.

It was the first time I realized the importance of madness in this world of surrenders; for there are times when only the madmen continue to fight.

3

I drew the job of asking Sam, as I got along better with him than anyone else in the Bay. Trouble was, I got along better simply because I *never* asked him anything—it was a silent agreement I had made with him.

Sam's cabin looked just the same as the first time I had seen it; about to fall down. I think more theoretical money had changed hands over that cabin than any other single item, including food. There was a running wager about the exact date of its collapse, and as no man was fool enough to bet over two months in advance, this wager was constantly being renewed. I myself owed over a thousand dollars on it, a debt contracted before I became crafty enough to realize that the law of gravity was just another sleight-of-hand trick by God.

Month after month, bet after bet, Sam's cabin continued to stand, taking the shock of the winter storms that roared across the bay, storms that sometimes lashed spray as high as the door itself. It shook, shuddered, wobbled, creaked—and stood, enduring. Perhaps men build houses in their own image; Sam, too, never seemed likely to last out the next heavy wind, but there was some mysterious rigid core in them both that fended off all natural disaster. I once heard that man gets not what he deserves, but what he resembles. Perhaps that is the answer.

When Sam let me in I felt as though I were forcing a door with false credentials. He always let me in, and I was the only man at the Bay who could say as much.

"Well, Sam," I said.

As was his habit, he had scurried back away from the door after opening, and now sat before the fireplace with his hands clasped. I sighed. It was a bad day to be talking to Sam, he was very shy. It came and went in spasms. I sat beside him on the bench, involuntarily clasping my hands in imitation of his.

"Well, Sam," I said again, cheerful. "Thought I'd like to talk to you a bit." I watched him out of the corner of my eyes, but he didn't seem to take offense. However, neither did he answer.

I cleared my throat. "You know, Sam, you know Means is dead."

He winced, and I knew I had made a bad beginning. I wanted to say that nobody blamed him for Means' lung fever, but it was so absurd I couldn't. Finally I just blundered ahead, on the theory I couldn't do any more harm than I already had.

"That leaves us in a pretty bad spot here, Sam. I guess you know."

"Yus." He wrung his fingers together, like twisting a cloth.

"We were talking, some of us, and I—we thought if we had a boat of our own—I mean, you can see that would solve the problem right there."

He said nothing.

"What do you think about it, Sam? You think that's a good idea?"

He thought about it a long time, trying to work out what he had done wrong. "I suppose," he said worriedly.

"We thought we might build one."

"Pretty hard thing to build a boat, Ben. Build it right, you know."

"That's kind of what I was leading up to, Sam. We don't know much about it. I mean, hell, you know us. Vaughn and me and Thomas and the rest." I laughed a little to put him at his ease.

"Got to have stuff to build a boat," he said reflectively. "I mean— there's stuff you got to have for a thing like that."

"We figure as how we could get the stuff, pretty much." I told him how it had come up, with my joking about the old *Shark*, and then about the grounded vessel at Netarts Bay.

He looked up at me in sudden surprise. "Ben," he said. "Ben, you ain't talking about a boat, you're talking about a real *ship.*"

"Well, there you are, Sam, that's our whole trouble. Hell, we're so dumb we don't even know what to call it."

He unclasped one hand and scratched the side of his nose, staring into the fire.

"I'll put it to you square, Sam. I'm not talking very good today. The way it looks, we either get a ship or leave the Bay. Since we got no money, that means we got to do it our own selves."

When I put it that way, so briefly, I was astonished at our ignorance. A handful of farmers who didn't know a ship from a boat, jumping with both feet into an art that had been perfecting itself for two thousand years or better. It was so utterly mad I could hardly believe my own voice.

"But we can't do it without you, Sam. That's the whole story right there, we can't do it without you. You can see that."

He bobbed his head briefly.

"You ever think about building again, Sam?"

After a moment's terrifying indecision Sam got up from the bench and went to the back corner of the cabin. There was a kind of cabinet there, a cabinet with real doors. It looked as solid as a mountain, and I had occasionally played with the notion that it held the house up. I had never seen inside.

Sam took a tiny brass key from his pocket. He glanced once at me, hesitated, then unlocked the big doors and swung them open. I almost fell off the bench.

There were six shelves inside, and each was lined with a row of small, perfect sailing vessels. The firelight rippled golden along the polished hulls, striking sharp lights from tiny brass fittings. In the darkness of the corner there was an incredible mystery about these swimming reflections almost lost in obscurity. A drawing in fire of a beauty so perfect your eyes would not hold it all. Each was a tiny, wooden— perfection, was the only word. In the rickety cabin the models were as out of place as diamonds in a pig wallow.

Tenderly little Sam lifted one down from the top shelf and brought it over to me, cradling it between his two hands like a small and precious living creature. He gave it to me, then turned abruptly and walked to the door. He stood on the threshold, looking out across the broad flat of the bay to the entrance bar where the breakers rumbled and scattered white spume.

When I had it in my hands I felt as though the breath had been knocked out of me. I was suddenly dropped into a different world, and had my first tugging awareness of the beauty men found in ships; the sweep of cutwater and bowsprit, the tall dignity of the masts webbed in cordage, the rich, pregnant curve of hull. I had never really seen a ship before. The large floating shapes with sails were not part of my life, did not move me. But the model, held in my hand, made it somehow possible for me to comprehend.

I could scarcely believe it had been made by a human being. My own hands felt clumsy and grotesque in comparison. I looked at the precision of the tiny fittings, the thread lines like spider webs that flew taut from the spars and running gear, crossing and re-crossing, complex as the patterns of a rip tide. The hull was made of individual planks, fastened with what seemed to be thousands of tiny nails that must have been smaller than a needle point. Ahead of the wheel there was a kind of little pulpit, with a compass. Lying on this housing was a sextant, less than half the size of my fingernail. As I turned it in the light I saw a tiny glinting reflection. In this instrument I could probably not even pick up in my gross fingers, Sam had put a glass eyepiece.

Little Sam came back from the door. "That's what you call a schooner," he said softly.

I gave him the model, and watched awestruck as the little man carefully placed it back in its shelf cradle and relocked the cabinet doors. He came back and sat down again to stare into the fire.

"Well, Sam," I said hesitantly. "That's—that's pretty fine work."

"Got lots of spare time," Sam said. "Like ships, I do."

"I—yes, I guess I can see that, all right." There were no words.

"You take a schooner now," Sam said reflectively. "Schooner ain't too hard to handle. Small schooner, a man could learn to handle easier than some. Man that didn't know nothin' to start with."

"Well, that's us, I guess." I still felt as though I had been kicked in the belly by a mule. After actually holding the model in my hands I was more miserably aware than ever of how perfectly that described us: "men that didn't know nothin'."

"Look, Sam. I'll tell you honest. We got no skill. But we'll *work* for you. We'll work hard. We'll do what we have to do."

Sam stretched his neck, birdlike. He surveyed the ceiling, seeming to count the cracks.

"We'll *work*," I said again. It was all I *could* say, all I could offer.

Sam bit his lip and jerked his head once, looking into the fire with an expression of pain. "Hard," he muttered. "Too hard, you got to *know*."

"You're the brains, Sam, and we're the hands. We'll work for you like your own hands. Sam, listen, we got guts, we'll work like you never seen human men ever work. We need it so bad, Sam. Is that enough?"

He shook his head. "No."

For the first time in my life I got angry at Sam. "You're wrong," I told him flatly. "It's enough."

He was startled by my tone and looked up, scared.

"Sam, I'm sorry. But it's *got* to be enough. It's all we got."

He looked back down at the fire.

I got up, feeling miserable. I tried to think of what Vaughn would say, tried to think of something as convincing as Vaughn always was, and I couldn't. I wasn't made that way. I went to the door, thinking I had thrown away our only chance just because I couldn't talk right. It didn't seem fair. It was too important to be spoiled for a thing like that.

"I wish—I wish you'd think it over anyway, Sam. It means a lot to us. It means everything."

He reached forward and got the poker, stirring up the coals.

"Ben," he said. "You're crazy. It's impossible."

"All right. We're crazy. Maybe when you want the impossible it's better to be crazy."

He sighed long. He stood the poker carefully back against the fireplace wall and finally turned to me.

"We'll build it," he said.

Chapter Four

At first it was like the beginning of a love affair. We tended to go around grinning foolishly at each other and running out of words at critical moments, because we shared a secret that nobody else could touch. We were going to build a Ship.

Vaughn's maniac declaration of war on the world Outside had something to do with it, too. We took a fierce and vengeful pleasure in our secret strength. For the first time I understood some things about the Revolution; things the history books left out. One fact that never gets written down is the feeling a man suddenly gets in his belly that he can *change* the way things are. With the strength of his back and arms and brain he can make things different, and he doesn't have to put up with it any more, whatever "it" may be. He knows he can fight, and he secretly knows he will survive anything. There is no other feeling like that known to humankind.

I think the key to it is the vast conviction that you can push past all normal limits, and still survive. Man is by nature a victim. A victim of the weather, the terrain, other men. But when he knows he can survive anything—he rebels, and is no longer a victim. He feels the power of his own surviving in his belly and it makes him wake up in the middle of the night and turn under his blankets with a secret smile. For the first time he realizes there is more to living than merely submitting.

So the building of the Ship began as love and hate at once. A man who has had that double charge explode in his belly no longer has room for anything else. He can think of nothing but the image and center of the storm that boils in him, and in our case that storm center was the Ship. She swept everything else out of existence. From the moment we understood the idea, the Ship was more real to us than the rocks of the coast, more real than the waves that rolled in from a thousand miles to destroy themselves against the unmoving continent. She was more real than hunger or cold, food or warmth or any of the trivial things that happen to a man's carcass in the course of a day. And all this occurred before we had even begun work, before we had thrown our bodies into this thing that resembled at once an act of love and an act of war.

Work we had. None of us could have guessed how *much* there would be; none of us, except possibly Little Sam, had any idea of how complicated it was, how terribly hard it would be, how insane we were even to try. And by the time we learned, it was far too late. The image of the Ship had us by the throat and shook and shook and drove us beyond ourselves and there was nothing to do but see it through or die. The world turned simple for us; build it or die.

It was almost the middle of May before we could begin even the preparations. The day after I talked to Sam it started raining. It continued then for nearly two weeks, a good Oregon spring rain that made it difficult for a man to tell if he were still on the beach or had wandered off into the ocean. It set our nerves on edge, and we accumulated enough tension of waiting to give the first day of actual work a half-hysterical tone. Vaughn was the only one who didn't mind. He said if the rain continued we could sail straight into the Willamette Valley over the mountains, which would be a saving of time in the end.

My first job was as packer, working with Eb Thomas. Eb had a claim back toward the foothills and four horses, which we were to use to bring the hardware down from the wrecked *Shark*. In the two rainy weeks that preceded the trip, Eb and I spent a good many hours arguing about the route. Both of us being firm of mind, we came near to not going at all. By the time it was possible to set out we were well on the way to being life-long enemies. My personal conviction, which changed very little with time, was that Eb Thomas was a butt-headed fool that couldn't find his ass with both hands.

Once on the trail much of our disagreement smoothed out, as it happened that both of us had been totally wrong about the country we had to cross.

It was a full two days' march up to the wreck, and we got there in the late afternoon. I had never seen the *Shark* before, just heard of it, and I was surprised. I had in my mind the picture of half a ship, lying tilted over on the shore, and it wasn't anything like that. There was no ship at all. It was a little disappointing from the standpoint of scenery, but there was no denying it was more convenient for us.

When the people from up north at Clatsop Plains came down to salvage the copper bolts, they had stacked a lot of the iron junk up high on the beach, out of reach of the tide. There was a very considerable pile of iron knees that had held the deck planking to the frame, neatly lumped there for the taking, just like a store. I suppose I should have thanked them, but frankly I was now considering their salvage of the copper bolts as outright thievery. The wreck of the *Shark* was clearly *ours*, because we needed it. We later bought a few of those bolts in Astoria, and it was with a clear and bitter sense of paying for our own property.

There was no question of returning the same day, so we decided to spend the night right there and load up in the morning. There were only a few hours of light left and there was no use packing up just to unpack again. We figured a half-day extra for the return trip, and neither of us was looking forward to it. In honesty, some of that so-called trail over Neahkahnie Mountain was nothing but a figment of some Indian's imagination, and there is nothing harder to walk on.

Having decided to wait for morning we had nothing in particular to do for the rest of the day, so we just fooled around on the beach. We picketed the horses under some trees where they could get good grass and wandered off up the beach trying to find sand dollars that weren't broken. I invented an infallible principle of nature, which is as follows:

If the sand dollar is lying with the flat side up, it is always broken on the other side. If it is lying with the roundish face up, and whole, it is never broken on the other side. No one told me this, I invented it for myself. I have spent much time since then trying to figure out how to make some money from this principle of nature that only I know. I made a nickel that first day from Thomas, betting about it, but he quickly discovered I had a principle of nature on my side and refused to bet any more. That nickel is all I ever made out of it. I have often wondered how much that Newton fellow made for inventing gravity. I hope he did not find it as difficult as I to turn a principle of nature into ready cash.

We filled our pockets with sand dollars, and when we were fully loaded found that we had no particular use for the things except to find them. So we skipped them all across the beach in little contests. I suppose all this sounds useless, which it was, but we had nothing better to do for the moment and it is quite a pleasant way to spend your time.

Thomas was secretly furious at me about my principle of nature, but he wouldn't let on how mad he was. One of the reasons he was such a butt-head is that he considered himself educated. He had no more formal schooling than myself, but he was a great reader and was constantly claiming to have read books I didn't believe existed. And I noticed that when he talked about those books, he always described the pictures, which made me wonder a little.

In any event, he took vengeance on my principle of nature by giving me lectures on everything else. He would look at a cloud and say, "That reminds me of a elephant, doesn't it you?" And I would say "No," and he would go on and describe about the life of the elephant, as he understood it.

The queerest thing he told me was about an animal I had never heard of, that he called a "camelopard." (He was reminded of it by a piece of driftwood that looked like a piece of driftwood.)

"That's a beast that lives in Africa," he said, "and it's the damndest thing you *ever* saw."

"You never been in Africa, Thomas, why do you keep on talking about Africa?"

"If you ain't interested in learning about things, just say so. I saw this in a book in St. Louis. You want to hear about it or no?"

"I expect I'm going to."

"This here beast has got spots like a leopard, and a body like a camel and legs about eight feet long and a neck about ten feet long like a snake, only it's stiff. They can't bend it."

"Hell, that ain't possible, Thomas. Allow a couple feet for the body and that makes him twenty feet tall."

He nodded firmly. "That's it. I saw a picture of it. Twenty feet, I guess the big ones are maybe thirty feet or better up there. And that ain't the funniest, neither. Them beasts don't sleep, because they can't bend their legs to sit down or nothing. Everything's *stiff* on 'em. They just wander around all the time. How do you like that?"

"You're making it all up, Thomas. You do that all the time."

"And they got horns on them, just little bitty horns. It was a English book," he added, just to clinch the argument. "They made it in England, with pictures and everything."

"Well, if they can't sit down, and their neck's so stiff, just tell me how they get something to eat. Tell me that, will you, Thomas? What do they eat?"

"Maybe they don't eat, neither. Maybe that's the only animal in the world that don't eat, you ever think of that?"

That was so unreasonable even *he* could see. "Everything eats," I told him, sure of my ground. "You eat, I eat, and your damned African beasts eat."

He thought it over for a long time, and I could see I had him worried.

"I remember," he said finally. "They eat each other's heads, I remember now."

"Thomas, listen, where do you get such stupid ideas?"

"That ain't stupid, Ben, that's logic. That's all there *is* to eat way up there, is their own heads. That's what they got them little horns for, to protect themselves from each other. Otherwise they'd all die from having their heads eat off."

"By christ, I'll tell you if somebody was trying to eat *my* head off I'd want a damn *big* pair of horns."

"Sure, but if they could protect themselves *too* good, then they'd all starve to death. It works out just right. That's what you call nature's wonders."

I let him have his way, and I have never really found out the truth of the matter. If it is true that these beasts eat each other's own heads, I for one do not wish to hear about it, nature's wonders or not.

✳

In the morning we packed all the iron knees we could on our horses and set off. It would probably not have been difficult had we been expert packers, or even vaguely competent. But neither of us knew the first thing about it. We were learning as we went along, and I will say we learned a fair amount that first day. These deck knees were a sort of right-angle bracket shape, and very awkward for packing. At the time we thought the main thing about packing was to get the stuff on the horse, so we just loaded them into a kind of tarpaulin pack, laid the pack over the horse, jiggled a little to settle the load and tied it down. Thomas said he'd read how to make a diamond hitch and did several fancy things with the rope, none of which resembled a diamond in the least. Since I had no better ideas to offer we let it go at that.

It was already noon when we started up the V-shaped depression of Neahkahnie that the Indians called the Meadow of the Ocean Waves. The horses were all behaving in a very peculiar fashion by this time. Even Thomas couldn't make out their style and he understood them very well from having such a horselike mind himself.

"Thomas," I said, "what the hell's the matter with your animals?"

"Damned if I know," he admitted. "They never acted like this before."

They were—hunchy, is the only word I can think of. They twisted and stretched their necks and hunched their backs and made pathetic snuffling noises. Thomas was genuinely worried about it. In thinking over their condition he was silent for once, and we plodded up the base of the V toward the high cliff, fighting our way through the head-high salal and manzanita that choked the trail.

"Listen," he said suddenly, with such excitement that I stopped short in the middle of the trail. "Listen, Ben, when my horses get starved, like in snow or something, they eat each other's tails. Nibble 'em right off, they do."

"Well, it ain't snowing and they ain't hungry now, are they?"

"No, but it proves about them camelopards, don't it? I mean, if my horses eat each other's tails, why shouldn't them African beasts eat each other's heads?"

"God *damn*, Thomas. Haven't you got anything better to think about?" I was sick to death of those monsters and I'd had awful dreams about them all night. "You figure out about your own animals and quit worrying about all that other stuff."

"It's the breakers," he said, frowning. "It's the sound of the breakers that makes them nervous."

"Didn't bother them coming up," I said. "Why start now?" He had no answer for that one.

The trail around the cliff at Neahkahnie was much lower down than it is now, almost at the very edge of the bluff. It followed a little natural ledge around, and at one point you were practically hanging out over the ocean, five hundred feet up. It'll make no secret that the standard way to get around this particular point was to coon it on your hands and knees and nobody was ashamed of it. A few years before, an Indian boy from Clatsop Plains had fallen over there with a horse, and they said his ghost came back to haunt it. I wasn't interested in Indian ghosts, but I was concerned that my own didn't make an appearance too soon. However, with the packed horses we had no choice but to stay upright, and we took them across one by one.

It all went well until the third animal, which I was leading. I was side-shuffling with my belly up against the cliff and we were going very slowly, which was the only way possible. Thomas was waiting on the other side. This animal was particularly nervous and irritable and I was worried about him. I had reached broad ground on the opposite side of the passage, and was gently easing the animal toward me. Suddenly the damn fool hunched his back.

The cinch broke, and the pack of iron knees was loosened. It swung around under his belly, throwing him off balance. The animal's rear legs were just at the last of the narrow ledge, and he scrambled frantically. His rump seemed to move slowly out over the open as his hind legs flailed at the loose rock of the trail. The suddenly shifted weight of the pack under his belly pulled him steadily down. I hauled at the lines with all my strength, digging my heels in and hollering for Thomas. He rushed past me from behind, drawing his butcher knife as he came. With remarkable speed he slipped the knife under the pack ropes and cut it loose. The pack clanked once against the ledge, then went hurtling down toward the rocks and breakers below, followed by a trickling stream of rock.

Once relieved of the weight the horse was able to get purchase with his hooves, and with Thomas and me hauling for life we finally got him back up on safe ground. The poor animal stood there with his head down, shaking like an aspen leaf.

Thomas was rubbing him and talking to him and smoothing his coat, when suddenly he said, "Ben, look here at this."

The hair was all rubbed off the animal's back in random spots. They were not yet sores, but would have been before long.

"That's what's wrong with the horses," Thomas said. "Them iron things is poking hell out of them."

"Jesus," I said, looking at the nearly raw patch. "They must really be hurting."

"Damn! If you'd been more careful with the packing this wouldn't—"

"*You* packed this animal, Thomas. I remember."

"The hell I—well, never mind. Let's look at the others."

We stripped the fourth animal of his pack before bringing him over the ledge. We unpacked them all and looked them over. That had been the trouble. As soon as the packs were removed they lost their nervousness and settled down.

Fortunately none of the others was as badly hurt as the one who'd thrown his pack, the one Thomas had packed so badly. We distributed the three remaining loads into four, which would help some. Mostly we re-packed a lot more carefully, having learned that the first consideration in loading a horse is not the load, but the horse. If you can't get your animal comfortable he is not going to carry. Sooner or later he will get rid of the pack, and in this case we were lucky not to lose the animal as well.

Ever after this time that point on the trail was known as Kahnie's Toll Gate. This was how the custom started of throwing a coin into the sea there, as ransom for your crossing. You always had to leave something behind for that passage and it was better to do it voluntarily than have it taken away from you, as had happened with our pack and the Indian boy before.

This was our only difficulty with the animals on the trip. I will say, however, that by the time we reached the Bay again I knew much more about those crazy damned animals in Africa than I had any use for.

We got the horses unloaded and Thomas went off home to take care of the poor beasts. I went up to talk to Vaughn about the trip and tell him how it had gone. Thinking to amuse him I recounted our adventures in a light way, and told him how amusing old butt-head Thomas had been about everything. After about an hour I left, and as I was walking back to my own cabin I saw Thomas himself coming up toward Vaughn's. I figured he was probably going to complain about his horses, which had been his own fault for not knowing how to pack them properly. I was glad I'd gotten there first so Vaughn wouldn't get any erroneous ideas about the way things were.

The next day Vaughn decided I was too valuable a man to waste on just packing, and I went to work on the blacksmith shop. Vaughn himself went with Thomas, making four more trips to the wreck of the *Shark* after having taken one whole day to construct some sturdy pack-saddles. I couldn't say I envied him, and was just as happy to be working with somebody else.

Thomas was a right enough fellow in his own way, but he was just plain butt-head about practically everything, particularly when it came to nature's wonders. There are some things in this world it just does a man no good to think about.

2

The blacksmith shop went up very fast. With three of us working we built her in two days, and were a little proud of ourselves. It wasn't much to speak of, more like a shed than anything, but the roof was good and tight and we felt we had done a creditable job to get her up so soon.

A man we called the Bishop, whose name was Clark, was our blacksmith, and in the late afternoon of the second day of work he came wandering down to inspect his new property.

"Well, sinners," he said, "I'm happy to see the congregation improving its time with good works."

"Good work is right," I told him. "Look at her, a regular house."

"Good *works*, I said," Clark corrected. "It ain't the same. No mind."

He looked the shop over and the three of us who had built it watched anxiously. It seemed very important that he be impressed; after all, it was the first actual carpenter work on the Ship.

"Not too bad, brothers," Clark admitted. "In fact, a first rate job."

We grinned at each other, satisfied.

"When do you start on the wood?" he said.

"Wood? What wood?"

"For the charcoal."

I blinked and turned to my companions, who were just as mystified as I. "Well, Bishop—what exactly have you got in mind?"

"Brothers," he explained cheerfully, "a smith has to have fire to work his iron, don't you even know that?"

"Oh, hell, yes," I said. "Didn't even occur to me. But you can get that for yourself, can't you?"

"Somebody's got to tend to the burning, make charcoal of it."

"Well—I suppose we can do it. Or anyway we can get the wood in before it gets dark. How much you figure you'll need?"

Clark frowned at the ground. "Don't really know—have to find out how much work there's going to be. We best go see Sam."

So the four of us trooped unsuspectingly down to where Sam was laying out the ways, and asked him. He was different these days than any of us had ever seen him before. He was no easier to talk to, but the reasons seemed different. He was so lost in thinking about the Ship that he forgot to be shy.

"Sam," Clark said, "these sinners got my smithy set up right smart. Now they're going to make charcoal. You ain't got any idea how many spikes and bolts you're going to want, have you?"

Little Sam looked up. He was just as distracted as ever, but I noticed he didn't turn his eyes down as he did when he was in the shy way.

"Yus," he said after a moment. He took a long stick from the ground. He walked off about ten feet, dragging it behind him in the sand, and I swear I thought he'd forgotten and was going home. But he turned and made a right angle with the stick and drew a line about five feet long. He came back to us and completed the circuit, finishing with a rectangle about ten feet by five. I was nervous and embarrassed, as I always am when somebody does things totally beyond my comprehension.

"Well, Sam," I said hesitantly, "about them bolts and things."

Without taking his eyes off us, Sam pointed to the drawn rectangle.

"Bishop," he said. "You count the grains of sand inside them lines, all right? Then you make me a bolt for each grain of sand and twice that many spikes." He turned back to measuring some distance on the ground and forgot about us completely.

We fidgeted for a minute, looking at his back, then walked off. Finally Clark cleared his throat. He tried to talk in the same bantering tone, but he wavered some. "Well, sinners," he said. "I got the idea I'm going to increase my blacksmithing experience right considerable on this boat."

"Ship," I said. "How much wood, Bishop?"

He looked down at the ground in front of him as we walked back toward the smithy of which we were so proud. "For that many bolts? Not too much. I expect about half the forest in Oregon ought to do the trick."

And half the forest in Oregon was just about what we cut for him. We also had to build a kind of kiln to make charcoal of the wood, and it took us two days for that, same as for the smithy itself. It appeared as though things were going to be a little more complicated than we had them in our minds.

We built the blacksmith shop and we had to have charcoal, so we built the kiln. Then we had to have wood to feed the kiln, so we cut trees. Then we had to get the trees back down to the kiln, so we built a mile and a quarter of drag road. Then the trees had to be bucked up and split to fit the kiln. Then the fire had to be kept.

We had damn near every animal in the Bay working, men, horses, and milk cows. Eb Thomas had the beginnings of a little dairy herd, and they were transformed into oxen for a while, dragging the great fir and spruce logs down from my land. (I had offered some of my timber, thinking of it as a chance to get some free clearing done.)

This was not all for the blacksmith shop, of course—that required only half the Oregon forest. The other half we had to cut down for the Ship herself.

Then we scraped up cash money, and that was hardest of all. Sam, who hadn't left our little ring of mountains since he arrived there, made a trip up to Astoria to buy the tools we needed. Christ, we didn't even have the tools. We didn't have anything, except the image.

It occurred to me in later years that we duplicated the entire history of the world that May and early June. It had taken mankind as a whole several thousand years to transform itself from a bunch of vaguely associated farmers squatting on fertile land into a civilization capable of building a thing of such ungodly complexity as a Ship. We did it in a month.

These first weeks there was never any problem of order, or what we were to do next. There was so much that you couldn't finish one job and have a smoke before your next week's work dropped on your back. We seemed to be scattered all over, some of us miles back in the woods, others in Astoria, others down on the beach with Sam, setting up the ways, others down looking over the wrecked ship at Netarts Bay and negotiating with the Indians, who claimed it was theirs, others simply packing and carrying like so many mules.

You couldn't keep it all in your head, there wasn't any one thing that seemed more important than the rest. The ways themselves, where the Ship would stand, were only one tiny item in the midst of ten thousand. The complications we ran into with the blacksmith shop happened with everything. Every act bred a dozen others to back it up, and it all had to be done from scratch. It was like watching the swirling activity of a kicked anthill; you couldn't tell who was going where, or why, or what the *hell* he thought he was doing. You couldn't even tell one man from another after a while. You lost track.

Eating and sleeping both got irregular as hell. Most of us were batches, and this is dangerous in such a situation. You get to working and you forget to eat, you forget to sleep, and there's nobody to remind you. What's worse is that if *you* have missed two meals in a row you consider it a sign of weakness that somebody *else* wants to eat. By christ, you've gone without food and you're still working—that other guy can do as much.

And with the Ship, weakness was a form of treason; we couldn't afford the effeminacy of regular hours, regular food, regular sleep. A man who finally had enough and went off was followed by hostile glances from the others. He didn't *care* enough. He cared more about his lousy belly than about the Ship. We were contemptuous.

In time this evened out, of course, because it is not an efficient way to work. You can't go without food and get your work done properly. But efficiency was the only reason. We regretted having to eat and sleep—but the Ship demanded it, so we did.

The Ship had begun to drive us. She filled our minds and our bellies in a way nothing else could. She drove, haunted, cajoled, persuaded and bullied and threatened. And we worked for her. She was our nourishment, the image of her, and it was a magic thing that by its simple existence created energy out of nothing.

And as yet we had not put down one single piece of wood for the Ship herself. Not one. We knew the first piece to go down was the keel—we knew that much. And that was all.

The only man who had any idea what he was doing was Little Sam Howard. I do not remember him speaking to anyone in this first month of preparation, myself or anyone else. At least not often. But he communicated somehow, and what he wanted done was done. Or perhaps the Ship communicated what *she* wanted done. The distinction between men and image was becoming vague. It was all done, but I can say neither how nor why, and could not at the time.

Then—very suddenly, it seemed—the world drew in. It was like poking a sea anemone with a stick and watching it close abruptly. There was no one at Astoria, there was no one at Netarts. All the ants piled back into the hill, and for the first time there was a focus for all that had been happening at random.

The focus was a shy little man who was lately spending much of his time in his rickety cabin, staring at a model he had made and turning it over in his hands.

Chapter Five

1

The laying of the keel was set for June 18th. It was the Sabbath, but by common, if silent, agreement nobody mentioned it and we planned to go ahead pretending we had forgotten. At that point we thought nothing in the world could stop us. We were wrong. I have since wondered if our intention to begin on a Sunday was in some way a bad omen. In any event, we were suddenly stopped, and by an act of God. The night of the 17th we learned of the first deaths among the settlers. Our ring of mountains isolated us from much, but man's oldest companion had found his way in.

A man named Cornwall, from Missouri, had taken up a claim at the far north of the Bay. This was quite recently, I believe sometime during the previous winter. His cabin was not even finished yet, having no floor but the earth and only a blanket for a door. This was mostly because Cornwall was often away and had no time to finish it.

He was a married man, and a preacher. He lived up there with his wife and a son of about sixteen years of age. At first we had been pleased to see them come, as families were what we needed, but we soon learned that the Reverend Cornwall was not at all concerned with us or our little community. He was an "illuminated" and his cabin was simply a base of rest between preaching voyages. Often he would go all the way into the Valley, stopping at every cabin he ran across and preaching for his supper. As a result we saw very little of him and did not know him well.

He arrived at my house in the middle of the night, pounding heavily on the door. I lit a lamp and let him in. I knew the man by sight, but at first I did not recognize him. His face was slack and loose, and in the light of the camphine lamp his eyes had a strange, wild quality that frightened me. He was pale as a ghost, his face and clothing covered over with a fine veil of ashes. He moved slowly, as though his body were very heavy, and looked around him crazily.

"They're gone. God took them."

"Who?"

"My wife, my son. God took them to punish me. His will is mysterious."

This kind of talk has always made me nervous, as there is no reply to it, there is never anything to say. Finally I built up the fire a little and got the story from him.

On returning from a preach in the evening, he had found his cabin a mass of smoking, charred rubble. There was nothing left at all. The crazy fool had poked around in the still smoking cinders, burning his hands quite badly, and had found the burned bodies of his wife and son.

Fire was something we were all afraid of. At this time all our chimneys were of wood, there was not a brick or stone chimney closer than Astoria. Chimney fires were not rare, but they were usually caught before becoming serious. In this case, the victims had apparently been suffocated by the smoke before they wakened.

My first reaction to this tragedy was not humanitarian. I wondered only what it would mean to the Ship. Everything that happened in the world was related to the Ship in some way; else it made no sense, it was not understandable. What was the disaster of a lifetime for poor Cornwall was, for me, an annoyance, because I knew immediately it would mean a delay in the laying of the keel. I am not proud of this. But at this time—and for the only time in my life—I had a clear and solid understanding of Good and Evil. Good was what helped the Ship; Evil was what hindered it. I had a way to measure.

I was at the same time very sorry for Cornwall, but I didn't see what I could do. It is absurd for a young man who has no real notion of death to be comforting an older one who has just lost the only living creatures who mean anything to him. In brutal fact, the great enigma did not touch me at all, it simply embarrassed me and annoyed me.

While I did not realize it at the time, Cornwall was more fortunate than most, in some respects. He had satisfactory answers to the most terrible of questions posed by death; Cornwall knew *why*. God had taken them away, and it was punishment for his sins. The significance was clear, and he was left with only the grief of his loss. No matter how intense, grief is not as shattering for a man as that wild incomprehension that shakes his understanding of the world.

As soon as it was light I took Cornwall with me to Vaughn's place, which seemed the natural thing to do. He could help no more than I, of course, but I wished to share the responsibility of this man's pain.

There was nothing any of us could do, and yet the tragedy could not be simply ignored. In the end a half-dozen of us returned with Cornwall to his cabin, paying some obscure moral debt with simple physical movement.

The journey was useless, of course, and unpleasant in the extreme. From what Cornwall told us, both his wife and son had been overcome not in their beds but in the middle of the single room, probably while trying to reach the door. It seemed odd that with no more than a blanket for a door such a suffocating density of smoke could accumulate, but this was obviously what had happened. We had no way to judge, as Cornwall had dragged the bodies from the ashes and they were lying some little distance from the cabin when we arrived. None of us had ever seen a burned human being before, and it was this that made it so terrible. The crown of the son's head was also crushed, probably by a falling roof beam, but whether it had occurred before or after his death was impossible to tell.

We buried the two of them in a place chosen by Cornwall, apparently at random, and he prayed over them. It was an awful sight, this broken man on his knees by the freshly turned earth, his body covered with the gray of the ashes and his face marked only by tiny lines of flesh color where his tears had washed away the soot and ash. It was like something from the Old Testament, there was an unreal cruelty and agony about it. In that moment it was easy to believe in a God of vengeance.

Cornwall turned us all away and remained weeping at the graves. We were not reluctant to leave; there are some things a man should not see, as it makes the rest of life seem futile.

I have found one thing about death, one thing of which I am sure. In my every contact with death since that time, I have found one element of the ridiculous. No one ever notices, because of their preoccupation with the serious. But I have come to look for it, and it is always that element of absurdity I remember later. Perhaps I am a cold man.

In the case of the poor Cornwall family it was a frying pan, a heavy cast-iron frying pan. It rested in the exact center of the ashes, undamaged and face up. It almost looked as though it were being heated on a fire too large for it, or as though all the ashes had miraculously boiled out of that single pan. It was centered with such absurd precision I could not get it out of my mind, and all the way back to my own cabin I thought about that frying pan, lonely and still and perfect in the midst of desolation and mortality.

2

The disaster slipped away from our minds very quickly, and it kept us from working for only one day. At that, some of the men went ahead anyway. William Hendrickson and Peter Morgan both worked while we were at Cornwall's place, and the rest of us were slightly envious.

Just after we had finished with the blacksmith shop (and kiln and road and hauling and cutting and burning) we had set up a frame for a whipsaw, or rather pit-and-frame. In principle a whipsaw is simple enough, but in practice we found it like everything else; full of unexpected complications. The pit was about seven feet deep, and the log to be sawed projected out over the edge. The sawyer stood down in the pit, under the log. His job was to haul down on the huge saw, and when he had finished his stroke the blade was drawn up again by the spring. In this case the spring was a flexible sapling mounted upright in the framing members. This sapling had to be replaced from time to time as it lost its spring or broke, and there was competition among the men as to whose spring would last the longest. Once the blade was well started in the log it tended to go straight, but getting the start was difficult. I will say here that William Hendrickson and Peter Morgan sawed out every timber and plank in the Ship on that rig, from keel to decking. They worked like fools, and were able to average about three hundred feet a day.

That first day, the laying of the keel, set a pattern that was to be repeated for all the rest of the time. We arrived at the ways ready to pick up the keel and lay it down where Sam said. We figured we could at least get started on the framing by noon.

Sam was there at the ways ahead of us, and he had brought his model along. There were no more plans than that. It was almost impossible to believe, but Sam claimed that every piece that would go in the real Ship was in that model, and it was a question of scaling up.

He had it sitting on a big fir butt near the ways, and we all crowded around in awe. He had taken off the deck and part of the planking, so we could see inside. It was like a picture of a person's insides I had once seen, full of mysterious objects and curves and connections I did not understand. I had a moment of panic, considering that complexity, and I do not believe I was alone.

"Well, Sam," I said. "The big day. Let's get that keel down."

Sam nodded abstractedly. I looked around the ways and saw no lumber that looked like the keel I had vaguely in my mind.

"Yus," Sam said. He paced nervously up and down beside the timbers, muttering to himself.

The rest of us stood and watched him. Finally he stopped the walking and turned to face us. He looked at everybody in turn—I think he was searching for a glimmer of intelligence—and finally directed his words to Vaughn and me, who were standing side by side.

"I think we can scarf her in three," he said hopefully.

Neither Vaughn nor I said anything, and it made Sam reconsider, frowning.

"Maybe take four?" he said in a questioning tone, as though we had suggested it. "Yus, four. Thirty-seven and a half feet."

Vaughn cleared his throat. "Sam," he said. "What does scarf mean?"

He had more nerve than the rest of us, Vaughn did. I'd have gone ahead and scarfed it *without* knowing what it meant rather than ask. At this point I was obsessed by a fear of offending Sam or discouraging him.

"Half a dozen kinds," the little man said. "More. I flat-scarfed the model, you can see that, but we best hook-scarf here." He looked up apologetically. "It's just that the model's so small and all . . . "

Vaughn and I bent over the model, peering inside to see if we could see anything that looked right off like a flat scarf. The rest of the gang shuffled their feet and looked embarrassed.

"I seen a Chinese scarf once," Sam said meditatively. "No nibs at all and no angles. Just a sweet curve. It was real nice."

Finally Vaughn sighed, glanced at me, and straightened up. "Sam," he said quietly, "we best get it all straight right now. There ain't a man standing here that knows anything about a scarf except you wrap it around your neck. We're here to work, you know that, you seen we're willin' to work. But we don't know nothing. You got to be the brain for us all, you got to tell us *everything*, like babies."

Strangely enough, Sam was neither surprised nor disappointed. "Yus," he muttered apologetically. "Yus, you tol' me that before. I forgot. I'll tell you." He looked absently at the ways, more to avoid meeting our eyes than anything else. "Yus," he said again softly. "We'll build her anyway, we will."

"What'd you say, Sam?"

"Look here." Sam took a long scriber and pointed down through the open deck of the model, touching the keel where an almost imperceptible line of joining showed.

"This keel's spliced together out of different pieces. That's what you call a scarf, the splice. It runs diagonal across the timber. If you make a flat diagonal, you got two shim edges, and that rots out. We'll nib the join, and there's another nib in the middle for holding fore-and-aft movement. That way she can't slide." He drew a little design for us in the dirt at the base of the stump:

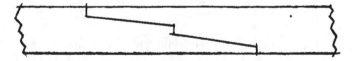

"We got to fit it together *perfect*, then," Vaughn said.

"That's it." Sam bobbed his head.

Vaughn frowned. "That there's real cabinetmaker's work," he said.

"That there's shipwright's work, Vaughn," Sam said. "You said you was here to work if I told you what to do. I'm tellin' you, then. And I'll tell you a scarf joint's about the easiest thing you'll have to do. You make up your mind right now."

Sam's tone was amazingly strong for him, but Vaughn did not take offense.

"All right, Sam," he said quietly. "There ain't no question, there's never been no question. How do we start?"

Sam looked at Vaughn, then at me, then at the rest of the crew. He seemed to consider the whole problem all over again. Fifteen men watched him as a cat watches a fly on the wall. He was not even aware of us. Suddenly he squatted down on his haunches, still holding the scriber absently in his hands.

"Each scarf got to span at least two frames. The length is at least five times the thickness of the timber. The nibs got to be one-eighth the thickness of the timber, the center one, too."

"Why?" I said without thinking.

"That's the rule," Sam said, standing up. "That's the way it's right."

"I mean, is that—"

"You build a ship the way you build her," Sam said. He turned away from me. I had never seen him this way. He talked different, he moved different, nothing was like the Little Sam whose gnomish face I had first seen ducking out of sight behind a gray window. He walked over to the timbers and kicked one of them.

"Thaler!"

"Yes, Sam." I jumped.

"Get an ax."

I grabbed an ax as fast as I could and ran over to the timber. "I'm going to show you how to make a scarf joint, Ben."

And the first chip that flew was from my ax. I realized it just as the chip hit the ground, and I had such an explosion of happiness in my belly I couldn't believe it. I hastily grabbed the chip up and stuck it in my pocket. Sam was scribing lines on the squared-off timber, showing me where to make the next cut. I saw him through a kind of haze. The first stroke was mine. Me, Ben Thaler.

3

All this activity did not fail to make a grand impression on the Indians. From the first day we were provided with an attentive audience, and at times it was difficult to constrain them to act merely as audience; they wanted to help. Until firm rules were established they tended to wander all over, poking interestedly in every corner, pointing and chattering to each other like so many squirrels. Their own custom was that any work in progress was subject to scrutiny and comment by everyone else, and they could not understand why we objected to the criticism, which was undoubtedly intended to raise the level of our work.

After some time I got used to being on display and thought no more of it. Except for once, quite a bit later, when the frames were almost all up. I was in the interior of the hull and happened to glance out through the framing, whose members were about ten inches apart. An old squaw was lifting a baby up so the child could see better. It was the exact gesture I had seen made by a white woman at a monkey cage. Looking out through the frames—holding them, in fact, like bars—I had a rather uncomfortable sensation for a moment.

We had no difficulty with "our" Indians, as their chief Kilchis was very cooperative. This chief, or *tyee*, as they called him, was one of the strangest men I have ever encountered. For one thing I think I have never known a more intelligent man of any color. Secondly, he was clearly Negro by race. He stood perhaps six feet three and weighed well over two hundred pounds. As these coastal people are small of stature he towered over them like a mountain. I don't believe there was one who reached as high as his shoulder. I never had a satisfactory explanation of how this obviously African gentleman came to be ruling a tribe of Indians on the Oregon coast. They had several wholly unreasonable traditions to explain it, but at root they were totally indifferent to his origins as long as he was a good chief. In any case, I have noted that Indian traditions serve a certain purpose, and literal truth is not the important consideration. It is the same with us, I believe, as history tells us only what we have already made up our minds to believe. But the Indians were more openly uninterested in the truth, or perhaps their idea of it differed from our own.

Kilchis had very exact ideas of what he expected from the whites, almost as though there were a contract between us all. In fact, I believe this was the case, as he often asked me when the white *tyee* with the beard was going to return. Some years in the past he had apparently been visited by a white man, and an agreement had been reached between the two of them concerning the settlement of the Bay. What had happened in the interim I do not know, but the great black man expected the agreement to be kept. As he was scrupulously fair there was no great problem. I have often wondered what became of that bearded white *tyee*, and pondered on the fragility of man's schemes.

Kilchis himself came often to the Ship, and he was allowed to inspect whatever he liked. I will never forget his enormous frame, draped in a bearskin robe, stooping among the timbers to examine a join or standing back to observe the whole. I was very fond of the old fellow, and I think we all were. He was a very worthy man, and I firmly believe that had he been white he would have made a far better President of the United States than many of the scoundrels we have had in that office.

But to return to the Ship. In the weeks that followed my first, magical ax-blow I was thrown into a world of such complexity that I nearly drowned in it. Little Sam seemed suddenly to have lost his ability to speak English, and instead communicated only in a wholly mysterious language, a jargon of terms—and actions to match them—that was infuriating and baffling. In moments of fatigue and depression I clearly remember having the strong impression that Sam was inventing words out of personal malice. It did not seem possible that such an enormous body of language and detail could exist without a man even having a notion it was there.

At first Sam himself could not work; he was kept running from first light, explaining this, demonstrating that, pointing out something else. We "shipwrights" were an enormous burden to him, and I almost think he could have done it faster all by himself. In time, of course, we no longer had to ask for instructions between each stroke of the ax, and it went better.

The first few weeks I went home at night aching in every tendon, with my head swirling in a fog of unfamiliarity. It was not surprising that a skilled trade should have its secrets, its special techniques. What astonished me was that it was *all* secrets, all special. Every movement was prescribed, every stroke of the adze had been perfected through the years until there was one proper way to do it, and no other. I do not believe there were two pieces in the entire ship of the same shape. Everything was unique, formed with meticulous care according to certain rules and criteria which often escaped me.

Take, for example, the frames themselves. Each frame was built up from seven precisely cut elements called futtocks, laboriously fitted together in a series of overlapping joints to form a double thickness from the floor futtock to top timber. And no two of them alike. Only one frame in the entire hull was permitted to have square edges, what Sam called the "dead-flat timber." All the others had to be beveled off to fit the curve of the hull forward and aft of the midships frame, and it all had to be calculated with a nicety of precision I found almost incomprehensible. Sometimes it seemed I had spent the best part of my life leaning over the sand while Sam drew pictures and explained patiently.

"Ben, it's just logic. The hull curves fore-and-aft, right? The frames got to fit the curve, is all. Look." And he would draw.

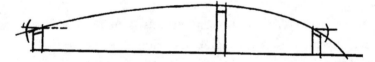

"The dead-flat timber can be square, but the rest got to bevel."

And that was merely *one* bevel, to fit the curve of the hull fore and aft. Each frame also had another, varying from top to bottom. Anywhere from four to six degrees difference of angle that must be faired into a smooth curve for the planking to follow. Each individual framing member was such a complex series of subtle curves that a man couldn't hold it all in his mind—and yet it made a whole. When a frame was finished you could look at it and see that it was a beautiful thing.

"Beautiful" was a word Sam used often, in the same way he used "rule": as an ultimate argument from which there was no appeal.

"That's the way it's beautiful," he'd say. "There ain't nothin' ugly in a ship."

"That's the way it's beautiful . . ." It was the final criterion of all, I suppose, but I was still young enough that it made me a little uncomfortable. I felt like a man going through a ritual, an unvarying ritual performed according to the ancient, fixed laws of the goddess. Questioning after "practical" reasons for everything eventually came to seem a kind of heresy, even to me. It was done this way because the priests had always done it this way since the world began. It was what pleased the goddess.

When the first panicky strangeness had worn off I settled down to the work with a grim joy. I learned that an ax could be used with precision to hew a line with the exactitude of a saw. I learned to love the sweetly double-curved shipwright's adze, so puzzling in the beginning. At first I couldn't even figure out how to grab hold of the damn thing, and yet when I learned to swing it between my spread legs the handle's complex curves fit the motion perfectly and allowed the smoothing cut to go with perfect accuracy and grace.

And the goddess began to live. Because of us or in spite of us or independent of us, I didn't know. But she began to live and grow and take shape before our very eyes, and we became a part of her mysteries.

We were almost halfway through the framing when Sam fell in love, or went mad.

He was running from one side of the Ship to the other, checking that Number Twelve was square with the keel both vertically and horizontally. As the ways themselves were slanted for the launching, true vertical would not do, of course. A small triangle of wood, the angle-board, was held to the back of the frame. It was so cut that when the plumb bob suspended from its peak hung straight along the back edge of the board, the frame was vertical to the keel. Then it had to be horned in.

Why this was such a satisfying experience, I don't know. The horning batten was a long strip of lumber fixed to the sternpost on a pivot. It was simply swung in an arc like a great compass, and when both edges of the frame were on the same arc it was square across the keel.

When Sam sang out, "All right, boys, we'll horn 'er," I got a bumpy feeling of excitement and anticipation. Then the long batten was swung and Sam fussed with each side of the frame until he was content and called, "All right, boys, tie 'er down, now." And Number Twelve was done and solid and somehow perfect, and the anticipation was satisfied until the next frame was lifted into place.

It was while Number Thirteen was just being hauled over that Sam fell in love. The two of us were standing beside the hull, absently watching the frame come. I suddenly heard Sam gasp, and my first thought was that he had spotted something wrong. We had already had to remake two frames because they didn't satisfy him.

He grabbed my elbow, and I followed his eyes. He was looking beyond the Ship at our perpetual group of spectators. There were at this time around a dozen. Four or five were "our" Indians, the others were a group who had come up from Netarts Bay to see what we were doing with the old hulk they'd sold us for twelve dollars.

"Ben," Sam said, "Ben, who's that?"

"Who's what, Sam?"

He clutched my elbow even tighter, until it hurt. "Over to the side, standing over to the side."

I looked, and recognized a young fellow I knew, a boy of about twenty named Cockshaten or some such. I hadn't seen him since just before we'd laid the keel, when he'd come up trying to swap for a knife.

"That's just Cock Hat, Sam," I said, puzzled. "You seen him around surely, he's one of our people."

"No," Sam said tensely. "No, Ben—the woman, the woman."

"Expect that's his woman," I said, shrugging. "I heard he got a girl up from one of the tribes down the coast. It was a couple of—Sam—Sam, what's the matter?"

"My god," he whispered, "my god."

He sounded so strange he scared me. I looked closer at the woman, but there was nothing in particular to notice about her. She was about sixteen or seventeen, I guess. Anyway young enough she hadn't gotten too sloppy yet. Typical coast Indian face, broad and flat, dumpy short legs like all canoe people, long black hair falling loose and greasy around her shoulders. Just an Indian girl like a dozen others in the village.

"My god," Sam whispered again, and his voice sounded half strangled. "She's—she's beautiful."

"Who?" I asked stupidly.

Sam jerked his hand away from my elbow as though he'd been touching a snake. He suddenly looked up at me, unbelieving and hostile. He stared at me with such pitiless intensity that I had to look away.

After a moment he turned away again, almost dazed, and looked back at Cock Hat and his woman. Cock Hat was pointing at something.

"Sam—Sam, what's got into you? What's the matter?"

He didn't answer, but started to move very slowly toward them. He didn't even seem to be aware he was walking.

"Sam!" He was really scaring me now, he didn't seem to be in control of himself. I didn't know what to do if he'd suddenly gone crazy.

"Listen!" Vaughn hollered in a big, petulant voice. "Are we going to hold this thing all *day?*"

The three men had by this time raised Number Thirteen frame into position and were waiting patiently for Sam to horn it. Sam stopped at the sound of Vaughn's voice, but he did not turn. He stared so intently at Cock Hat and the girl that I almost expected to see them disappear.

Just then two of the Indians from Netarts started a lively argument about something or other, and Cock Hat and his woman went over to see what it was about. They merged into the small group of gesticulating men. Sam watched them go, standing immobile with his fists clenched. He didn't know what to do. He was ripped between the imperative of horning the frame and the even more violent need to look at the girl. I ran over to him, and he shook my hand off.

"Sam, listen—" I started.

"Get away, you," he said viciously. "You don't *see.*" He bit his lip and looked down at the ground. "You just can't see," he said again, softly.

"Well, hell," Vaughn hollered sarcastically. "I don't care if we get this frame up or *not*. We *working* today or not, is all I'm asking you."

"Take it easy, Sam," I said. "Jesus, take it easy."

He started to walk slowly toward the Ship, his fists still clenched at his sides, his arms stiff.

"Well, it's about *time*," Vaughn said. "I thought you was *never*—"

"Shut up, Vaughn," I said. I was half panicky. I didn't understand what was happening and I wanted it all to stop.

"Listen, Ben, you don't have to—"

"Just shut *up*, Vaughn. Just don't say *anything*." I almost pleaded with him, and he looked at me with puzzlement. "Listen, Sam," I said.

Sam shook his head, looking at the ground. "You don't *see*," he repeated. "She's—perfect."

"It's just an Indian girl, Sam, hell, there's—"

He wasn't listening. "She's the only perfect thing I ever seen in this world," he said, almost to himself.

It was the only time I'd ever heard him use the word. I suppose I should have known it meant trouble, but it was so unreasonable I couldn't take it seriously; I was just panicky. The girl was only a girl, no different from any of the others who drifted around to watch us work.

Sam horned the frame, but his mind wasn't with it. He had a haunted look, he didn't seem to care. And after Thirteen he said he was sick and going home. So we all quit work, though there were still a good two hours of light left. Vaughn and the others had missed most of it, and were very sympathetic about Sam's being sick.

"He best take care of himself," Vaughn said. "Without him we're lost. Do him good to rest a little bit."

"Yes, I suppose."

"He really drives himself, Sam does."

I don't remember what I said, just something to fill up the silence. We all drifted off home. By the time I'd gotten to my cabin I'd about convinced myself that I was imagining things. There was absolutely nothing about that girl that could get Sam so upset, it was something he had in his mind. Maybe he *was* sick, that was the only reasonable explanation.

I was still young enough to look for the reasonable explanation. And stupid enough not to realize that there is no creature on the face of the earth so dangerous as a man who is searching for perfection.

Chapter Six

There is no question but that framing is the best part of building, the most beautiful part. Each day produces something new to be seen, a new growth, something of mysterious significance you only half catch out of the corner of your eye.

As a child in its first years changes with baffling speed, so the Ship grew in framing. Before your eyes the squalling bundle of flesh becomes an infant, then a child, then a young person, and it all goes so incredibly fast. Later it slows, and there is no visible change from one month to the next, and later still, from one year to the next.

But in the beginning all life is consumed with a wild eagerness to fulfill itself, to take its proper form. All else is swept aside in the hurricane pressure to *grow*, an irresistible rush toward finality.

With the Ship it was the same. The complexity of curves and angles that grew steadily from the stacks of rough-cut lumber were transfigured by the simple act of making them a part of the whole structure.

In becoming necessary to the whole they lost their uniqueness, and became something even more. The wing of a bird, no matter how graceful its lines, fulfills itself and becomes real only as part of the bird. These intricately shaped pieces of wood were the organs and muscles and limbs and skeleton of the Ship and achieved their meaning only as part of her body. There was no way to avoid the conviction that she grew like any other life, rather than being constructed.

In the end we became merely witnesses at a miracle, as a mother is witness to the miracle of birth. We were necessary, as is the mother, but past a certain point the life that is rushing to create itself becomes the unquestioned master; the mother has no choice when labor has begun, we had no choice. The goddess was using us to birth herself. We were no more than the instruments of her self-creation.

There was a satisfaction I cannot describe, participating in this miracle. Isolated, each frame with its staggering complexity of curves and angles and fairings and joints seemed almost arbitrary. Beautiful but incomplete. But when it was horned in and trued along her keel, each stroke of the adze was transformed into an unchangeable necessity. No curve overwhelmed you by itself; but as it became a part of her body the beauty grasped you by the throat and made it hard to breathe. How this could continue undiminished, day after day, I do not know. By any reasonable standard I should have been far beyond the point of sensing beauty.

For I paid—as we all paid—in the coin of an aching back and a mind wracked with fatigue. A kind of fatigue different from any I had ever known. It was the first time in my life that my working day was spent making only one sort of motion, the long swing of the ax and the shorter stroke of the adze. Suddenly the burden of my working hours was thrown on one set of muscles, and it broke me.

Night brought no relief, for it was filled with images of the Ship. When my body ceased building at dusk my mind began, working through the darkness of the night, following the spidery, fevered trails of dream. She filled me, she dominated me, twenty-four hours of each day. Waking and sleeping became ambiguous terms without real signification; the only reality was the Ship, the magical rite that consumed and fused us all. I had never known what it was to work.

The summer days were long and rich, and we worked whenever there was light to see. Fourteen, sixteen hours at first. But we knew the days were imperceptibly shortening as the season drew on, and the knowledge drove us even harder to profit from the light we had. At the end of the day I was no more than half alive, but rebelled fiercely against the necessity of stopping in the failing light. By the pre-dawn glow that silhouetted her frames against the pale sky I was already restless and anxious to get my hands on the tools again.

As the framing moved steadily on, Little Sam looked like a haunted man. His eyes were vast and dazed and circled with dark as though someone had thumbed soot into the sockets. I heard no more about the woman, and so forgot her as best I could. I could not see what she had to do with the Ship, and was impatient to wrench that useless image from my mind, to fill myself wholly with the goddess. And in any case Sam's condition called for no particular sympathy, nor did it even seem remarkable. We were all about the same, we were all haunted men. The condition of any individual was irrelevant, unless it interfered with his work. Sam worked as before; that was the only reality I was willing to acknowledge.

We burned. We had been converted into the white-hot instruments of the Ship, and the only meaning to life was work. The madmen of the goddess, and we accepted it joyously, and all the rest was no more than the rustling of wind in the beach grasses.

About midway in the framing I had quit going home at all. There seemed to be a huge emptiness in the cabin, something missing. Almost as though someone had died, and I kept expecting to see her there. What was missing was, of course, simply the physical presence of the Ship, and that was easily solved. I took some blankets down by the ways and installed myself in her very shadow. It was too close to the water to be entirely comfortable. The frequent night fogs crept through my blankets and I was chilly even in the summer nights. But the compensations—the compensations were worth any amount of damp.

When I turned restlessly in the night and opened my eyes—she was there beside me. I saw her by moonlight and starlight and in the dying glow of my fire. I saw the fog drifting gray and silent among the black bones of her frame. I saw her in a thousand ways none of the others had ever seen her. And when there was no light at all, she was there. I felt her, there, looming up out of the blackness into blackness, the beauty and the power of her, and I could sleep more content. I saw her in the first light of morning, while the rest of them were rubbing sleep out of their eyes and thinking about something to fill their bellies and looking at the dead lumber of their cabins. I kindled my own fire and warmed us both a little from the night. I never had to take my eyes off her. And when the others came back to her, I had the secret satisfaction that I had never left her. I was more faithful than they.

It made them furious that I had thought of it first, of course. They funned me a lot, told me I was too tired even to go home, told me my cabin had burned down or was getting mildewed or half a thousand other things that didn't move me at all. But they knew I was right.

The first one that finally gave in and admitted it was, of all people, that butt-head Eb Thomas. It was one night just at dusk, a dead moment of peace and content when we looked over what we had done during the day and thought about tomorrow. To my recollection we had just tied in Number Seventeen.

Thomas drifted over to where I was sitting and thumped himself heavily down on the ground beside me. Ostentatiously he hauled a handkerchief out of his pocket and wiped his forehead.

"Whoo, what a day," he said.

"No worse'n any other," I told him right out. I glanced over at him to let him know I wasn't about to listen to any more stories about his head-eating beasts in Africa.

"I'm beat right down to the boots," he said.

I didn't say anything. He wasn't any more tired than anybody else, he was just feeling sorry for himself or something. When he saw I wasn't going to go along he got right down to business.

"Say, Ben," he said casually, "you wouldn't have maybe an extra blanket lyin' around, would you?"

"No, I got no extra blanket, what do you think? I ain't running any hotel down here, you know."

"Well, hell," he said, getting his back up. "Don't get nasty. I was just *asking* is all."

"Well, I'm just telling you: No, I got no extra blanket. I don't know why you should expect me to keep a inventory of blankets around, Thomas."

"I don't expect *nothin'* of you," he snapped, losing his temper the way he always did. He never really forgave me for not believing his lies and for not telling him my principle of nature about the sand dollars.

"Well, you sure act like it," I told him plain. "Coming around asking for blankets just like you expected it."

He saw he wasn't getting anyplace like that, losing his temper, so he put on real friendly. "Don't get mad, Ben, I didn't mean nothin'."

"Well, am I right or not?" I asked him. "I mean, why should I have blankets around just like that?"

"Sure Ben, you're right," Thomas said, "but you don't have to be nasty about it."

"What do you want a blanket for?" I said, even though I knew just exactly what he was getting at.

"I'm too tired to go home," Thomas said. "I thought I'd just stretch out down here."

"It's cold and wet," I told him flat. "You'd catch your death, particularly without no blanket."

"*You* been sleepin' here a week or better."

"I *want* to."

"Well, maybe *I* want to, too," he said.

I guess it must have sounded like we were arguing or something, because Vaughn came over from the other side of the hull.

"Listen, can't you guys even *talk* to each other without getting in a fight every damn time? What's it about?"

"It's about the blanket," I told him.

"What blanket?"

"The blanket Thomas hasn't got."

"What do you want a blanket for, Eb? You got blankets."

"I want to sleep here because I'm tired, is all," Thomas said. "I just asked Ben polite if he had another blanket and he got nasty."

"Listen, Vaughn," I said. "Am I running a hotel here? Did I ever say that? I mean, who the hell would *expect* me to have a blanket except *him?*"

"You just don't want anybody else to sleep down here is all," Thomas said. "You think you can keep her all to yourself."

"Who's getting nasty now?" I asked him.

"Well, is it true or not? Is it?"

"You're mad because I thought of it first, that's your trouble."

"That ain't the point. You don't want anybody else to sleep down here, is that true or not, just tell me."

"I thought of it first."

"We're all workin' just as hard as you, Ben. We got just as much right to sleep down here as you have. You ain't God or anything, you know."

"Now, listen," Vaughn said in a reasonable tone. "Every time you two get within twenty feet of each other you get in an argument. We can't *have* that all the time. If Eb wants to sleep here he can sleep here."

"Ben wants to keep her all to himself, he thinks he's God or something."

"Listen, I never said anything about that. I don't give a good god *damn* where you sleep, Thomas. You can sleep out on the breakers for all *I* care about it. All I ever said was very simple, that I didn't have no blanket."

"Who needs *your* blanket?" Thomas said, jumping up. "I got blankets, I can get a blanket any time I want it."

"Listen," Vaughn said. "If you're both going to sleep down here you got to sleep on opposite sides of the Ship, all right? And you got to promise me you won't talk to each other. Will you promise me that?"

"I thought you was too tired to go home, Thomas."

"Don't you worry about me, Ben Thaler," he snapped. He turned around and started fast for his place, which was better than three miles back.

Vaughn sighed. "Jesus. You guys. I never saw anything *like* you two."

"He's going to get hisself so tired out he won't be fit to work."

"No, but listen, Ben. You know he's right. If him or any of the other fellows want to sleep down here, they got a perfect right to do it. Even if you did think of it first. The Ship belongs to all of us. Now you got to admit that's only fair."

There was nothing I could say without looking as stubborn as that Thomas, so I didn't say anything at all. Vaughn sighed again and went away.

Thomas came back about two hours later. It was pitch dark, and he made himself a little fire on the other side. It was actually to my advantage, for the shadows of the frame were silhouetted against the fire in a way I hadn't seen before, and seemed to move by themselves when the fire flickered. It put me in such a peaceable mood I took him over a piece of meat I had left, so he could have something to eat. He'd been so furious mad he'd forgotten to bring anything, and of course he was too butt-head to ask.

2

Within a few days there were half a dozen men sleeping down at the Ship. After my first disappointment I didn't mind, and I even took a certain satisfaction in it. With us all there we started working earlier in the morning; that much more work accomplished for which I was, in a way, responsible. I missed that lovely morning time when I could just sort of wander around her all alone, but that was the way it was, and I got used to it.

The evenings were quite pleasant, usually at least two or three fires going, lighting her from different angles, and men moving from one to another visiting. It was a companionable little society, and since Thomas and I had other people to talk to we didn't argue. We never had any disagreements except when we were talking to each other.

Everyone was dead tired after the day's work, and there was a peaceful atmosphere of somnolence and fatigue, like the last few moments before you drop off to sleep, while your mind is wandering aimless and free, without strain. I myself had found that it was easier to relax with the Ship near, and I think everyone felt that way.

Neither Vaughn nor Little Sam slept by the Ship. Vaughn's cabin was the nearest of any, so it was practically the same. He said he could see her out his window with the fires and all, and he liked it that way.

Sam, though, I couldn't figure Sam out. He had been so strange for the last little while that nobody could figure him out. I guess no one tried very hard to find explanations for Sam. He was one of the unpredictables of the world. It did no good to think about it, and made me nervous into the bargain. So I didn't, and neither did anybody else. He had a right to do anything he wanted as long as it didn't hurt the Ship.

It was quite late one night when I heard someone coming up to my fire. I had rolled up to go to sleep, and the fire itself was burning down. I watched sleepily as my visitor threw another stick on, and when the yellow flames licked up the sides I saw it was Vaughn.

"You awake, Ben?" he said quietly.

"Yeah, I guess so." I rubbed my eyes. "What time is it?"

"I don't know. 'Bout midnight, I guess." He poked at the fire absently.

"What the hell you doing up?" I said. "You're not going to be fit to work tomorrow. Why ain't you asleep?"

"I was," he said. "I got woke up."

His voice was funny, and I was by now awake enough to see the expression on his face. I sat up suddenly. "What's the matter, Vaughn?"

"Listen, Ben, we got trouble and I don't know what to do about it."

I glanced over at her, but in the light of the fire I could see nothing wrong. "Trouble? What trouble?"

"It ain't with the Ship."

I relaxed. It couldn't be very important. "What, then?"

"Listen, Ben," he said. "You remember old man Cornwall's cabin that burnt down?"

"Sure, we had to hold off on the keel for a day."

"It wasn't a chimney fire. I mean, it wasn't an accident. It was an Indian that done it."

"An Indian? You mean—that woman and boy was killed by—Vaughn, that ain't reasonable."

"That's what happened."

"How do you know for sure? And why the hell didn't you speak up then?"

"Hell, Ben," he said. "I didn't know till tonight myself. And keep your voice down anyways. Kilchis come tonight. It was one of his people. He just found out, too."

"God, Vaughn. What are we going to do?"

"I wish to hell I'd never found out," Vaughn said miserably.

"You and me." I was suddenly aware of our position here, in a way I'd never even thought of. Twenty or thirty white men and a few families; that was all there was on the whole coast between Clatsop Plains and California. And a good dozen bands of Indians, maybe two dozen. I suddenly felt very small. As long as there was no trouble, it didn't matter, we just got along as well as we could. But now there was trouble and it had to be straightened out one way or another.

"We'll never catch him now," I said hopefully. "That was almost a month ago, we hadn't even got the keel laid."

"We don't have to catch him," Vaughn said, twisting his mouth unhappily. "Kilchis picked him up as soon as he found out."

"What does Kilchis say?"

Vaughn shrugged. "Says he wants peace and order in the Bay. Says he agreed that crimes against the whites would be punished by white law and crimes against his people would be punished by his people."

"My god, does he want this man *hung* or something?"

Vaughn shrugged again. "He wants peace, that's all he says. He says he's done his part, he'll give us the man. Then it's up to us."

"Fine, god, that's just fine. And the framing's almost done."

"Listen, Ben," Vaughn said. "Come along, will you? Kilchis says we have to come get this guy. And he wants to make a bargain."

"All right. But jesus, Vaughn, I don't know what I can do. Can't we just let it go? Anyway, until she's done?"

"No, you know we can't."

And we couldn't. Once it had come up we were stuck with it, and the choices open were not encouraging. If we hung this man, what kind of effect would it have on the surrounding tribes? That was unpredictable. If we didn't hang him—that effect was predictable, we had the experience of the first Valley people to go on. It meant simply that if one man could kill the whites and get away with it, so could everyone else. We were one tiny bubble in a sea of Indians, the Nehalems and Clatsops up the coast, the Yaquina and Alsea south, the Kalapuya inland, the Klackamas and Kelawatset and god knows who else. The bubble could be broken in one night, and if our revenge came later, in the form of the Army or whatever, it would be of very little interest to us. We would all be dead, and the Ship lying half-finished on the ways. The Indians would chop her up for firewood. It was a thought that made me physically sick.

No matter what we did, we were wrong. I think I was more resentful than afraid. The Cornwalls had meant nothing to us, nothing at all, we scarcely knew them. We had no interest in avenging their death, or in justice or anything else of the kind. Not when it meant risking the work.

None of us had even seen the preacher since that terrible scene at the graves. Probably he had wandered blindly back into the Valley, carrying his burden of guilt and punishment, and we were just as happy to have it that way. The sole thing we demanded of the world was to be left alone to work on the Ship, and now even that was cast in doubt. I would have given a hundred dollars never to have heard of this thing.

As we trudged gloomily through the night toward Kilchis' lodge, Vaughn explained to me how it had come about. The Indian, whose name was Estacuga, had been on his way north to trade off some blankets with the Clatsops. He had stopped at the Cornwall cabin for water just at nightfall. Inside, he noticed a barrel of vinegar, which he took to be whisky, and asked for some. This was refused and he was asked to leave. He made camp a little distance away, but in the middle of the night he sneaked back into the cabin. This was not difficult, as there was only a blanket for a door. While he was trying to get the barrel open the old woman woke up and attacked him with a frying pan. He got panicky and killed her with his knife. He killed the boy too, stabbing him and crushing his skull with the frying pan. In this scuffle Estacuga himself was hurt pretty badly, being hit with the heavy cast-iron pan on the face and head.

He was badly frightened when it was all over and set fire to the cabin to cover the traces of the murder. He then went on up to Clatsop Plains and traded with the people up there. When he returned his wounds had not yet healed, and he went to a man we called Indian Jim, a sort of doctor, or *tamanawis* as they call them. Estacuga made up some story of falling down a hill.

Indian Jim treated him for a long time, but the wounds did not heal. Finally Jim decided that his patient had a *Boston sick*, a white man's illness over which his magic had no power. He told Estacuga that the only way it could be made right was if he told everything that had happened. Estacuga told him the whole story, hoping to get well. Kilchis heard it from Indian Jim, had the man brought to his own lodge, and then told Vaughn.

So now he was ours, and we had to decide which risk to take.

3

There were five or six lodges of Kilchis' band clustered on a point by one of the rivers that ran into the Bay. The long squat shapes were almost indistinguishable in the night, the flatness of the roofline being the only sign to distinguish them from the blocky, dark silhouettes of the Coast Range hills. The lodge of the *tyee* himself was set off a little distance from the others.

A slave woman let us through the door-hole and motioned us to the fire that burned toward a back corner. The smell of smoke and dried fish was heavy in the obscurity. Above our heads the drying racks were crammed with strips of salmon and some jerked deer. The customary sleeping bench ran around three sides of the lodge, but the tyee's was made of cedar planks rather than earth, and the space beneath was used for storage. Hundreds of bundles, neatly wrapped in skins or reed mats, testified to Kilchis' wealth.

Kilchis himself was waiting for us near the back, sitting on the sleeping bench with his legs drawn up beneath him. He was a ponderous and frightening figure, like something carved of rain-dark slate. He was utterly motionless as we approached, but the flickering of the fire across the planes of his face gave an illusion of constantly fleeting expression.

"*Klahowya*," he said, and motioned us to sit by the fire.

The old slave woman who had let us in brought a wooden platter and put it before us. There was a large wooden bowl in the center, full of nearly rancid whale oil, and two individual platters containing strips of dried salmon. We dipped the salmon in the oil and got a strip down somehow.

"*Nika ticky howh katsuk nika tillicums*," Kilchis said. "I want peace among my people."

"The Bostons want peace, too," Vaughn said.

"The Bostons are my people now," Kilchis said. "I am *tyee* in this Bay."

I looked at Vaughn to make sure I had understood. It was the first time it had ever occurred to me that Kilchis might feel responsible for *us*, simply because we lived on his land. Questions of responsibility had never entered my head; we just tried to get along and didn't think much about it.

Kilchis leaned forward. "Your ways are not ours. Your law is a law of animals. One is killed, you kill another. You do not pay blood money or blankets to the family, which is right."

"It is a very old law with us," Vaughn said, embarrassed.

"Our law is old also," Kilchis said quietly. "Our law is to stop the killing."

He leaned back again and waited a long time before he spoke. "You will kill this man Estacuga?" he asked, gesturing with his hand.

For the first time I noticed a blanket-wrapped bundle on the sleeping bench a few feet away. It was so completely motionless I could not believe there was a living man beneath it.

"There must be—a trial," Vaughn said. "That is where people talk and decide what is to be done."

Kilchis nodded. "And then you will kill him?"

"If the trial decides he has done this thing he will be punished, yes."

"He had told me with his own tongue he did it," Kilchis said.

"In our law there must be the talking first, to decide," Vaughn said obstinately.

Kilchis shook his head with puzzlement, then lifted his massive shoulders in a gesture of resignation. "You follow your law. I have brought the man to you."

"Kilchis," I said. "What will happen if the man is punished?"

He looked at me, not understanding.

"What will your people do?" I said.

"Listen, Ben," Vaughn said to me in English. "Don't bring this up."

"It's better to know, isn't it? Better than wondering?"

Vaughn thought about it a moment and sighed. "I suppose so," he said discouragedly. I turned back to Kilchis.

"If this man Estacuga is hanged, will your people make war on us?"

"War? I want peace here," he repeated slowly. "There is no war when a crime is punished."

"But our—law, our punishment is more hard than your people's. If by our law he must die with the rope, what will your people say?"

"I am *tyee* here," Kilchis said. "It is not for the people to say, but for me. I agreed with the other Boston who was here before, he who had *tupso*, the beard, that crimes against your people would be punished by your law. I agreed that. I am *tyee* here."

Vaughn looked at me. It was better than we had any reason to expect. It did not solve the problem of the other tribes, but it was better than nothing.

"Was the man alone?" Vaughn said.

"No. There were two women with him. One of my wives." He pointed to the slave woman. "They have done nothing. You will only punish him who did the thing."

"If they were there, can we—"

Kilchis leaned forward again intently. "This thing I will say. The man who did the crime will be punished, and that is justice. But you cannot punish one who has done nothing. Then there would be trouble. There would be anger, and the other bands would not listen to me. Punish the guilty, that is justice. Punish the not-guilty is war. You must understand this."

"No one will be punished who has done nothing, Kilchis. But—can this woman tell what she saw there? That is part of our law."

Kilchis thought about it. "Yes. She can do that."

Vaughn nodded. "Then we are agreed."

"Kloshe, hyas kloshe," Kilchis said. He looked at us closely before he continued. "Now I give you this man to keep peace. In return I ask you a thing to keep peace."

"Ask us?"

"You must keep Tenas Sam away from my people."

Vaughn looked at me, then back at Kilchis. "What about Sam?"

"He is *sullics*, Tenas Sam. He is mad. You must keep him away from my people now, or there will be trouble."

"What has he done?" Vaughn said apprehensively. I was holding my breath out of pure fear.

"It is the woman of Cockshaten, Star of Morning."

"I don't understand, Kilchis. Ben, do you—"

"Tenas Sam makes my people afraid," Kilchis said, leaning forward again. "They are frightened, because he is *sullics*. He wants Cockshaten's woman, he wants to buy her. This is a long time ago, now."

"Holy jesus," Vaughn breathed. "Ben, do you know anything about this?"

"No, hell, nothing like that. It's just a girl, Vaughn, I never—"

"Cockshaten does not want to sell his woman," Kilchis went on. "But Tenas Sam will not listen."

"Kilchis, I swear. We don't know anything about this."

"That is why I tell you," Kilchis said patiently. "He is of your people and you must keep him away. He frightens my people and they do not like it. They want him to go away."

"How, frightens them how?"

"He is not like other men, Tenas Sam. He comes every night to the lodge now. He comes into the lodge and he stands over my people. He says he will kill everybody. He says he will bring the Boston soldiers into the Bay and kill all my people and he will take the woman."

"That's—that's impossible, Kilchis. Sam wouldn't—"

"That frightens the people, what he says. Sometimes he makes loud cries in the lodge at night, and the people cannot sleep. Sometimes he makes strange noises like animals, and weeps like a woman. Sometimes he stays outside the lodge and makes scratchings on the wall."

"Oh, god, oh my god," Vaughn said, putting his head in his hands.

"My people do not want to listen to him talk about killing. When he comes to the lodge and looks at the woman they are frightened. Sometimes he sits all night looking at the woman. When he makes the terrible sounds and scratching on the wall and talks about killing, the people are frightened. They want him to go away."

"Why have your people done nothing to him?"

"They are frightened. He is *sullics*, he is not like other men. They do not wish to touch him, but they do not want him around like that."

Vaughn turned to look at me, and his expression was panicky. "Ben, what are we going to do now?"

"I don't know, Vaughn. Jesus, I don't."

Kilchis waited patiently while we spoke English, then said, "I give you Estacuga. You must keep Tenas Sam away from my people."

"We'll—we'll talk to him, Kilchis."

"He is one of your people. I want peace here. I do not want *sullics* men screaming in the night like animals and taking our women."

"Yes, I understand, Kilchis. We'll—try."

Vaughn sounded helpless, as we both felt. We were shocked by Kilchis' description, as though he had plunged us in cold water. I was full of an incredible dread when I thought about Sam, creeping down to an Indian lodge in the middle of the night, crying out, scratching on the walls, weeping.

We left the lodge, leaving Estacuga with Kilchis until the morning, when we could decide what to do about a trial. After what he had told us about Sam, the trial of a murderer seemed minor.

"Well," Vaughn said, laughing nervously. "Now we know why he don't sleep down at the Ship."

"Listen," I said. "I saw this woman—Sam acted awful strange. But I didn't know anything about the rest of it."

"He's lucky he's still alive, Sam is."

"They're terrible superstitious, the Indians. I guess we're all lucky nothing happened before we found it out."

"Hah!" Vaughn snorted. "Listen, you take a man who does those things Kilchis says he's been doing. You figure you can just say, Sam, you better quit now?"

"He's just trying to scare Cock Hat into selling him the girl."

"Still. It takes a pretty—unusual sort of mind to take that particular line."

"What the hell's *wrong* with him?" I said.

"He's in love," Vaughn said. "Ain't it sweet?"

"The hell of it is—Vaughn, I even *seen* this girl. Christ, that's what I can't understand, I seen her, and there's nothing to see."

"Real women ain't no problem," Vaughn said. "It's when you get an idea of a woman in your head that you're in trouble."

"Well, we're all in the kettle now."

"You know," Vaughn said thoughtfully, "if there's one thing in this world I don't want to suffer for, it's another man's illusions. I got enough trouble with my own."

Chapter Seven

I was glad the Indians were as ignorant of law as we were. The trial of Estacuga would have been open to criticism. The plain fact is, we had no law at all in the country at the time and didn't know how to go about it. We were so uncivilized we couldn't even convict a man of a murder he freely admitted.

Early the next morning the whites drew straws for office. I drew judge, Warren Vaughn got to be attorney, and Joe Champion was foreman of the jury. Most of the rest of the Ship crew were members of the jury.

At the time it seemed perfectly natural that the trial should be held down by the Ship, though looking back I can't see any good reason for it. But she was the focus for everything, and we couldn't get away from her. The judge's bench was the huge fir butt next to the ways. Vaughn brought me down a chair from his cabin.

There were even more people gathered for the trial than for the laying of the keel. I think the entire population of Kilchis' band was there, and the majority of the whites. Some other Indians from the surrounding tribes came to watch but Kilchis sent them away. He said this was a concern of the Bay people, and was nobody else's business. I was greatly relieved by this, as the presence of hostile strangers would have complicated the affair in ways I didn't like to think about.

We were all nervous and on edge as it was, but we had agreed we had to go through with it as best we could and get this man condemned, preferably before noon. We wanted to have the rest of the day to work, though as it turned out we didn't.

When everybody was gathered Kilchis went off to get the prisoner. The jury and the spectators, all of whom were sitting on the ground, fidgeted around and muttered to each other. Vaughn walked back and forth, also muttering, but to himself. I expect he was rehearsing his speech. Joe Champion got on my nerves worse than anybody. He had taken his usual non-active posture with his hands clasped on top of his head, staring up at the sky with his mouth half open. He could do this for hours, absolutely motionless, unless you gave him something definite to do. He strongly resembled an idiot, and every time I followed his glance up in the air to see what was falling, so did I.

"Damn it, Joe," I said. "Can't you pay attention?"

"Attention? Is somethin' happening?" He looked at me in puzzlement, his damned elbows sticking out at the side of his head like ears. I had to admit nothing was going on, and irresistibly Joe turned his eyes back to the sky and opened his mouth.

My bench was not the best in the world, either. There is no possible way to put your knees under a stump. I had to sit off to the side with the stump under my right arm, and that chair teetering precariously on the uneven ground.

After a while the Indians got bored, too, and started wandering around the Ship, which was only a few feet away from my bench. This infuriated Vaughn, who was working himself up to a rousing condemnation anyway, and he hollered at them to get away from the frames. There was, altogether, an enormous amount of noise. The jury muttered, all the Indians were chattering like squirrels. Since there was nobody left in the village itself, all the dogs had followed the parade and there must have been a hundred and fifty of them. Like all the Indian dogs, these mongrel pups had terrible, shrill, yapping voices that never stopped. They were also extremely ugly; waddling, fat little creatures who were kept that way for feast days. These dogs swirled in and around and about the Ship, the judge, the jury, and the spectators like a swarm of bees going in all possible directions. Yapping, yapping, yapping and snarling and whining and howling when they got close enough to someone to be kicked.

At last Kilchis appeared with Estacuga walking beside him, and the two of them slowly came up to the Ship. It was the first time I had seen Estacuga except under the blanket, and he was a terrible sight. The whole left side of his forehead seemed to be split open, and his eye was still puffy and swollen. I expect there must have been a number of bones in his face broken, and he seemed to have trouble moving his jaw. He showed no particular pain, but he was such a pathetically beaten sight I felt sorry for him. The day was extremely warm, even that early in the morning, but Estacuga was completely wrapped from shoulders to ankles in the same Hudson's Bay blanket that had covered him the night before. Kilchis made him sit down ahead of the spectators, just in front of the stump that served as my bench. The jury and Vaughn and I looked at him, and he looked back at us all in turn without saying anything.

"Well, let's get started," Vaughn said finally. He seemed to have lost a lot of his spark when he saw how badly beaten the poor Indian was.

"All right," I said. "This court is now in session." I slammed the stump with one of our carpenter's mallets, which produced no noticeable effect on the noise.

"Listen," I said, "can't you shut up those *dogs?* They're going to drive us all crazy." Vaughn asked Kilchis in the Jargon.

Kilchis nodded and said something in his own language to the crowd. Most of the squaws and slave women got sticks and pieces of scrap lumber from around the Ship and methodically started clubbing the dogs, who simply ran around in circles and howled and yipped. After this the women sat down again, and the dogs returned to yapping in their normal voices. It had looked like a brutal massacre while it was going on, but it changed nothing. The rest of the trial took place with the dogs racing and staggering about and barking at each other and us, so that from time to time you had to shout to be heard.

"All right, Vaughn, which are you going to do first, the prosecution or the defense?"

"Christ, Ben, I can't—I mean, Judge—I can't hear myself *think.*"

"Well, I can't stop them, can I? I tried, didn't I?"

"All right, all right," Vaughn said discouragedly. "I guess I'll do the prosecution first."

I slammed down the mallet. "Who's your first witness?"

"That wife of Kilchis, that woman that was there."

"Call the first witness, then."

Vaughn asked Kilchis. "Estacuga is here," Kilchis said. "Why do you not ask him?"

I looked at Vaughn, and he just shrugged. I was sure we had to have witnesses and testimony to make it official, but there wasn't any real reason Estacuga couldn't testify first if he wanted to.

"All right. Well, Estacuga, what do you have to say?"

He stood up in front of the stump, clutching his blanket. As he rose the blanket edge flipped open briefly and I stared. In one hand, hidden beneath the blanket, he had a huge butcher knife.

"*Vaughn*, come here!" I said.

Estacuga started to make his speech, but he stopped when he saw we weren't listening.

"Jesus Christ, Vaughn. He's got a knife under that blanket a mile long," I whispered.

"Well, what do you expect *me* to do about it?" Vaughn looked pale.

"Take it away from him."

Vaughn half laughed. "The hell with *that*, I don't want to get cut."

I looked at the jury. Joe was watching the sky. There was nobody else I thought would be inclined to do it.

"Well, we sure as hell can't have a trial on a man with a butcher knife."

"Kilchis," Vaughn said. "This man has a weapon."

"What man?"

"Estacuga. He's got a big knife under his blanket."

Kilchis said something rapid in the Salishan dialect they used, and Estacuga murmured a brief answer.

"He says it is his own knife, he did not steal it."

"You have to take it away from him," I told the *tyee*. "We can't do this trial on a man that's fit to murder us with a *knife.*"

He said something again, and this time Estacuga answered at greater length. It was awful to watch how carefully he had to move his jaw to speak, and how much it obviously hurt.

"He wants to keep the knife," Kilchis said. "It is his knife and it makes him feel better to have it. He will give it to you when you hang him."

"Yeah," Vaughn muttered. "But *where*, is what I want to know."

"Kilchis—"

"This is finished," Kilchis said impatiently. "We are not here to talk about this knife."

Vaughn sighed and shook his head. "Get on with it, Ben. We'll just have to go ahead."

"I sure don't like it."

"You don't have to," Vaughn said.

"All right. Estacuga, what do you have to say?"

Estacuga spoke in the Jargon this time, having prepared his statement beforehand. "*Nika mamook memaloose Boston klootchman*," he said. "I killed the white woman." Then he said the same about the son, and sat down.

"Did you burn down the cabin, too?" I asked him.

"*Nowitka*," he nodded.

I looked at Kilchis, who appeared to be satisfied.

"All right, call the first witness," I said.

"He said he has done it," Kilchis objected. "Why do these other things? Punish him and we will all go home."

I explained as best I could that it was the Boston law to do things with witnesses and testimony, and there was no help for it. Kilchis was annoyed, and I resolved to get the thing finished as fast as I could. His cooperation was the single thing we had in our favor, and I didn't want him angry at us.

The slave woman came out of the mass of seated spectators, and with Kilchis as intermediary we questioned her. Because of the languages it was a clumsy process. The question was framed in English, Vaughn translated it for Kilchis into the Jargon, Kilchis translated into Salishan for the woman, who spoke only her own tongue.

"Where were you the night Estacuga killed the white people and burned down the cabin?"

"She was with Estacuga," Kilchis said. "I told you that."

"No, we have to ask *her*," I said.

Kilchis asked her, impatiently, and turned back with an expression of triumph. "She was with Estacuga."

We questioned her some more and in the end we learned what no longer surprised us much, that Estacuga had killed the white people and burned down the cabin. By this time I was embarrassed about the whole trial. Kilchis obviously considered it useless. And while he knew no more about legal procedure than we did, there was no question but that he knew all there was to know about justice.

I was doggedly going to go ahead and question the other woman, when there was a sudden movement among the Indians, a kind of shiver as though a cold wind had come off the bay. I thought they were staring at me, then realized they were looking behind me.

I turned, and there stood Sam Howard, his blond hair flying around his head, his eyes wild and soot-dark.

"Hullo, Sam," Joe Champion said.

I turned quickly back to the crowd. I spotted Cock Hat, but not his woman, and was relieved. Sam said nothing, just stared with that maniac look to him. The Indians watched him intently, moving restlessly, but not speaking. For the first time even the side conversations had stopped, and there was no sound but the yapping of the dogs, which we had almost ceased to hear.

Sam moved up beside me without turning his head and stared down at Estacuga. The Indian looked up at him, and suddenly scrambled to his feet.

I grabbed Sam's elbow and said, "Sam, he's got a knife."

Sam shook me off without hearing and went to stand right in front of Estacuga. He was as small as the Indian, and for a moment they faced each other in silence. I was sure Sam was going to get cut. I suddenly thought what that would mean to the Ship, to have Sam hurt, and jumped up myself, knocking over my chair.

"Sam!" I said. "Listen, don't—"

"You wasn't alone, was you?" Sam said in English.

Estacuga looked around in panic, the wildness of his stare almost equaling Sam's.

Kilchis and I reached the two of them at the same moment, Kilchis taking the Indian's arm and pulling him away, me grabbing Sam.

"Sam, you'll get yourself cut! Think of the Ship, Sam, he's got a knife!"

"He wasn't alone," Sam said angrily. "Ask him. He wasn't alone."

"All right, I'll ask him. But you come back here, Sam. Jesus, think of the Ship if you got cut."

Sam let himself be pulled back to the judge's bench and I set the chair up again by the stump and pounded with the mallet. The day was already so hot I was sweating through my shirt.

"Ask him," Sam kept saying. "Just ask him."

"Estacuga, were you alone that night?"

"*Wake.*"

"Who was with you, then?"

Estacuga pointed out Kilchis' slave woman and the woman in the crowd I hadn't gotten around to questioning yet.

"This is all finished," Kilchis said. "The women did nothing."

"Ask him," Sam said again. "Ask him why he don't tell the truth. Cock Hat was there and helped him kill them people."

"Sam, listen—"

"ASK HIM ASK HIM ASK HIM!" Sam's fists were clenched at his side and rivulets of sweat were running down into his eyes. He looked so wild and crazy he scared us all.

"Was—was Cock Hat with you?"

"*Wake, wake,*" Estacuga shook his head definitely.

"He's lying," Sam said. "Cock Hat killed them people. I know."

He stared around the crowd until he picked out Cock Hat. When Sam's eyes met his the Indian squatted suddenly to his heels and began to trace aimless patterns in the dirt with his finger.

"There he is," Sam said, "the murderin' bastard. There he is, he's even wearin' old man Cornwall's clothes. Look at him."

Cock Hat was in fact wearing a shiny satin vest, but we had all seen him in it before.

Kilchis had come over to stand by the bench, where he was close to Sam. He glanced at the little man out of the corner of his eye. "What does he say?" Kilchis asked me.

"He said Cock Hat is the murderer, he has the old man's clothes."

Kilchis stared at Sam for a moment, trying to decide what to do. Then he looked at the crowd and said in the Jargon, "Where did Cockshaten get his shining clothes?"

Cock Hat stood up straight at the sound of Kilchis' voice and pointed to Estacuga. "Cockshaten bought the shining clothes from Estacuga, with other things. He paid two blankets."

"What other things?" Kilchis said.

"A coat, pants, and an iron kettle for cooking," Cockshaten said.

"Where did these things come from?" the *tyee* asked.

"From the cabin of the Bostons that Estacuga burned."

Kilchis lowered his head for a moment, like a bull about to charge. Then he said, "Those things will be returned to the Bostons, for they were stolen things."

"Will Estacuga return my blankets?" Cock Hat said.

"No. You will pay the blankets as money to the Bostons for buying things that were stolen from them. That is my word, that is just."

"That is just," Cock Hat said reluctantly, in formal agreement. He obviously didn't like it, but there was no appeal from Kilchis' judgement.

I had not caught all of this, despite the fact that Kilchis was speaking the Jargon for our benefit. Vaughn had been explaining in English.

"No," Sam said suddenly. "No, he don't get off that easy, the murderer. He was there. He done it. I know he did."

"Sam, please," I begged him. "Don't be crazy, don't make trouble."

"ASK HIM!"

"All right, Sam, all right. Cock Hat, were you with Estacuga?"

"No."

"Make him prove it. Make him prove it."

"Sam, he can't prove he *wasn't* some place."

"Make him prove where he was."

I asked.

Cock Hat thought for a long time, counting days on his fingers, asking people in the crowd. Finally he brightened. "Cockshaten was at the Nestucca River. There was a whale ashore, and Cockshaten went to trade for oil. He took blankets and salmon."

"That is right," Kilchis nodded. "There was a whale ashore there. "

"Wait a minute," I said. "Wait—" Then I began to count on *my* fingers. "The day we laid the keel—it would be two days before that . . ."

"What are you figurin', Ben?" Vaughn asked.

"Cock Hat is right," I said finally. "Three days before we laid the keel he came to my place with blankets and salmon and wanted to trade for a knife. He said he was going to the Nestucca because there was a whale ashore there. He *couldn't* have been with Estacuga."

"Yes," Cock Hat said. "Yes. I wanted a knife from you. You said you would buy a knife from *me*, if I had one."

Another of the Indians offered the information that Cockshaten had brought back whale oil from Nestucca, so there was no question.

Vaughn wiped his forehead. "All right, it's settled."

Sam looked at me. "You can't be sure. It was a long time ago."

"No, I'm sure, Sam. Honest to god. It was three days before we laid the keel, and the murder would've been the day after. There ain't no doubt at all, I'm sure of it. He was fifty miles away."

Sam's eyes were so strange I couldn't meet them for long. He stared at me, and he stared at Cock Hat. Suddenly he turned and charged off toward his place without saying another word.

Joe Champion clasped his hands on top of his head and surveyed the sky. The Indians relaxed and started talking to each other again, and I could suddenly hear the annoying yipping of the dogs. I felt weak and shaky, I felt like a man who has just slipped off a cliff and caught himself in time, there was a tingling thrill of falling in my toes.

"We're going to have to talk to Sam or something," Vaughn said worriedly.

"Sufficient to the day the trouble thereof," I said. "Or something like that. Let's get this trial over."

We convicted Estacuga, and just at the moment Joe Champion was saying "Guilty, I guess," Vaughn had a stroke of absolute genius. He jumped up excitedly and had to calm himself before he could speak.

"The victim will have to be sentenced and punished by regular law," he said. "We could do the trial all right, but we have to have regular law for the rest of it."

"What are you gettin' at, Vaughn?"

"Listen, Ben, the nearest regular Territorial District with law and all that kind of stuff is in the Valley, ain't that right? The Yam Hill district? They got a sheriff and all."

"Ha! Them Yam Hill boys *need* law worse'n most. They're a rough bunch."

"No, listen, what I'm sayin' is, the Bay here sort of belongs to the Yam Hill District as far as legal goes. We got to turn the victim over to the District Court in there. We should've done that in the first place, but I didn't think of it."

It was perfect. If we did not do the hanging ourselves, as far as the Indians were concerned it would be the Yam Hillers who were responsible for it. We'd satisfied justice by having a trial and condemning him, but we wouldn't have to take the blame for the hanging if it were done in the Yam Hill District. It was the way their minds worked, and it got us out clean.

"Vaughn, jesus, man, you're a legal genius."

"I am, I am!" He was so excited he was almost hopping.

Kilchis asked what was going on and we explained it to him, how it was Boston law, etc., etc. All he said was that the Boston law took an awfully long time to take care of things, but if that was what was necessary it was all right.

So. It had worked out after all, in spite of our forebodings. We would be left to work in peace. A couple days' delay at most and we could get back to her. Three of the jurymen and I would escort Estacuga into Lafayette, where there was a regular Territorial Sheriff.

The whole crowd broke up, and there was no complaining from anybody. Kilchis was dissatisfied that it had taken so long to conclude the obvious but it was still over and done with by noon.

I hung around the Ship, looking at the framing, and it seemed a month since I'd touched her. Missing one mornings's work was enough to do that to me. I was running my hand down one of the bevels, feeling the smooth change of angle and counting in my mind how easy the planking would go over a bevel as beautiful as that. Cock Hat came up beside me and touched me on the shoulder.

"Mahsie," he said. *"Hiyu, hiyu mahsie."*

"Hell, nothin' to thank me for, Cock Hat."

"You not speak—he kill me, the little man."

"Hell," I said jokingly. "It didn't cost me nothin'. A man's life is a man's life, after all." It embarrassed me a little to be thanked for simply telling the truth. What else did he expect?

"Mahsie," he repeated, smiling. *"Nesika kahkwa tillicums.* We are the same people." It was a damn nice thing to say, and made me a little proud.

He left then, and I looked back at the incredible complex beauty of the framing members with the hot midday sun pouring down and molding them with gold and deep purple shadows.

2

I loafed around her the rest of the day, not doing too much, smoothing out a joint here and there, checking that the treenails were tight and flush in the futtocks. The trial had left me empty and restless. I suppose it was the sudden succession of terrible apprehension about Sam and the equally strong relief that Vaughn had found us a way out. I was really ashamed of what Sam had tried to do, and I suppose he was, too. He was really out of himself, there. When he realized he had actually tried to get an innocent man hanged he would be so humiliated with shame and guilt he would probably be in a terrible state about it for a week. I felt sorry for him. It's an awful thing to lose control over yourself; awful afterwards, when you can think about it.

The next morning the three jurymen and Estacuga and myself set off for the Yam Hill District. I was happy to see that Estacuga had given Kilchis the knife after the trial, as I would not have cared to escort a wild Indian with a knife through the broken country of the Coast Range.

This was the first time I had been Outside since I came down to the Bay, and I was pleasantly surprised. The numbers of people that had come through in the last couple of years had left a very respectable trail. It was an entirely different history from my first trip, my nine days of confusion and misdirection. By starting at first light we had crossed the spine of the range and were nearing Lafayette by late evening, around eight o'clock.

Estacuga had said nothing during the entire voyage. He was about as miserable as it is possible for a man to be. Whenever we stopped to breathe a little, or to take a bite to eat, Estacuga covered himself over with his blanket, face and all, and lay still as a corpse. When the time came to go again, he got up without protest and went on. He acted as though he were already dead, or perhaps his wounds hurt so much he was incapable of anything else. In any case his lack of apparent emotion was a blessing for us. I don't know what we would have done had he screamed and cried and tried to get away. And I can tell you that if I were going to *my* hanging, I would scream and cry and try to get away.

By the time it was full dark we were in the house of the sheriff, one James Quick. Mr. Quick was a regular Territorial Sheriff, that is to say he had been sent in there by the Provisional government. He was not one of the Yam Hill boys. These fellows in Yam Hill were probably all fine boys, but they were the scum of the earth. The district was a kind of dump heap for every individual who was not able to get along anywhere else. I remember in Oregon City when a drunk got mean or vicious we used to say, "There's a boy for Yam Hill," and if it kept up he usually ended there. I have always been afraid of toughs like that, because you never know what they're going to do next, if you don't understand their kind of mind.

The Yam Hill boys always had ten times as much trouble with the Indians as anyone else, and it is my belief that they provoked this trouble with their violent ways and a never ceasing hatred of the Indian. It was the Kalapuya people around there, and I had always found them very inoffensive. Nevertheless, there was so much hostility that a bunch of the Territorial Militia was permanently barracked there to take care of emergencies.

With this high feeling against the Indians in the District, our arrival with the prisoner caused a great deal of excitement. The news went around the country like a brush fire. Between our arrival and midnight there were seven or eight of the boys there at the Sheriff's house. As I have said, Mr. Quick was an honorable man and not one of the Yam Hill boys.

"Well, boys," he said, "we'll lock him up good. You just give me the papers and she's as good as done."

"What papers?" I said.

"The commitment papers."

"Well—we got no papers. We just got *him.*"

"You said you had a court down there at the Bay," Quick said. "Didn't they give you no commitment papers?"

"Well—to tell you the truth, it was a kind of informal sort of court, Mr. Quick."

"Who's your justice of the peace down there?"

"I was. Anyway, I was the judge. We drew straws. We don't have any statute down there or anything."

Quick frowned. "You know, this ain't regular, Mr. Thaler. I mean, I'm just a sheriff, I can't accept to arrest a man without no papers to commit him."

One of the Yam Hill boys, named Wallace I believe, grunted like a bear. He was a big, heavy man with a beard, and very surly.

"Papers, papers," he muttered belligerently. "God damn, Quick, you're the pickiest man I ever see. Hang the sonofabitch and have done with it."

"Law's law, Wallace." Quick said, sighing. "I got to have papers."

"Well I say hang the sonofabitch and have done with it," Wallace mumbled. "Jesus, papers. Goddam schoolmarm you are, Quick."

"You tend to your business, Wallace, and I'll tend to mine. You been in my lockup more'n any man in the District, but you ain't any smarter for it."

"Hell, you ain't *s'posed* to get smart in a lockup! That's what they got *schools* for!" Wallace roared at his own wit. "Don't you even know *that?* That's what they got *schools* for, is to get smart. You ain't *s'posed* to get smart in a lockup!"

"Well, Sheriff, what do we do?" I asked him.

"All I can tell you is I got to have commitment papers. You'd ought to have them signed by the foreman of your jury and your judge and the arresting officer and all. And witnessed. Particular, I don't want any trouble on account yours wasn't a regular court or anything."

"Now wait a minute," Wallace said heavily. "You ain't going to let this bastard go *loose*, are you? It ain't ever' day a man gets a chancet to hang a Siwash, not legal anyways."

"I suppose I could go back and get some papers. I don't really know what to do."

"Goddam shame to let a dirty murderin' bastard like that go *loose*," Wallace grumbled.

"Wallace, you shut your trap or I'll lock you up with him."

Wallace roared again. "*That* ain't such a bad idee," he said. "That way we'd know for sure the sonofabitch wouldn't come out alive!"

"Well, Mr. Thaler," Quick said to me. "I think you'd better get me them papers. That way there won't be any trouble with the government. I hate like hell to make you go back, but it's my job I'm thinking about. I don't want any more trouble than I got, on account of irregularity or anything."

"I b'lieve you're goin' to let that boy *loose*," Wallace muttered. "That ain't justice. You call that justice? Hey, Quick?"

"Never saw you worryin' so much about justice, Wallace," Quick said impatiently.

"Oh, hell, I ain't *worryin'* or anything. But I tell you, I sure do like to see them dance around, them red bastards. Hey, you!" He hollered at Estacuga. He pretended to have a rope around his neck and bugged out his eyes and stuck out his tongue and made strangling noises. When Estacuga turned away without saying anything Wallace broke up in roars of laughter and slapped his thighs.

"Listen, boys, what do y' say we take him out and string him up now? Right *quick*. We do it *quick*, how do y' like that?"

"Shut up, Wallace!"

"No, listen, Quick," Wallace said, gasping for breath. "We do it *quick*, how about that?"

One of the other Yam Hill boys spoke up for the first time. "No, you know, Wally's right. Be a goddam shame to let this boy go loose on account of some papers."

I stood up. "Listen, I'll get the papers. I can get back here in a couple of days. All right? Mr. Quick, you can keep Estacuga till then, can't you?"

"Ezgakuga, what the hell's *that?*" Wallace said.

"That's his name."

"Hell, they ain't got names, the sonsabitches. They's all Mr. Siwash to me. Hey, Mr. Siwash!" He went through his little strangling act again. He was the most easily amused man I ever saw, Wallace was.

"All right," Quick said. "I'll lock him up until you get back."

"Hey, wait a minute. What if somethin' happens to this here guy? I mean, what if he busts a leg or something? What if he can't even *write* them papers? Listen guy, c'n you *write?*"

"Good enough for that. Or if I can't, Vaughn can."

"I'm just worried something happen to you is all," Wallace said happily. "I mean, then they let this bastard *loose*, or something."

"I'll leave first thing in the morning and then be back day after tomorrow," I said.

"All right," Quick said. "But one o' your boys best stay here, so's I ain't got the responsibility of holdin' him without papers."

None of the three men with me was very enthusiastic about staying in Yam Hill any longer than he had to. If this was civilization, we much preferred the Bay. But finally Peter Morgan agreed to wait there until I could get back with the papers. Quick put Estacuga in his "lockup," which was just a sort of woodshed attached to his house. The Yam Hill boys went on home, grumbling about what a shame it would be to let him go *loose* after all that trouble. The rest of us rolled up in blankets lent us by the Sheriff, and in the early morning I set off again for the Bay.

We set a good two-forty pace and reached Vaughn's before dark. Vaughn pointed out that if I'd said Morgan or one of the others had been foreman of the jury I could have saved the whole trip and made out the papers right there. But Joe Champion had been foreman, and it had never even occurred to me to say anything different.

Vaughn being good with words, he made out the papers in a couple of hours, and I signed for judge. Vaughn himself signed "Joe

Champion," because, as he said, it saved a lot of trouble. It depressed me, since it made all my trouble seem for nothing. Since Joe's signature was illegal anyway, *anybody* could have done it. Vaughn said the *signature* wasn't illegal, just the "X."

Joe couldn't write, so somebody else would have had to write the signature. It didn't seem so serious to forge just the "X."

In any case the effort was not wasted, as I didn't make the return trip after all. Peter Morgan came trudging in about midnight, looking pale and scared.

"Don't bother goin' back, Ben," he said. "They came and got him this morning about an hour after you left."

"Who?"

"That big bastard with the beard and about a dozen others."

"What did—"

"What the hell do you *think?* Strung him up high and short. They got a good laugh out of it, I guess."

Vaughn cleared his throat and looked down at the floor for a moment. "Well," he said hesitantly, "anyway, there wasn't any doubt he was guilty or anything. I mean, it ain't like—"

"I didn't see it, even," Morgan said. "They run me out, same time they got Estacuga out of the lockup."

"What'd Quick do?"

"Hell, I don't know," Morgan said. "I tell you plain, Ben, when that bunch said 'Frog,' I jumped. I don't want no trouble with that kind. Sam'll tell you about it, he prob'ly saw it."

"Sam? Little Sam? What are you talking—"

Morgan looked up in surprise. "Didn't you pass him on the trail?"

"No, hell—"

"Yeah, well Sam pulled in about fifteen minutes after you'd left. I figured you'd of met him on the trail."

"Vaughn," I said, "did Sam say anythin' to you about going Outside?"

Vaughn shook his head. "Not a damn word. I ain't seen him since the trial."

"He looked real tired, Sam did," Morgan said. "He must of walked all night."

Chapter Eight

W e went back to work the next morning. Sam had not returned, and the way he had been lately none of us was willing to wait; he might not get back until tomorrow or the next day. We couldn't tell what was in his mind, and nobody could stand the idea of another day without work.

We had put up enough frames under Sam's guidance that we were pretty confident we could do it alone. I myself felt a certain desire to try out my wings. There was a kind of sneaky satisfaction in going ahead on our own, as I suppose a baby must feel when he takes his first step without the supporting pressure of his mother's hand.

We got Number Twenty up in pretty good shape, though it seemed to take an enormous amount of time; much more than when Sam was there. I don't know why, really; there were as many men working. But we checked and re-checked everything like maniacs. We had already had to remount two frames that didn't satisfy Sam, and he had checked them *himself*. None of us wanted to risk an imprecision that would bring down his wrath and make us do it all over again.

So I doubt that any frame in the history of shipbuilding has been horned and trued as carefully as our Number Twenty. It made us all very cheerful to see her standing there, even though it was already afternoon when we finished. This one we had done by ourselves. There wasn't so damned much to framing after all; you just had to work careful, work like a shipwright.

"All right," Vaughn said. *"Now* we're sailin'!"

"Hooraw boys," Thomas said. "Let's get Twenty-one going now."

Vaughn and I were doing the horning together, checking each other so there couldn't be any mistake. While we waited for Twenty-one we contemplated the beauty of the Ship. Our frames ran six to eight inches in thickness and were around ten inches apart. The effect was that the hull looked almost solid if you squinted your eyes and allowed a little in your mind for the air spaces. We could see her as she would be when the planking was on, a full and graceful whole.

"By god," I said, "for a pack o' farmers we're a pretty damn good bunch of shipwrights."

"I don't believe I ever saw a hull go up any faster," Vaughn said contentedly. "And there's been days we haven't worked, neither."

"Yeah, but those days still count," I said.

"No, they don't count. You figure by the number of days actual *work.*"

"That don't tell you nothin', Vaughn. You got to figure all the time it takes from beginning to end."

"Just the workin' days," Vaughn said definitely.

"That don't make sense. S'pose you work two days and get up three frames. Then you take a year off, then you put up another frame. You only worked three days, right?"

Vaughn frowned. "Yeah, but—"

"But it's took you better'n a year to get up four frames, that's the way you got to figure."

"A *year* to get up four frames! Hell, we can do that in a few days! "

"Vaughn, god damn you, you ain't *listening*. That's what the whole trouble with you is, you never damn *listen.*"

"I'm listening, I'm listening. You said a year to put up four frames. Now isn't that just *exactly* what you said?"

"Yes, but—oh, never mind. Sometimes you're worse'n Thomas, you're so damn butt-head and you never *listen.*"

Vaughn shrugged.

"Anyway," I said. "You never saw a ship built in your life before. How do *you* know whether this is goin' up fast or not? Maybe some guys get the framing done in a week, for all you know."

"First it takes you a year to get up four frames, and now you get the whole thing done in a week. Listen, Ben, there's something wrong with your *mind*. You got a mind like a grasshopper."

"You said that before."

"Then why don't you *do* something about it?"

"Hell, I can't do anything about my mind, you idiot. Anyway, just because you say it don't make it true. And anyway—"

"Hey, you guys!"

We looked around and there stood Twenty-one ready to go, with Thomas and two others holding it and looking impatiently at us.

"You come to work or not?" Thomas demanded bitterly. "What the hell you talkin' about, anyway?"

"Talkin' about Ben's mind," Vaughn said.

"There ain't all *that* much to it," Thomas said. "How can you—"

"Listen, Thomas, you funny bastard—" I started.

But he had just caught on that he had said something funny and went into hysterics.

"Hell," he said, gasping for breath, "I mean, a subject like that, you ought to be able to finish up right quick."

"All right, all right. Come on, we got a ship to build or not?"

So Vaughn and I horned it in while Thomas chuckled obscurely at his own wit.

"All right, tie 'er down," Vaughn called, in an unconscious imitation of Little Sam's high voice. The frame was blocked into position and Thomas began to bore for the driftbolts in the floor futtock.

"You know," Vaughn said, "Sam tells me they got a regular Wood Borers' Association in the shipyards back East. Them guys don't do nothin' but bore."

"I ain't surprised," I said. "When we get down to the deadwoods and got to have three foot of dead straight bore she's going to take a little doin'. It's a regular trade, know how to do that just right."

"Main thing, you can't force your auger," Vaughn confided, as though he'd founded the Wood Borers' Association.

The driftbolt was, naturally, the wrong one. A driftbolt has to be two and a half times the length of the pieces it joins. That's the rule, and this was too short by a couple of inches. Finally Thomas scrabbled around and hollered at the blacksmith shop loud enough that the right bolt appeared by magic and we tied down Twenty-one.

"There she is, boys," Vaughn said majestically. "All right, let's have Twenty-two up here."

"Oh, no," I said, unable to believe my eyes.

"What do you mean, oh, no?" Vaughn said irritably. "You can see it for your own self, can't you? Come on, boys, let's—"

"God, Vaughn, look!"

He looked, but she was square and trued with the keel.

"What's the *matter* with you, Ben? You got a mind like a—"

"It's backwards. We put her in backwards."

"—grasshopper. Oh sweet jesus, we did." He walked over to the frame like a sleepwalker and put his hand on it tentatively, as a man would touch a hot stove.

"The bevel's facin' the wrong way."

We were well back from the midships timber and the frame bevel was quite pronounced. But instead of slanting back toward the stern it slanted forward toward the bow.

"How could we *miss* it?" Vaughn kept saying, "how could we *miss* it?"

"You was so damn busy talkin' about Ben's so-called mind," Thomas said.

"You was there all the time, too, Thomas," I told him.

"It ain't *my* job to place her," Thomas said. "I hold and I drill, that's what *I* do. *You* guys're the experts about bevels and like that. To hear you talk, anyway."

"All right," Vaughn said dispiritedly. "Let's not argue, let's just take her down and start again. How *could* we . . ."

So we took her down and then there wasn't enough time to remount her that day because we ran out of light. It gave us a start because it was such a stupid thing to do, such a terrible stupid thing. We were less confident of our solitary ability when we finally got her back in the next morning.

"Listen, one thing we got to agree on," Vaughn said the first thing, before we'd even started work.

"Let's agree to put 'em in frontwards," I said. "That'll solve a whole lot of our problems right there."

"No, listen," Vaughn said intently. He'd obviously given this a lot of thought during the night. "Nobody says anything about this to Sam, all right? Nobody says one word, we fix it and that's all there is to it and Sam don't have to know. All right?"

He didn't have any trouble getting unanimous agreement, and Twenty-one went back in right and we were all relieved when it was done.

"All right, bring up Twenty-two," Vaughn said. "We had a bad start, boys, but that's a good sign. Today we'll really roll, and surprise Sam when he gets back."

"Wait a minute, Vaughn," I said. "Come here a minute." I was studying the model of the Ship, checking position and shape of the next frame.

"What's the trouble?" Vaughn said apprehensively.

"None yet. But look here. We're on Twenty-two, right?"

"Right."

"Well, Twenty-two ain't a vertical frame. Count 'em your own self."

He counted the frames in the model. And I was right. The last frames both fore and aft are not vertical with the keel, but incline forward or back. Twenty-two was the first of the inclined frames aft, and it had to slant back toward the sternpost, just a little. After Twenty-two each frame slanted a bit more until the very last, the fashion timber, had to be canted so it just came to the end of the main transom.

"Well, that just means we're really movin'," Vaughn muttered. "All right, boys," he addressed the crew. "We've finished up the squares and we're going to start on the cant-timbers now."

"Yeah, but *how?*" I said.

"There must be another angle board to true the cant-timbers," Vaughn said hopefully.

"Sure. But where?"

Vaughn poked around in the piles of scrap lumber and found half a dozen triangular shapes, any of which might or might not have served to indicate an angle for one of the cant-timbers. He suspiciously examined each one, turning it over and over in his hands. Then he dropped them all disconsolately in a pile.

"Listen, did he say anything about having the angle boards for the cant-timbers made?"

Nobody remembered if he had or not. Every day we were so busy with the day's work there was no chance to think about what came next, what would be required for it, and whether or not it was prepared. When the time came everything was ready, always. When a new gauge or angle was necessary, Sam had it. He took care of things like that.

"It's in Sam's head," Thomas said morosely. "Like ever' other goddam thing about this ship."

And he was right, of course. Without Little Sam we had accomplished only one day's work, and done *that* wrong. The second day—we couldn't even start, couldn't even pick up a tool. In spite of the model, in spite of the frames, in spite of the work, there was no such thing as the Ship. She existed—really existed—only in Sam's head. The rest of it was merely a hint, a handy reminder of the dream.

"Well—I guess we may as well face it," Vaughn said. "Without Sam we don't amount to a whole hell of a lot."

"That's about it."

"What the hell's he doin' Outside, anyway?" somebody asked irritably. "He belongs here with the Ship."

"Well," Vaughn said with finality, "there's nothing for it. We'll quit for the day and maybe he'll be back tomorrow. He can't stay away from her very long."

In fact it seemed totally bewildering that he should be gone, and silly to boot. There was nothing to do Outside that could interest a man; the Ship was here. But gone he was, and we dragged off home though it wasn't even eight o'clock in the morning yet. A whole damn day stretched endlessly ahead of us. I didn't know what to do. It had been so long since I'd had to *decide* what to do with my time I'd forgotten how to do it. You got up and you went to work and that was all there was to it. Having to make a decision about spending my energy seemed a completely new experience to me.

What I finally did was, I sat on my doorstep in the morning and I took a nap in the afternoon by the Ship, and cursed the emptiness of such an absurd and useless day and hoped Sam would get back soon.

2

I had lazed around so much during the day that I was exhausted by nightfall, and went to bed just after dark. I slept so thunderous heavy all night I could hardly wake up when Indian Jim came around in the early light, pushing and hauling at my shoulder.

"What—what's it?" I said, sitting up and untangling my blanket. My eyes felt puffy and heavy from all the unaccustomed sleep. I glanced up at the silhouette of the frames against the lightening sky and marveled all over again at how—

Jim tugged at my shoulder. "You come, you come quick."

"All right, all right, don't push at me so." I hauled on my pants clumsily and reached for my boots. I have a trouble, which is that when I first wake I am a little bit simple. I liked to spend those first drifty moments looking at the Ship, and Jim's insistence was annoying. It finally occurred to me to ask *why* I had to come. As usual I had been doing as I was told, on the assumption that anyone who could talk was in a better position than I to know what I should do.

"Bad. Very bad. *Hiyu cultus.*"

"Yeah, but *what?*"

"Tenas Sam is come back. With all the Boston soldiers. They say they going to kill us all."

I knew then it was just a realistic dream, and it relieved me. There was no possible way for the white soldiers to be here, there'd never even been one in the Bay. They had their hands full with the settlers who didn't get along with their Indians.

Still—the chill of the dawn was so distinct it worried me a little. "How many Boston soldiers are there?" I asked Jim.

"Many, many. Two thousand."

It was reasonable enough, for a dream, but Indian Jim might simply have picked the number at random; Indians do not have a very precise idea of such things.

"I get Vaughn and the others," Jim said. "You go on? You not let them kill everybody, all right?"

Jim took off fast for Vaughn's place and I continued down the beach toward the village. After a minute or two I began to run, and by the time I first caught sight of the blue militia caps I was completely awake. Awake and sick with dread.

There were not two thousand, but there were enough. Perhaps twenty, perhaps a few more, I didn't stop to count. And they weren't exactly Boston soldiers. It was the Yam Hill crowd, wearing blue military caps.

They were spread negligently in a semicircle around the lodges, rifles on full cock and pointed square at the doors. There was one man in full military uniform and I ran for him. He was talking to another huge bear of a fellow whose back was turned to me.

As I ran up, panting, the huge man swung around sharply and lifted his gun. It was Wallace, big dirty beard and all. He relaxed when he saw it was just me and said to the military, "Well, lootenant, here's the Judge right now, just in time for the hollering."

The military stuck out his hand and said deferentially, "Lieutenant Anderson, Judge. Hope you haven't had too hard a time."

"I'm no judge," I said. "Listen, my god, what are you doing here?"

"Say, boy," Wallace said, shoving his big black beard at me. "You never come back with them papers. I was worried somethin' happen to you."

"Lieutenant, what in god's name are you doing? You'll get us *killed.*"

"Now, Judge, don't worry about a thing," the lieutenant said, very sympathetic. "I know you've been going through hell here, but the situation's in control now. Don't you worry about a thing."

"Hell, no," Wallace said. "We'll take care of ever'thing. Listen guy, I was real worried you'd busted a leg or somethin'." He exploded into his great guttural laughter and the lieutenant looked at him curiously.

"Yeah, you were so worried you hung Estacuga," I said.

"Well, hell. When you didn't come back and *didn't* come back, we figured as how you was *lost* or somethin'."

"You took him half an hour after I left."

"Was that it?" Wallace said with ponderous surprise. "Don't exackly remember me. Never did have too good sense o' time, you know." He bellowed again. "Listen lootenant, you're going t' love the judge, here, he's a real comical guy."

"Judge," the lieutenant said, "you really should have sent word sooner."

"Word? Word? What are you talking about?"

"You know Oregon's a full-fledged Territory now. The day's past when you have to defend yourself against these red savages all alone. That's what the Army's for. You can call on the government now."

"We never defended ourselves in our lives—"

"I imagine not," the lieutenant said sympathetically. "Isolated as you are here—it must have been hell, Judge. Believe me, I know these beasts. You should have tried to get word out to us. When we heard the Killamooks had gone on the warpath and were massacring your people down here, why naturally we came right away. We'll take care of everything." He put his hand on my shoulder. "That's what the Army's for, Judge, you know that's why you pay taxes and all."

"Warpath? What are you talking about, *warpath*? And you call this rag-tag bunch of ruffians an *Army?*"

"Don't worry, Judge, it's all official. These boys are militia. They ain't regular Army but they'll fight and die for this Territory with all their hearts."

I stared at him. I couldn't believe my ears. Here he stood on his own two feet in the middle of Oregon, talking about Indians on the warpath and fighting and dying and probably Old Glory and liberty next.

"Lieutenant, how long you been in this country?"

"Fifteen months," he said proudly. "Got nine to go."

Fifteen months and he still thought he was living in the middle of a newspaper thriller. Or something. I didn't know *what* kind of world he was living in, but I knew it wasn't the same as mine. Warpath . . .

"Look, Lieutenant, I can't explain everything—listen, we're building a ship here, we can't have any trouble. We just *can't!*"

"Hell, boy," Wallace said. "That's what us volunteers is *here* for. In case there should maybe any trouble come up."

"What the hell *are* you here for? Just tell me, please tell me."

"Why, we figure to finish up this here little job that we started with Mister Siwash up to home," Wallace said. "Listen lootenant, you see what I mean he's a real comical guy, the Judge? I mean, I think he's got a little bit hysterical from all the fear or somethin'."

"We're here to protect you settlers from the savages," the Lieutenant said. "And to discipline them. You know, so they won't massacre you any more," he added by way of explanation.

"Protect us from *what*? We don't need protecting, we do fine. Get out of here, you're going to get us all killed!"

"Like I was sayin' to the lootenant, I b'lieve you're a little bit hysterical or somethin', Judge. If you guys is in such a dead-ally danger to get killed, why you need pertectin'. Now ain't that right?"

"Now, Judge, don't worry about a thing. We'll make an example of this man, and you can go ahead and build your boat in peace."

"*What man?*" I shouted. "That's what I'm asking, *what man?*"

"Mister Siwash," Wallace offered.

"I didn't get the name just exactly," the lieutenant said dubiously. "Cockahatty or something like that."

Vaughn came running up then, looking worried, and Joe Champion was just behind him and I saw Eb Thomas bouncing like a rabbit down the beach.

"Ben, what's going on here?" Vaughn said. "What are these men doing here? Indian Jim said—"

"It's the Yam Hill crowd," I told him helplessly. "They say they came to discipline the Killamooks."

"*Disci*—for what?"

"Lieutenant Anderson." The military introduced himself politely. "Surely you can see that we can't let this murderer off free or your lives will be menaced from now on."

"I thought they hung him up to Yam Hill," Vaughn said, bewildered.

"This here's what you call his complice or somethin'," Wallace explained. "We're fixin' to hang him, too. Then you boys'll be safe." He got a big kick out of making us safe, and laughed and laughed.

"They're after Cock Hat," I said.

"Oh, god." Vaughn looked at me for a long moment. "Where's Sam?" he said finally.

"I haven't seen him."

"Listen," Wallace said, poking my chest with his thick finger. "That little feller's the only one o' you boys got any guts *at* all. Why, wasn't for him you could of all been massacreed in your feather beds, like the lieutenant says."

"Where is he?"

"Oh, he's around," Wallace said negligently, grinning.

"Listen, Ben," Vaughn said. "For christ's sake, find Sam and talk to him."

"You find him," I said. "I'm going to talk to Kilchis."

"Jesus, *I* can't talk to Sam, you know that."

"Find him and hold him, then," I said. "I got to see Kilchis." I started away from the lieutenant toward Kilchis' lodge, across the clear space that separated the ring of rifles from the village.

"Wait a minute," the lieutenant said. "There ain't nobody allowed in them houses."

"Did you tell the *tyee* what you're here for?"

"We didn't get the chance. They all run to into the houses when we came," Anderson said. "One of the boys' guns discharged, by accident."

"Scared as birds, they was," Wallace said. "*Boy*, they run. Bang, *bang!* 'n' off they go. I want to see a couple o' them Siwashes dance on the air a little bit."

I gave up talking and started back toward the *tyee's* lodge.

"Hey, come back here, Judge!"

"Shoot me," I said. I knew they wouldn't, but I had a bad chill when I heard Wallace mumble, "Hell, why not?"

I turned around, but he was just grinning at me with his rifle butt-grounded and I went on.

"Kilchis!" I hollered when I got near the lodge. "It's me, it's Ben Thaler!" There was no answer for a moment. I had a terrible creepy feeling with all those rifles pointed at my back and held by Yam Hill boys.

Finally I heard a voice from inside the lodge say, "*Chako.*"

I stooped down and pushed the skin flap away from the door and went inside. It was so dark after the brightening dawn light I had to stop to let my eyes get used to it. I guess I had expected to find the Killamooks all huddled inside terrified. The women and children were toward the back, silent, but certainly not panic-stricken. What really scared me was the men. They had slightly lifted one of the planks that formed the wall, raising it against the withe binding and propping it open. Through the crack a good dozen rifles rested. I bent down and peeked through the slot and I could see every one of the whites, standing out in full view like shooting marks. Vaughn was gone, but the lieutenant still stood talking to Wallace. It would have been finished in ten seconds if Kilchis gave the word to fire. What made me shiver was that a minute before I'd been out there myself, covered by one of these same rifles.

The lifted board let in a long flat shaft of light, striping the dark faces of the young men and making a broken line of white on the sand of the floor. Kilchis stood behind his men, and the light made a slash of brightness across his legs. There was too much brilliance, the eye couldn't hold both the brightness and the dark, shadowy lodge. After looking out the firing slot I was half blinded again, and couldn't make out the expression on Kilchis' face as he stood watching me.

I thought of half a dozen things to say and all of them sounded so stupid that I finally blurted out, "Are you going to shoot them?"

"Not if they leave my people alone. What are the Boston soldiers doing here?"

"They've come—they've come for Cock Hat."

"Cockshaten has done nothing to them. I want peace here."

"We all want peace—"

"Soldiers are not for peace. They are for war."

"Kilchis, I don't know what's happening here—"

"The Boston soldiers come and catch the people bathing in the morning and shoot their guns and point them at us. They frighten the people. I want them to go away. You tell them."

"Just don't shoot, Kilchis. We can work this out, we can do something. But as soon as someone is hurt, there is no stopping."

"We are not *sullics* here. The Boston soldiers are like the sand. If I kill these there will be ten thousand tomorrow. I know all this. I want them to go away and we will live here in peace. Have we ever hurt your people that there was no payment? Estacuga has been punished, he is dead, the runners say so. That is finished."

"We can get it settled between us, Kilchis, we must talk openly—"

"What there was, was between Bay people and it is settled now. We live in peace with your people, Vaughn and the man who lives in the tree and even Tenas Sam. We have never done harm. You live here and you do not bother my people except for Tenas Sam when he comes at night. But he is *sullics*, mad, and not to blame. Why do they come and point their guns and say they will kill us?"

"Kilchis, I don't know. We must talk about it, or there will be killing, by mistake."

"I will talk, I do not want more killing in my Bay."

"We must have Cock Hat here to talk also."

He was silent for a moment. "Cockshaten is not in the Bay. I sent him to Nestucca to trade. This was a long time ago, when you judged Estacuga."

One of the young men turned and said something rapidly in Salishan, and Kilchis questioned him briefly. He turned back to me.

"Klakwun says Cockshaten has returned, in the night. He is in another lodge."

"Bring him to talk, Kilchis."

"The Boston soldiers will kill him."

"No, Kilchis, it can be settled. I promise you no one will be killed. Bring Cockshaten to talk and it will be over soon and the Boston soldiers will go again."

He thought about it, frowning. His massive face twisted in a grimace that was frightening, like the folding of a mountain chain before your eyes.

"I will bring him, then," he said finally. "You must tell the Boston soldiers not to shoot me when I come out."

"All right." I was feeling almost dizzy with relief.

When I lifted the skin flap and went out, half a dozen rifle muzzles swung to point at me. It was still early in the day, but my shirt was already pasted to my back with sweat. I was in such a state I didn't even feel anything in particular at the sight of all the muzzles.

Wallace was cheerfully suggesting that they set fire to the lodges and shoot 'em like rabbits when they came out.

"Well, Judge," the lieutenant said, "You're a courageous man, go right in there with those savages."

"You're pretty courageous yourself, Lieutenant," I said. The men to either side of us were listening attentively. "There's about a hundred of them savages in that lodge, and every one of 'em has a rifle trained on a white man's belly."

The lieutenant looked around him, wide-eyed and panicky, and finally hollered in a wavering voice, "Get into cover, you men!"

Those who had heard the conversation had not waited for his order. I never saw so many men wanting one tree. In a few seconds everyone but myself was crouching grimly behind whatever cover was nearest. I was both furious and disgusted.

"For christ's *sake!*" I hollered, "if they was going to shoot you they'd of *shot* you! Oh, god, you stupid—" I stopped. It did no good to holler at them. Nothing did any good.

I explained to the lieutenant that Kilchis was going to bring Cock Hat for a talk, and he cheered up a little. Peace-parleys with Indians on the warpath were just his style. He gave the order not to shoot, and I called for Kilchis to come out.

He stooped through the door and walked off toward another lodge without even looking at us, standing straight and striding in the early morning sun like a real king. He didn't even bother to see if there were rifles pointed at him or not. I don't believe I ever respected a man so much in my life as at that moment. And I was damn glad he was on our side. Once we got the Yam Hill crowd out of here we could settle back down.

After a few minutes he reappeared at the door of the other lodge, with Cock Hat following him. The two of them came up to the lieutenant. Kilchis offered his hand to shake. Lieutenant Anderson looked at it.

"There is blood on your hands," the lieutenant said. "There will be no shaking of hands until the blood is gone." I wondered where he had read *that*.

Kilchis said nothing, not understanding English, but his jaw moved and I could see he was angry at the refusal.

"Is this the man?" Anderson said, pointing at Cock Hat.

"Hell, I don't know," Wallace said. "I just come to *hang* him, I wouldn't *reck*anize the bastard. He'll do good as any."

"Yus," said a voice behind me, tight with strain. "That's him. That's the murderin' savage right there."

I hardly recognized him. His face was even thinner than the first time I'd seen it behind his gray window. His eyes were haunted and circled with dark, and his hair flew wildly in all directions. He held his body stiffly and bent slightly forward as though about to dive, and his fists were knotted tightly at his sides.

"Sam," I said. "What in god's name have you *done?*"

He didn't even look at me. He kept staring at Cock Hat with that crazy wild stare, the whites of his eyes showing all around the pupils.

"Yus, that's him. Hang him, now."

"Sam!" I looked over his head at Vaughn, who had come up just behind. Vaughn looked dazed, and only half aware. His eyes were frightened and he spread his hands loosely in a gesture of helplessness; he had tried.

"Well, now, all right," said the lieutenant, regaining some authority in his voice. "Listen, I want your people out here where I can see them. I want no sharpshooting. Leave their guns behind."

"He don't speak English," I said. "Tell him in the Jargon."

"I never learned that beastly tongue," Anderson said with a certain pride.

"You been here for—"

Vaughn interrupted to translate for Kilchis, who stared at the lieutenant for a long moment. Then he looked at me, and I nodded. Finally he made a quick, resigned gesture with one hand and silently went to his lodge. One by one the young men came up, glancing apprehensively at the armed whites.

"Put down your arms," Anderson said. "We come in peace. The Great White Father in Washington has sent us to—"

"Forget it," I said. "None of them speak English. The oration's wasted. And they ain't got any arms, can't you see that?"

"Don't they have an interpreter even?" Anderson said. "The Sioux always had an interpreter."

"Maybe they like speeches better," I said. "Listen, just forget about the newspapers, will you? This is real."

"Yeah, hell," Wallace said. "Let's hang him and get it done with."

"You're the first sonofabitch I'd hang," Vaughn snapped. "We got to live with these people. You can go home and rot in Yam Hill, we got to *live* here."

"What the hell's so special about here?" Wallace said, looking around. "Just a dumpy little bay is all, what the hell's so special about *here?*"

"Now boys," the lieutenant said. "We're here to do a job, not argue with each other. Mister," he said firmly to Vaughn, "a man'd think you didn't need help, you talk so big."

"Oh, jesus christ," Vaughn said. He covered his face with his hand, dazedly. "My god," he muttered. "You don't know what you're doing."

"*We* know what we're doin'," Wallace said, and roared with laughter again. "We're a hangin' Mister Siwash in the m-o-o-r-ning!" It was a little song that amused him.

"Mr. Howard," Anderson said. "You're sure this is the man?"

Through all the conversation Sam had continued to stare at Cock Hat, who simply looked at the ground.

"Yus. That's him. He killed the preacher's family."

"Sam, think what you're doing," Vaughn pleaded. "Think what you're *doing!*" Sam gave no sign he'd heard.

"Lieutenant," I said. "Listen. This is a private quarrel. We can settle it ourselves. We been *through* all this one time, it's all settled. Cock Hat didn't have nothin' to do with it, he was fifty miles away."

"That ain't what the other Mister Siwash said," Wallace broke in. "Afore he lost his voice *en*tire, that is."

"That's right, Judge," Anderson said to me. "That other fellow admitted it. This here Cockahatty was in on it, too."

"Admitted it, admitted it to who?"

"T' me," Sam said. "He tol' me. He said, Cock Hat done it, too. He tol' me."

"Sam, Sam, you're lying!"

Finally he turned to look at me, and his face was totally without expression, even the wildness was gone. "He confessed. He tol' me," he repeated. "Cock Hat was in on it, was him as killed the woman. Raped her, he did, raped her and killed her."

"The dirty beasts," Anderson said.

"Bunch o' damn murderin' rapin' bastards," Wallace muttered. "Hang the sonofabitch high and short. Watch him dance. He won't rape no more white women. Cut his balls off and make him eat 'em."

"You can't defend a man who's done that to a white woman," Anderson said, his face dark. "And if that other Indian confessed to it—"

"It's just *Sam* says he did," Vaughn said. "It's just Sam's word, and he wants this man's woman. That's the story right there."

"Well—" The Lieutenant hesitated. "Anyhow, Mr. Howard's a white man, and I think we can take a white man's word, can't we?"

"I heard it, too," Wallace offered encouragingly. "Ain't that right, Howard? Hell, I wasn't more'n fifty 'r a hundred yards away when you was, ah—talkin' to Mister Siwash on the rope." He laughed, but the lieutenant didn't catch on.

"You see, Judge, there's two men as heard it. I—I will admit there's some funny things about this case, but you can see how it looks pretty bad for this here boy."

Vaughn was explaining everything rapidly to Kilchis. The **tyee** frowned and said in the Jargon, "Cockshaten has done nothing, this was all settled before when you judged Estacuga."

"He done it," Sam said. "Raped her and killed her. He's got to hang." He turned to the lieutenant, almost pleading. "You got to hang him, you *got* to hang him."

"Oh, we'll hang him all right," Wallace said. "Ever'body's just talking up a big wind first, like to get ready."

"God *damn* you and your Yam Hill crowd!" Vaughn said. "Why don't you go home and leave us *alone?*"

Wallace laughed. "Hell, it'd be a cryin' shame t' make this whole trip for nothin'," he said. He looked at Cockshaten and the smile drained from his face, leaving his cheeks slack above the blackness of his thick beard. "I come t' see Mister Siwash hang," he said evenly, "and I ain't goin' home afore I do. You chicken-liver little boys best stay out of this or somebody's liable to get hurt."

"Yus," Sam said. "Yus, stay out of it. You, Vaughn. You, Ben. You stay out of it."

Suddenly Vaughn wheeled to me. "Ben—tell them! That's it, you tell them! *You* saw Cockshaten, and he was going to Nestucca. You can *prove* he didn't do it."

"Christ," I said, "I never even thought—things're goin' so fast—"

Sam twisted to me, faster than a fox. He lunged out and grabbed my shirt front, shoving me back several steps with the violence of the movement. He pushed his face up close to mine and his eyes were bright and feverish.

"Tell them, Ben," he whispered, and his voice was like the distant thin rasp of a saw. "Tell them, and I'm gone tomorrow. You know, Ben, gone. No ship. You can't build her without me. It's through. You back me up or it's all through."

"Sam, don't—"

"Well, Judge," the lieutenant said impatiently. "How about it? I mean, if you say so, that's all there is to it. This is a crazy kind of business anyhow, I don't understand it . . ."

He went on babbling a little more, but I didn't hear him. Sam suddenly snatched his hands away from my shirt front and stood rigid as a wire, staring up at me. At that moment the hot fire-circle of the sun cleared the Coast Range peaks at the east and the blinding new light flooded into my eyes. I could see nothing, my vision drowned in the hot golden flare. I was cut off, suddenly alone in my mind.

"Listen," Anderson's voice came faintly. "What are you two whisperin' about? Judge, if you can prove this boy didn't do it, just say the word and we'll let him loose, but I want to get this thing over with."

I could feel the warmth of the sun on my face, and I couldn't take my eyes away from the brilliance, as though the shock of it had paralyzed me. Queer, amorphous shapes in red and black swam back and forth in my mind, and all I could think was that the terrible impact of the sun was like the beauty of the Ship, it burned and burned.

"Come on, Ben," Vaughn said. "Tell them."

"Tell them, Ben," Sam said into my ear. "Tell them you don't remember."

At last I looked away from the sun, but when I turned my eyes down to the dark ground the flaring, blinding image still floated somewhere, more real than the earth and sticks.

"I don't remember," I said.

Chapter Nine

There was a long silence. I tried not to think.

Finally Wallace muttered, "Take him," and there was a small shifting movement and the Yam Hill boys closed in around the two Indians like a fist.

"Now hold on here a minute," Anderson said. "Seems to me as how there's some doubt here and I don't want to go rushing off with something that ain't perfect and legal."

"Listen, what the hell you *want?*" Wallace complained. "There's two white men as says he did it and nobody as says he *didn't*. I mean, what the hell do you . . ."

While they were arguing I met Vaughn's eyes. He was looking at me open-mouthed with shock. He came over to where I stood just outside the ring of men, and spoke quietly.

"Ben," he said, "Ben, what are you doing? You said before that Cock Hat was at Nestucca. What do you mean you don't *remember?*"

"Vaughn, listen—"

"You're as crazy as Sam." He shook his head in bewilderment. "Ben, they're going to *hang* that boy if we don't stop it."

"Vaughn, *listen* to me for once! Sam'll quit us. He'll leave the Ship. Do you understand me? He'll leave the Ship."

"But jesus christ, Ben, a man's life—"

"He told me. We trade Cock Hat for the Ship, he means it. What's more important, Vaughn? One man's life or the Ship? Suppose a guy got killed *working* on her, it'd be—terrible, but we'd go on. It's the same thing, Vaughn, we can't let her go. Not now."

He shook his head miserably. "My god, Ben, I don't know. I just don't know. Kilchis, the Indians . . ."

Anderson and Wallace had resolved their squabble and the lieutenant's voice raised authoritatively. "All right then, you men. We'll vote on it, and then it'll be official."

"Vote on it?" Vaughn said. "What do you mean, you can't vote *facts.*"

"It's a jury, like," Wallace said.

"All right," Anderson said, "everybody in favor of hanging this boy come over by me. Everybody *not* in favor, step over there."

Slowly there was a little movement. One by one the Bay men stepped to the side, except for Sam Howard, who remained standing by the lieutenant, staring at us. Vaughn and I stepped over with the others, and Vaughn rapidly told Kilchis in the Jargon what was happening. Our group was pitifully small, Vaughn and me and Thomas and Champion and half a dozen others. The twenty-odd Yam Hill boys outnumbered us by two to one without any trouble.

The two small knots of humanity confronted each other. The Yam Hill boys grinned at us like wolves. The Bay men were sullen. They—we—were confused and apprehensive.

"Well, that's clear enough," the lieutenant said. "Guilty he is."

Kilchis looked at the lieutenant and the Yam Hill boys clustered around, then turned to look at us. He turned slowly and began to walk back toward his lodge, motioning his young men to follow.

"Hey, come back here," the lieutenant said. "Listen," he said to Vaughn, "you tell him to come back or we'll shoot."

Vaughn told him, omitting the threat.

"I will not watch this thing," Kilchis said quietly.

"The hell you won't," Wallace muttered, swinging the barrel of his rifle gently to and fro across Kilchis' figure. "Lootenant, is this here a objeck lesson like you said, or not? I mean, I ask you, what they going to learn from this here objeck lesson if'n they don't see it?"

"No, you're right," Anderson said, thinking about it. "They should all watch."

Wallace gestured quickly to some of his boys. "Run them rabbits out o' their hutches," he grinned.

Half a dozen of the Yam Hill boys went off toward the other lodges, and in a moment there was cursing and shouting from the inside. Triumphantly they herded the whole population of the village out into the open at rifle point. Most of the young men had been in Kilchis' lodge, and the small milling crowd was made up almost entirely of old men, women, and children. The dogs ran wildly around the outskirts of the dense pack, yapping and snarling at everybody.

"That there's more like it," Wallace said with satisfaction. "What the hell's a hangin' without a audience anyways?"

"What'll we hang him on?" the lieutenant said absently, looking at the fringe of trees around the edge of the clearing.

"Looka there," Wallace said, pointing to Kilchis' lodge. The ridge timber projected out from under the eaves by several feet, overhanging the door. "Why, they even got us a gallows ready," Wallace said. "They must of knowed we was comin'."

"Wait a minute," I said. "You can't hang him on the *tyee*'s own lodge."

"Now listen, Judge," the lieutenant said. "I don't believe you understand the seriousness of this. This here execution has got to impress these savages. This is perfect."

"I can't watch this," Vaughn said. "I'm going home." He shook his head and started to turn.

"Say, boy," Wallace said, swinging his rifle barrel casually as he turned to face Vaughn. "That's a real bad idee, there. Here we come all the way down to do you a favor, an' you don't even want to watch? No, no. That's a bad idee." With his left hand he reached absently up to scratch his cheek. The rifle, cradled negligently under his right arm, was fixed as though by accident on Vaughn's belly.

Vaughn compressed his lips and looked down at the ground.

"Vaughn, you better come," I said.

He came over slowly, as though he were being dragged on a chain.

"That's better," Wallace said cheerfully. "All in the family, boys. Come on, come on!"

The Yam Hill boys opened up their circle a little and prodded the Indians with their rifle barrels. The whole crowd, sixty or seventy people, milled slowly toward the front of the *tyee*'s lodge. The Bay men were simply lumped in with the Indians, and the Yam Hill boys herded the whole mass like a reluctant troop of sheep.

"Come on, there, let's move, come on!" Wallace kept everything under control. He liked to see people flinch away from him, and jabbed the muzzle of his rifle at them, touching them gently on the ribs and grinning at the scared expressions he provoked when the cold metal touched flesh. The crowd was dense and tightly packed, and it might have been an accident that he jabbed me too, but I did not think so.

"God damn it, man!"

"Whoops, sorry, Judge," he said. "Took y' for a Injun, I did." He bellowed with laughter and Kilchis turned to look at us. I couldn't meet his eyes. He turned away. I did not know how I would explain what I had done. And yet I felt very little remorse, only fear of what was to come.

When the herd had been massed in front of the lodge, one of the Yam Hill boys brought up the rope, and a cord to tie Cock Hat's hands behind him. The rope was thrown over the ridgepole and settled around Cock Hat's neck.

"Well," the lieutenant said, "ask him if he's got anything to say."

"*Mika ticky mamook wawa?*"

"*Wake.*"

"Tell you what," Wallace said. "I'd like t' see this here boy confess."

"What difference does it make?" I said. "You're going to hang him anyway."

Wallace swung the muzzle of his rifle around again and said pleasantly, "No, we'll just see if he's got any more guts than that other one. Jack, come here."

One of the Yam Hill boys gave his rifle to another and came over where Wallace was standing holding the end of the rope. Wallace stood his rifle on the butt against the wall of the lodge.

"We'll just try her out for strength a little," Wallace said. The two of them hauled back on the rope. The knot tightened under Cock Hat's ear, and they lifted him until just the tips of his toes were touching the ground. He began to strangle, and his toes stretched down toward the ground for support.

"Wallace, you damned animal! Let him—" One of the Yam Hill boys stepped up beside me with his rifle cradled across his forearms. He didn't even look at me, his attention seemingly fixed on the dangling form of Cock Hat, but the barrel was almost against the side of my chest.

They held him there until his eyes were bulging and his face had purpled. Then they dropped him suddenly. Cock Hat fell to his knees in the dirt, coughing and gasping.

"*Mamook wawa,*" Wallace snapped at him.

"*Wake, wake,*" Cock Hat whispered.

"Don't torture the poor devil," the lieutenant said. "Let's hang him and get it over with."

"Now lootenant, you're new around these parts, you just don't get in the way. We know all about these kind o' doin's, the boys and me. All right, Jack."

They pulled back on the rope again, dragging Cock Hat up from his kneeling position. This time they brought him a few inches off the ground, and his legs twisted wildly, searching for support. Wallace watched intently. The crowd shifted from side to side, and there was a low murmur. Cock Hat's face swelled up and the veins of his forehead stood out like rawhide cords. Suddenly a gout of blood spurted from his nose, reddening his chest.

When they dropped him this time, he fell completely on his side, his hands still tied behind him. He thrashed on the ground, strangling.

"Loosen that knot," Wallace said. His companion stepped over to the writhing figure and spread the knot a little. The strangling sounds turned to retching, and the Indian began to vomit, staining the ground around his head with a foul mixture of blood and vomit.

"*Mamook wawa,*" Wallace said, watching the contorted face.

This time there was no answer at all, and Cock Hat continued to retch.

"Must o' been somethin' he ate as didn't agree with him," Wallace said seriously. He did not take his eyes off the helpless figure that twitched in spasms like a gut-shot animal.

"Wallace, I don't—" the lieutenant started.

"Shut up."

Wallace watched, fascinated. When Cock Hat had ceased to vomit, he finally looked up. "My god, he's stubborn, this one," he said.

"Well," Jack said, "you know that other one didn't confess till we'd run him up three times."

"Yeah," Wallace said reflectively. "Yeah, that's right. Well, third time's a charm, boys." He yanked sharply on the rope, jerking Cock Hat's head off the ground and letting it slam back again. "He's real limp, ain't he?"

One of the old women in the front of the crowd began to wail, the high, shrieking death-song that cut across our ears like the sound of breaking glass.

"Shut her up," Wallace said absently, and one of his boys jammed the muzzle of his rifle hard in the old woman's belly, making her gasp for breath.

Cock Hat was struggling awkwardly to his feet. With his hands tied behind his back he had to lever himself up with his head, moving like a crippled bird. Wallace grinned, watching him. When Cock Hat was standing erect he began to speak. His voice was low and rasping, barely audible.

"You can hang me," he said in the Jargon. "You have the power. Hang me, then. The sun will rise tomorrow and the fish will come into the Bay. The moon will be bright. Summer and fall and winter and spring will come to the Bay without me."

"What did he say?" Anderson asked.

"Sayin' his prayers," Wallace said. "We'll give him another little bit for good luck. All right, Jack."

This time they brought him well off the ground, leaning back on the rope with all their weight. Cock Hat's body began to jerk and twist again, his legs flailing out crazily as he strangled, twisting the rope and turning him around. Abruptly, from behind Wallace, a figure darted. The gnomelike body of Little Sam hurtled the few feet of clear space and he dived at Cock Hat's waist, throwing all his weight. Cock Hat's head jerked suddenly to the side as his neck broke. The last enormous spasm of his body threw Sam off, and the little man fell on his back. Instantly his body contracted, curling into a tight ball, rigid and motionless.

Cock Hat's spasms ceased. The limp and suddenly shapeless form swung wildly from the momentum of Sam's dive. Finally it settled in a small irregular circle, twisting on the rope like a pendulum coming to rest. The village dogs still ran yapping around the silent, fixed crowd, and one sneaked tail down into the clearing to lap tentatively at the pool of blood and vomit.

After a moment Wallace said, "Well, well. I guess he ain't going to confess. Tie this rope off, Jack." He went over to where Sam lay curled on the ground. He nudged the motionless form with his toe. "You shouldn't ought to've done that," he said, conversationally. "We could o' kept him goin' another ten minutes."

I ran over and took hold of Sam under the armpits. "Get the hell out of here," I said to Wallace. "Come on, Sam." I tried to pull him up. "Come on, Sam, you did right. It was the right thing to do."

His body was like wood, completely stiff, as rigid as though it had been carved of one piece. As I struggled to get him up, something bumped me from behind, and I said, "Get the hell out of here!" I looked back and saw the body of Cock Hat swinging gently away from me.

"Listen to that, will you!" Wallace bellowed. " 'Get the hell out of here,' he says. Hey, listen Judge, he can't hear you! Holler louder!"

The body came swinging back and I moved out of the way as the loose form swung past me so slowly I thought it would never pass. It smelled foul.

"Sam, come on."

Finally Sam began to uncurl and loosen a bit. His eyes were blank and unfocused. I helped him back to the cluster of Bay men. "Vaughn, get Sam home, for christ's sake."

Vaughn nodded and took him from me. It was like exchanging a sack of potatoes, an object.

Kilchis stepped up to Wallace. "You go. You have killed him. You go."

"Hell, yes," Wallace said. "Nothin' to do here." He looked with satisfaction at the still-rotating body of Cock Hat. "There's Mr. Siwash the way he looks best, right Jack?" He laughed in Kilchis' face. He laughed at the crowd and at us, he spat out his contempt for us all in one great roar of laughing. Still chuckling he picked his rifle up from the wall and deliberately plowed straight into the crowd of Indians. They separated to let him pass. The Yam Hill boys all followed, making the Indians give way before them, holding their rifles carefully and grinning.

The Lieutenant came over to me. "Well, Judge," he said. "I don't think you'll have any more trouble. These savages respect a show of force, that much I can tell you. Wallace got a little rough, but at heart he's a good man. He knows what these people respect, and I think it's better that way. If you need any more help, just call on us." He stuck out his hand and I turned away.

"I must say you're a strange man, Judge. After we—"

"Get out of here," I said. "Just get out."

He turned and set off in the wake of Wallace and his crew. The Indians turned to watch them go, and when the whites had disappeared around the first bend of the river trail, they turned back to look at Kilchis. One of the young men said something sharp and gestured to the lodge, where their old muzzle-loading fuzees had been left.

Kilchis spoke softly, but deliberately. I did not understand what he said, as he was speaking Salishan, but the young man did not move toward the lodge.

"Kilchis, let me talk to you," I said.

"Yes," he said. "Yes, I must send my people home." He spoke to the crowd, very shortly. They began to drift off toward the other lodges slowly, glancing back at the hanging form of Cock Hat.

Kilchis did not go back in his own lodge. He started walking down the edge of the river to the little point where it emptied into the Bay. I followed after. He walked heavily, his huge shoulders hunched and the bearskin robe swinging about his knees. He did not speak until we had reached the point. For a moment he stood still, looking out across the flat expanse of water to the rumbling line of breakers that stretched across the mouth. Then he sat down, his back against a rock, and stared absently with his hands resting limply on his knees.

"Kilchis, you've got to understand—the Ship—"

"It is not the Ship, it is Cockshaten. Now there will be trouble. There will be much anger on the coast now. The bands will be angry."

"What—what will your own people do, Kilchis?"

"They will do as I say. But we are few. The Nestucca and Yaquina and Alsea are many. I do not know what we can do."

I didn't understand what he was saying.

"Kilchis—what I did—you've got to understand why I—"

"You did what was possible," Kilchis said. "We could do nothing. Not with the guns. But—the other bands, they will think only 'Boston.' They will not know that you are the people of my Bay. I saw what happened. I saw them point the guns at you, and you talked in your language, and they hit you with the guns. I saw. But the other bands will not know."

I realized then that Kilchis did not know I had condemned Cock Hat with my silence. It had all been in English. He thought we had been desperately arguing to save the man.

"Kilchis—"

"Now there will be trouble, and we must make a defense, for the other bands will be angry. I wish—I wish the Boston had not come to my Bay."

A defense for us, for the whites. Because we were people of the Bay and had tried to save Cock Hat, who was a man of the Bay. All that was more important than any question of Boston and Siwash.

I could find nothing to say. I did not tell him I could have prevented it. It was impossible. Cowardice, lust, or obsession, I don't know. But even at that moment the thing that was strongest in my mind was the Ship. We had to finish the Ship, and it made my own guilt petty, trivial. The only thing that was real was the Ship.

We were silent then for a long time. Finally I said, "Kilchis, the woman of Cock Hat, Star of Morning. Get her away from here. Send her to friends or relatives, but get her away from here."

"Star of Morning is no longer in the Bay."

"Where is she?"

"She is with the Nestucca, she is married to one of the Nestucca men."

"I—I don't understand, I thought she was Cock Hat's woman."

"That is why Cockshaten was in Nestucca until now. He sold his woman to one of the people there. She is no longer of the Bay."

"*Sold* her? But I thought—"

Kilchis gestured impatiently. "I sent him to do this."

"You *made* him sell her to the Nestucca?"

"Yes. I did not want the woman in the Bay. This was just after you judged Estacuga, and I saw the face of Tenas Sam. I sent her away, because I did not want any more trouble here. I wanted peace."

2

I was almost afraid to go home, because I had to pass the Ship. She was now all that remained, the only thing of certainty in a world that was falling apart around us. Cockshaten was dead uselessly, the Killamooks were thrown against the other bands, Kilchis prepared to defend "his" people and his Bay against the anger of the others. Everything had exploded, like a fistful of powder thrown into a campfire. And now even the woman was gone, as though she had never existed. It was all pointless, it was all meaningless, there was only the insanity that boiled without result. Except for the Ship. For, while it had begun with the woman, it finished, as everything in life finished, with the Ship. For whose lust had Cockshaten died, Sam's or mine? I didn't know. I couldn't straighten it all out in my mind. And I did not know how far Little Sam could be blamed for his actions; there was something terribly wrong with him. I had never seen a man stiff like that. But I—I was sane and healthy, I was responsible for my acts and perhaps Sam was not.

In the end it all revolved around the Ship; every life in the Bay, brown or white, was in some way tied to the Ship. Everything else was insubstantial; the swirling mystery of Sam's mind, invisible, a woman— was she real? I could not even remember her face—gone. Somewhere. Cockshaten dangling above a pool of vomit and blood, but out of sight. The anger that was to come—from somewhere I could not place. It was all invisible, all unreal. The only thing to cling to was the solidity and reality of the Ship. You could see her, you could touch her. And above all, you could work. Your days could be made meaningful and real, with tools in your hands. Your life could have some significance. As long as the Ship held, as long as you could lose yourself in the image we were bringing to life. Without that, none of what had happened had any meaning; it was insanity and chaos and waste. And so I was afraid to see her again at that moment. I was afraid she would be only shaped lumber after all, a cargo vessel under construction. If the image did not hold, we were all insane, our lives were futility.

When I topped the little rise of the beach, I deliberately did not look, not right away. I let my eyes scan the forest inland, and only gradually slip down toward the Ship. It made my breath catch in my throat when I finally let myself look at her fully, squarely. She was— beautiful. There is no other word, and it is not enough.

She drowsed in the warmth of the morning sun. The raw wood of her framing glowed in the early light like the flesh of a sleeping woman, flushed with joy. The sweet curve of her cutwater was a throat proudly raised and her flanks were firm and strong.

I swallowed my excitement, and went down to her. Close, she was even more beautiful. I rested my hand against a frame, running my palm down the softly curving bevel that changed so imperceptibly I could not be sure at any point it was different from before. It swelled gently under my moving hand like the firm swell of a woman's thigh, and faired smoothly into the keel. The join was soft as skin, as perfect as the hollow between the soft curve of groin and thigh.

I rested my face against the frame, and it had been warmed by the sun like a living thing. I stood there for a moment with my eyes closed, simply letting the form of her possess me, allowing myself to sink into a sweet and oceanic sensation of fulfillment, repose.

It was all right. She was there, and all the rest of it faded from my vision until it was no more than an annoying barb in the back of my mind. She was there, and nothing else mattered. She was perfect. The rest of them couldn't understand her the way I did, they couldn't *see*. I didn't care about it one way or the other. As long as I had her, it was enough. She was the only perfect thing I'd ever seen in the world.

As soon as I came in sight of Sam's cabin I saw Vaughn sitting at the door with his feet stretched out and almost hanging over the edge of the tiny bluff. The door was open, and Vaughn was leaning back against the frame with his hands in his pockets and his head down.

"How is he?" I said. I peered into the cabin and saw Sam on the cot near the back corner. Or rather, I saw a bundle on the cot which I took to be Sam. He wasn't moving. The light from the little window made a square on the blankets, that was twisted out of shape by the lump that was Sam.

"Is he all right?" I asked Vaughn, sitting down beside him.

"Damned if I really know, Ben," he said. "*Damned* if I do." He shook his head and stared down at the toes of his shoes. "He—he's real queer, like. He scares me, to tell you the whole truth."

"He say anything?"

"I ain't *asked* him anything," Vaughn said. "I brung him back and put him to bed, but I ain't asked him anything."

"But at least he ain't stiff like he was down at the village."

"He got stiff again just after I put him on the cot, maybe ten minutes. He just laid there stiff, staring up at the ceiling. I didn't know *what* to do, Ben. Then after a while he loosened up. He goes from limp to stiff, it seems like. I never saw anything like it."

"Me neither."

"I guess he must've took quite a shock to his system or something, when he did that with Cock Hat."

"I suppose," I said. I didn't really know. "I don't understand any of it, Vaughn, I'll tell you plain. I don't even know why he done that."

"*I* figure he didn't want to see the poor bastard tortured any more. That's what I figure," Vaughn said. "That Wallace, he's a real mean sonofabitch."

"You know, Cock Hat's woman is gone. Kilchis made him sell her to the Nestucca. She ain't even in the Bay."

Vaughn looked up in surprise. "You mean—you mean what Sam— it was all for *nothing?* For *nothing?*"

"Looks like it. Anyway, he won't have her."

Vaughn thought about it for a moment, then shook his head. "My god, Ben, this is all like some nightmare. What's Kilchis say?"

"He says—he says he'll defend us."

"*Defend us?* After this?"

"Listen Vaughn, let me tell you. Kilchis figures we did what we could to save Cock Hat. He figures we're his people, and he's got to take care of us like all the rest."

"But it was Sam—"

"Kilchis says Sam ain't to blame, because he's *sullics*, he's not like other men."

Vaughn looked at me, then back at the ground. "Ben," he said quietly, "I'll say this just one time and there's an end to it. Sam or no Sam, if you'd of spoke up, Cock Hat wouldn't of been hung. That military even said so."

"Jesus Christ, Vaughn, you think I don't know that?"

"I don't see how Kilchis could—"

"He doesn't *know*. He doesn't understand that part at all. He saw them Yam Hill boys treating us just like the Indians, pointing their rifles at us and laughing and all. That's all he knows. He says we tried our best."

"And you didn't tell him."

"Vaughn, just for once try to put yourself in somebody else's skin. Sam told me straight out, Cock Hat or the Ship. What would *you* have done? Just tell me honest, Vaughn, I want to know."

Vaughn glanced absently in the direction of the ways. The Ship was far out of sight, but he stared intently as though he could see her.

Finally he sighed and turned away. "I don't know. Maybe the same as you, I guess."

I was surprised at the enormous feeling of relief that rolled up out of my belly. I hadn't known it was so important. "And—would *you* have told Kilchis? Ain't we got enough trouble without *asking* for more?"

"Ben, listen. Don't try to make me say you done right. It's done now, and we got to make the best of it. Maybe I *would* have done the same, I don't know. But that don't make it right."

"What I done, I done for the Ship. That's all. That makes it right."

"Ben, honest to god, I don't know what to think. I don't want to talk about it any more, all right?"

"All right, all right," I said. "I didn't want to talk about it in the first place. I want to forget it."

"I hope you can," Vaughn said.

We said nothing for a while. I heard a rustle inside as Sam shifted under the blankets.

"He's awake," I said.

"I don't think he's been asleep," Vaughn said. "He's just been— someplace else."

"What are we going to do about Sam, Vaughn? What are we going to do?"

Vaughn shook his head. "I'm fresh out of ideas, Ben," he said discouragedly. "*Can* we do anything? It's up to him."

"He can't stay like this."

Vaughn laughed shortly. "Tell him."

"I'll tell him," I said, standing up.

"What makes you think he'll listen?"

"He'll listen, maybe not to me, but he'll listen to her. He'll listen to the Ship. He's got to do it, for her."

"Ben, there's a limit to how far you can drive a man. I think Sam's past it. I don't think he's eaten for days, nor slept neither."

"I don't give a *damn* if he eats or sleeps. I want him to *work*. He's got to *work*."

"You ask too much."

"I ain't asking nothing. It's her that's asking. A man can always work. Even when he can't do *nothing* else, not eat or sleep, he can work. That's what a man's made for, that's what he can do."

I turned and went into the dimness of the cabin. Slowly Vaughn got up and followed me. There was a chair at the head of the cot, and I sat down. Vaughn stood behind me. I looked down at Sam's face, in the darkest corner. His light hair was spread out on the straw mattress like a cloud. His little pointed face was motionless, and the skin was a funny color, though it may have been the darkness that made it seem so. His eyes were wide open and unblinking and seemed to take up half the face. He had absolutely no expression that I could tell, he was perfectly neutral.

"Sam?" I said. "Sam, can you hear me?"

After a moment he said, "Yus. I can hear you." I was shocked. His voice was perfectly normal. It had lost the terrible edge of tension that had strained it before, at the hanging. It was soft, and a little shy. If I closed my eyes I could see him as he had been before we started building, with his hands clasped tightly, looking embarrassed at the floor. But his eyes remained up, staring blankly at the ceiling.

"Well, Sam, how you feeling?"

"I'm feeling all right."

"You look pretty tired, Sam."

He said nothing.

"I guess it's been pretty tough for you lately. But it's all over now, Sam."

He remained silent.

"Sam, listen. Did you, did you hear what I was saying to Vaughn?"

"No."

I rubbed the back of my neck, where it was getting stiff from bending over toward him. I glanced up at Vaughn, but he was no help.

"Well, Sam, listen. I ought to tell you that—you know, that woman, you know who I mean. She's gone, Sam."

Vaughn poked me suddenly on the shoulder, but I didn't pay any attention. I wanted to get it over with, I wanted it over and finished and forgotten so we could get back to work.

"Sam, look at me, will you?"

He turned his head to look at me. "She's gone, Sam. It's all over. Is it all right?"

For a moment he was silent, and I was afraid he had quit hearing. But finally he said, "Yus, it's all right." He turned back to gaze at the ceiling again. In a little bit there were tears in his eyes and they spilled over in a little rivulet that trickled down his temple into the light hair in front of his ears. For the first time he spoke of his own volition, without a direct question to answer. He didn't seem to be talking to me. Just thinking.

"It was—terrible," he said. "Terrible, terrible." Suddenly he clenched his eyes shut.

I looked up at Vaughn, but he looked blank. "What was terrible, Sam?"

"All of it. All of it. Everything."

"You did right, Sam. It was the best thing, what you did."

He opened his eyes again and turned his head slowly toward me. "What I did? What did I do?"

I looked at Vaughn again. He clenched his lower lip in his teeth and frowned at the floor.

"Ben?" Sam said. "Where is she, Ben? Where did she go?"

"She's—dead, Sam. I'm sorry. She was—drowned, I guess she was drowned down the coast is what I heard. I'm sorry."

"Drowned. No, she ain't drowned. Where is she, Ben?"

"That's it, Sam. I'm sorry, it's all over. There's no use thinking about it any more. You got to forget it, like it never happened."

He closed his eyes again and turned his head back. After the first tears he had not cried any.

"Sam, did you hear me?"

"Yus."

"What did I say?"

"She's dead. It's all over."

"That's right, Sam. I'm sorry, but that's the way it is. It's better that way, you'll see."

After a minute he said, "I want to sleep now. I'm tired."

"Wait, Sam—"

"For christ's sake, Ben, let him sleep!" Vaughn broke in.

"In a minute. In just a minute. Sam, listen, there's one other thing. And you listening?"

"Yus."

"The Ship, Sam. She's waiting for us. We got to get back to her."

"Yus, the Ship."

"She's there, Sam, I just saw her, just now. We're up to Number Twenty-two. She's waiting for us."

I leaned over closer to him. "Number Twenty-two, Sam. Can you see it in your mind? Try, Sam. Number Twenty-two, back toward the stern."

"Twenty-two's a cant-timber," Sam said. "Twenty-two's the first of the cant-timbers at the stern."

"That's right, Sam, you got it. *Think*, Sam. Get her in your mind. We're damn near to the transom, Sam, how about that?" I was getting excited, because I knew I had found the answer. If I could get the image of the Ship clear enough in Sam's mind, he would do it, he would work. The goddess would give him strength. He would get up and work because She wanted it, She demanded it.

"Sam, remember the nick I took out of Number Fourteen by accident with the adze? You remember when I dropped the adze on Fourteen?"

For the first time his forehead wrinkled, he frowned slightly. "Yus, I remember."

"We'll take it out, Sam. We'll take the whole damn thing out and make a new frame, if you want. Would you want that, Sam?"

"Listen, Ben—" Vaughn said.

"Shut up. Just be quiet!" I was getting to him, I could see it in his face and eyes, I was getting to him and I was winning. "Sam, how about it? We'll yank the whole damn frame and make a new one. She'll be perfect, Sam. Do you understand? She'll be damned god-awful absolutely *perfect!*"

"Yus. That nick—that was bad, that bothered me. I wanted to fix it right, but you all laughed at me."

"I didn't understand then, Sam. But we'll do it. We'll make her perfect. I understand about her now, I can see now."

He looked at me and slowly brought one hand out from under the blanket. He gripped my elbow lightly. "Ben," he said, "listen. There's a trunnel split on Number Twelve. It's the upper trunnel on the right hand side of the floor futtock on Number Twelve."

"We'll drill it out," I said. "We'll take that goddam auger of Thomas's and drill it straight out and put in a new one. All right?"

"They weren't dry enough. It checked on the end after it was drove in. It's been worryin' me."

"We'll drill the sonofabitch right out of there, Sam, by *god* we will. There won't be a piece in her that ain't perfect. Not *one* piece."

"Yus," Sam said. His eyes were bright now, as he thought about it.

I leaned over until I was practically whispering in his ear. "She's waiting for us down there, Sam, she's beautiful. I just saw her. The sun's on her now, you know how it sneaks between the frames? And stripes the keel with gold? That's the way it is now, Sam, right now. She's made of gold and blood, Sam, she's beautiful. You got to see her. We got to get back to work. Can you work?"

"Yus. Yus, I can work."

"Can you work tomorrow, Sam? Can we get back to work tomorrow?"

"Yus. We can work, can't we?"

"We can work, Sam. There's no men ever made can work like us. We can work like God himself, Sam."

"Yus. We'll do it. I'd forgot how beautiful she was. I'd forgot her somehow."

"She's there, Sam, just waitin' for us. I'll stay here and get you stuff to eat today and you sleep and tomorrow we'll go back to work."

"No," Sam said. "You go on. I can take care of it all right. You go on. I got to think, Ben, I got to plan. I ain't made the angle boards for the cant-timbers, yet."

"We looked for 'em, but we couldn't find 'em. You sure you'll be all right, Sam?"

"Yus, sure. You go on. I got to think."

He was staring at the ceiling again, but it was all different now. There was a light in his eyes, and his face shifted constantly in tiny changes of mood. He was puzzling Her out in his mind, he was going over every inch of Her body in his mind. I'd given him back the image.

I stood up. "All right, Sam," I said, casual as I could. "See you at the ways in the morning."

He didn't answer, he was thinking, he had Her in his belly again.

Vaughn and I left and went out front. He was looking at me strangely.

"Ben," he said hesitantly, "You're a hard man, Ben. You're a cruel man."

"Cruel? Me?"

Vaughn shook his head. "You'll kill that man, Ben. You can't drive him like that, you can't set him on fire and leave him to burn. He'll work himself to death over her, Ben, you know he's not fit."

"Let him die," I said.

"Ben!"

I turned to him. He couldn't see, he was one of the blind ones. He thought he knew it all, but he just couldn't see. "I'll kill him," I said. "I'll kill myself. And I'll kill you, too, Vaughn. But we'll get her done. That's why we're here. You stay out of my way if you don't want to die working. You blind—you terrible blind bastard!"

He stopped suddenly and I went on alone. I had too much energy pouring through me to go home. I went and got the auger and bored out the split treenail in Number Twelve and put a new one in to surprise Sam when he came in the morning.

Chapter Ten

I was burning high and bright that day. The flame of the goddess roared through me, making me exultant and ten feet tall. Getting my hands on a tool again was an enormous fierce joy. But the triumphant sense I felt also made me unfair in what I had said to Vaughn. He was willing to work, they were all willing; there was never any question. But it was impossible for me to believe that anyone else—except possibly Sam—really understood her, as I did. I could not believe that anyone else was as hopelessly drowned in her beauty as I. And as with all men who have a Vision, the others seemed half-blind to me.

Every time someone addressed a word to me I was afraid he was going to diminish the image. Afraid he would not be sufficiently enthusiastic, sufficiently powerful in his conviction. Afraid, in short, that She had not possessed him. Certain as I was in myself, I still did not want to hear anything that would make Her less important. Not even a minor complaint from some butt-head like Eb Thomas. I could not have tolerated it.

The whole crew was there in the morning before Sam, and that was enough to put me on edge. Everyone was nervous, a little jumpy. Our rhythm had been broken. We had been forced against our will to think of something other than the Ship, and it made us uncertain. For the time we were just a bunch of men again. We didn't know what to do, what was going to happen, where we were. Once back into it, we would be all right. It was the transition that made us wobble; all transitions are hard.

When Sam came he was pale. He said nothing to anyone, and we all watched him anxiously. We didn't know what the new pattern was to be. After Sam's—recent actions, there was no way to predict how he would be with her.

He stood off at a little distance, looking her over from bow to stern. I tried to see through his eyes, but she overwhelmed me with her beauty, and I could not know if there was anything that might dissatisfy Sam. Finally he walked slowly all around her, dragging the palm of his hand absently along the frames, sometimes stopping to check a bevel from floor futtock to top timber. He was almost somnolent, letting the rhythms of her body absorb him, creep into his veins and nerves. I noticed him glance quickly at Number Twelve, where I had replaced the treenail. He said nothing, but I was relieved to see a faint smile on his lips. At Fourteen he let his fingertips rest on the nick I had stupidly caused with the dropped adze. He rubbed it gently, as though he could make it right with the simple power of his desire that it be perfect.

"Maybe we can plane it out," I said.

He didn't answer me. He continued on around, touching gently, looking, evaluating. Finally he stepped off a little distance from the bow, and looked at her head on.

I couldn't stand it any longer. "Well, Sam?" I said.

He was silent for another moment, and said at last, "Well. Seems as how she's going up pretty fair, anyway."

There was another silence, until Eb Thomas threw back his head and howled at the sky. "Hooraw, boys! Let's move!"

Everybody grinned at each other and Vaughn said authoritatively, "All right, all right, come on! Let's have Twenty-two over here! Come on, move!"

We broke up like a flock of startled, happy quail. We were back to work. We were ourselves again.

It felt as though we had come home after a ten-year journey. Suddenly everything was familiar, and absurdly nostalgic. Hendrickson and Peter Morgan got the whipsaw running hot, and I never knew a man could miss a sound as much as I had missed that rasping whipsaw. I suppose a man born by the sea will never lose the necessity of the sound of breakers, and it was that way for me with the whipsaw. Life did not seem normal without that constant background to every act, every thought, every word.

We worked as though we could see a wick burning down to a keg of powder. In five days we had the framing absolutely completed. Not a little left to do here and a few touches there, but *finished*. Cant-timbers and all.

The keelson went in, fairing sweetly up against the deadwoods at either end and lying atop the floor futtocks. We tied her all together inside with the long and incredibly graceful strips of the bilge strakes and, up high, the deck clamps. That was more tricky, and we had to hold ourselves down a little. The exact deck height had to be measured on each frame, making allowance for the thickness of the deck itself and the beams. The deck beams would rest on the clamps, hooked with the iron knees we'd salvaged from the *Shark*. So the clamp, a long strip running all the way around, had to be absolutely perfect at each frame. Everything had to be perfect, so I suppose it was no more trouble than anything else. But, god! how we hated to go slow. We wanted to push, we wanted to dive, we wanted to run and jump and fly and get her *done*.

It was the seventh day after we re-started, the day we finished the deck clamps, that the wick burned all the way down.

I did not know how long I had been asleep when I felt someone shaking my shoulder. Blearily I looked up, trying to adjust the real shape of the Ship that loomed up beside me in the night with the image of her I had been dreaming.

Eb Thomas stood over me, looking worried.

"Thomas, what the hell's the matter with you? You're going to be too tired to *work* tomorrow."

"I heard something, Ben," he said.

I glanced at my fire, and there were still a lot of good coals, so I had not been asleep too long. Vaguely I could hear a little rustling as the other men sleeping by the Ship shifted under their blankets.

"I don't hear nothing," I said. "Thomas, go back to sleep. For god's sake don't be butt-headed in the middle of the night."

"No, Ben, I heard—"

And just then I heard it, too. The sound of a rifle. I came awake faster than ever in my life and bolted up, getting tangled in my blanket.

"You hear it?" Thomas said.

"Yes. What's going on?"

"I don't know," Thomas said. "That's what worries me."

Three more shots came, spaced irregularly. Then nothing.

"It sounds like it's down by the end of the Bay," I said. "Down the other side of Kilchis' village."

"Maybe them Indians got drunk and are shootin' up the place," Thomas said.

"They get happy-drunk, not shootin'-drunk," I said. "Anyways, I don't think there's any liquor in the Bay except at Vaughn's. And he don't give none to the Indians, Kilchis don't like it."

"What should we do?" Thomas said worriedly.

"I don't know. Anyway we better wake up the rest of them. If it gets any closer we might better go up to Vaughn's."

We went around to the other blankets, shaking up those who were still asleep. We built up my fire again and sat around it, listening to the darkness. After the isolated cluster of shots that woke me, there was nothing. The night sounds continued normally; the rumbling mutter of the breakers at the bar, the soft brushing sounds as fir tops moved in the light breeze. Nothing.

After about two hours of tense listening and low talk, we all went back to bed again. I was tired enough to go to sleep, but it was not a restful night.

The next morning we were due to start on the rail stringers. They had been cut to size, and there was little to do but mount them, and all of us could not work at once.

"Say, Ben," Vaughn said. "Did you hear guns last night?"

"Yes."

"What was it all about, do you know?"

"No. Sounded like it was down past the village. I don't think it's any of our business." I didn't want to think about it, in fact, and was willing to let the whole thing pass. I was afraid to find out something that might stop work again.

Vaughn frowned. "I don't like it, anyhow," he said. "I think somebody better find out what it was."

I looked at the rail stringers waiting to go up. I didn't think I wanted to know about the shooting bad enough to leave her, even though there wasn't much I could do today.

"Why don't we run down and see what Kilchis has to say?" Vaughn said.

"Go ahead."

"You come on, too, Ben."

"There's nothing *I* can—oh, hell, all right. I suppose we best find out. Sam! Hey, Sam!" I told him what we had in mind. His cabin was much farther away from the village than the ways, and he had heard nothing. He frowned when I told him about the shooting, but quickly lost all interest when somebody dropped a stringer.

"Break it!" he shouted. "Go on, break it all! I don't give a damn." He was his old self again these days, his old working self, which was all that mattered. The real man is the man that works; the rest is a masquerade.

"So Vaughn and I thought we'd go down and see if Kilchis knows anything."

"Yus. Yus, I don't need you for a while. Go ahead." He wasn't very interested in the problem, which was normal. I suppose there isn't much interesting about a gunshot, unless you happen to hear it yourself in the middle of the night.

We didn't even get to the village. About halfway there, Vaughn and I met Kilchis, heading up toward the Ship.

"Kilchis," I said, "we heard shots last night. Did anything happen?"

"I come to tell you," Kilchis said. "Is not—serious. Some of the Klickitat people come here last night. We send them home."

"Klickitats? From clear in the Valley?"

"There is much talk in the Valley," Kilchis said. "The Klickitats and Kalapuya are angry. Also the Clackamas. They say if the Killamooks do not rise to kill the Bostons, they will do it. They are *sullics.*"

"What was the shooting?"

"My guards caught them coming into the Bay. They shoot to tell them to go home again."

"What guards?" Vaughn said.

"Since those others killed Cockshaten, there are guards. There are some of the young men on the trail from the Valley. Others on the beach road. They will stay until the trouble is over."

Vaughn looked at me. We had heard nothing about guards.

"When will the trouble be over?" I said.

"In time. In time they will forget about it. Now they are angry, but they do not want trouble with us. They will try to sneak in to find the Bostons alone. We will keep them out. I was there last night, I talk to them, I explain. They are satisfied now, but there will be others. Now they go back into the Valley, they say they will kill the Yam Hill Bostons."

"Wouldn't mind if they did," Vaughn muttered. "That big bastard with the beard is behind all of this."

"How many of the Klickitats were there?" I said.

"Many, many," Kilchis said, frowning. "I did not expect so many."

"How many? In numbers."

"Ten, maybe."

"That—that doesn't seem like so many," I said. I wondered if he had the figure right, or was just picking one at random. I have never understood the way Indians think about numbers.

"You do not understand about this thing," Kilchis said. "There is no war, the *tyees* of the other bands will not permit a war over this thing. Between us, perhaps. But not with the Bostons, the Bostons kill too many people in a war. We would all die, then. This is a thing for the young men to get excited over. It will be small groups of young men who are excited and wish to show they are brave."

"That's what it was last night? Young men, excited?"

"Yes. No *tyee* would let his band be risked for such a thing. There are too many Boston soldiers in the country. I do not understand how you can have so many soldiers and still have people."

"There's—a lot of us, Kilchis."

"Yes," he nodded. "Like the salmon in the rivers. I do not understand where all the Bostons come from. It must be a very big country, much bigger than mine. Some of my young men, they have been to Astoria. They say they see all the people in the world walking toward them. And when they turn around, there are just as many going the other direction. Is that true?"

"Just about, Kilchis."

He frowned, and finally lifted his great shoulders in a shrug. "I do not understand where the salmon come from, either," he said at last. "They come, and that is enough. So it is with the Boston. I did not know there were so many people in the world. It must be very big."

"I'm afraid the salmon are a lot more use to you than we are," I said stupidly.

"Yes," Kilchis said. "Yes, that is true. We eat the salmon, and trade."

This was not a flattering comparison of value, but I suppose it was my own fault for bringing it out.

"Well," Vaughn said. "Then you don't think there's any great danger from the other tribes?"

"There is always danger when men are excited and angry. There will be shooting in the night. Your people who are far out should come in, for safety. The man who lives in the tree should come in, he is all alone. We will try to keep them out of the Bay, but we may not catch them all."

"All right," I said. "We'll bring him in. He can stay with me."

"*Hyas kloshe,*" Kilchis nodded, satisfied. "*Klahowya.*"

"*Klahowya,* Kilchis."

He turned and started back toward his village.

"God, what's he doin' out there in the middle of the night?" Vaughn said. "That's dangerous."

"He knows his trade pretty well. That's what being a *tyee* means, I guess. He's responsible." My mind wasn't on what I was saying. I had just had a glimpse of something that drove the attacking bands right out of my mind.

"I suppose I'll go help Champion move his kit in," Vaughn said.

"The hell you will!" I blurted out.

"What's the matter?"

"I will," I said. "I'll do it, and nobody else. He'll stay with me."

"Hell, you don't have to—"

"Listen, Vaughn, I'll do it. I been here better than two years now. I had a picture in my mind of the man that lives in the tree for *three* years, and I never seen it. I tried a thousand ways to get Joe to invite me up in his tree, but he never did, the stupid bastard. He's a butt-head, just like Thomas. Now I got the perfect chance, and I'm going to *see* it."

"Hell, Ben," Vaughn said. "There ain't all *that* much to it. It's just—"

"Don't *tell* me," I said. "For christ's sake don't spoil it *now.*"

"My god, I never knew you was so interested in Joe's tree. I'd of took you up a dozen times if I'd knowed you was so—listen, why didn't you ever *say* something about it?"

"I figured it would just happen real natural like," I said. "An' other times I was too busy to think about it. Anyway," I admitted finally, "to tell you the truth, I was kind of embarrassed to be so interested about that damn tree."

"By god, Ben," Vaughn laughed. "You're a strange case. You really are. Hell, it's just a—"

"Don't *tell* me, don't *tell* me! Vaughn, don't you ever *listen?* I don't want to *hear* about it, I want to see it with my very own eyes. I had that in my mind for three years, now I'm going to *see* it."

"All right," Vaughn said, real fast so I couldn't stop him. "But it ain't going to be like you got it in your mind."

He always had to have the last word, Vaughn. But I didn't care. For three years—not all the time, but regular enough—I'd had that damned picture in my mind of Joe Champion hanging by his knees up in his tree and looking around. After knowing Joe it even seemed probable. And if he didn't do it while I was there—by christ I'd *ask* him. It's not often a man gets a chance to compare the reality with his image of it. I intended to profit fully from the opportunity. It might never happen again in my life.

2

"So that's about how she stands," Vaughn said. "Chances are we ain't going to have too much trouble, but there's no point takin' too many chances, neither. Ever'body living far out better bunk up down here." He was standing on the big fir butt by the ways, his feet dangerously close to the model. Little Sam was watching him suspiciously, afraid he was going to break something. He didn't care about any of it, Sam. While Vaughn talked he glanced from the model to the Ship and back again, wanting it to be over so he could get back to her.

The crew had listened in silence to Vaughn's explanation of last night's shooting. Now there was a little shifting of feet and muttering, as they talked it over among themselves. I was apprehensive that someone might even say he was not going to work with the Indians rising, and I waited impatiently for the first definite reaction. I had half a notion that the first one would swing the rest.

Finally Eb Thomas cleared his throat. He had been frowning down at the ground. Now he looked around him at all the others, his expression half worried, half puzzled. "Well," he said. Everyone turned to look at him. I was panic stricken. It was just my luck to have a notorious coward like Eb Thomas be the first to speak. I think I'd have thrown an ax at him if I'd had one in my hands.

"Well?" he said again. "Let's get back to work. We been standin' around with our hands in our pockets for ten minutes."

I think I'd have kissed him if I'd been a little nearer. Or maybe not, but I was sure damned happy to see everybody getting back to their jobs, even if they dragged a little. It would be all right. When we were working *everything* was all right, we were full and happy. It was those tiny moments in between that were dangerous, when we had a chance to think.

Joe was standing near me, his hands on his head and his mouth half open, staring at the sky. I went over to him.

"Well, Joe," I said, friendly. "You can bunk up with me."

"That's real nice of you, Ben," he said gratefully. "I guess I best do that. I mean, I wouldn't want to get killed or anything like that."

"No, take no chances," I said heartily. "Tell you what. After work I'll just run up to your—place with you, and give you a little hand to bring your kit down."

"Oh, you don't have to do that," Joe said, embarrassed by my gesture. "There ain't that much to bring down."

"It's nothin', Joe, think nothing of it. It'll go easier with two, anyway. I mean, you can lower the stuff down to me, and I'll stand on the ground and catch it."

"Yeah," he said, looking at me funny, "but—there ain't all that much, Ben, I mean—"

I took him very gently by the shoulder. "Joe," I said, like a father, "don't argue with me. I'm going to help you whether you like it or not. Just don't argue with me about it."

"Oh," he said anxiously, "I ain't a arguin' man, Ben, you know that. But I just—"

"Fine," I said. "That's it, then. We'll go up right after work, all right?"

And that's just what we did.

I knew the general direction of his tree, just from comments I'd picked up in two years, but that was all. Once or twice the first year, when it was still hot in my mind, I'd gone out for little constitutional walks in that direction, just sort of looking around casually. All I ever got out of it was a crick in the neck from peering up into the branches to see if I could spot any sign that a man lived up there. I think I had never before realized that the whole damn forest was individual trees, and that a man could easily spend a lifetime looking up into the branches of each one. I'd finally given up that approach as hopeless. But the doubt and anxiety were almost over now and I was cheerful as a squirrel as we trudged up toward the foothills.

"By god," I said. "You know, Joe, it ain't every man that lives in a tree, I'll say that."

"No," Joe said thoughtfully. "No, that's right. I'm the only one I guess." He walked along like a mountain, his huge long legs eating up the trail like a brush fire. I almost had to trot to keep up. I could see how he'd be able to shinny up damn near *any* tree, even without a ladder. Even every night. After a while, I supposed a man got used to it.

"Listen, Joe," I said. "Tell me something. How's a man happen to get it in his head to live in a tree like that?"

"Oh, it wasn't exactly I got it in my *head*," Joe said. "I come down here, you know, I was the first one here, an' I didn't have no place to live. So a Indian took me out there and showed me this tree and said I could stay there. So that's what I did, Ben. I wasn't sure I was going to be here long, so it didn't seem like it was worth the trouble to *build* nothin'. And after while I got used to it, sort of. You know, that's the way it is."

"Yes sir," I said, "that's the way it is."

"You know, a man gets used to about anything, Ben, after a little while. Then he likes it. A man likes what he's used to, and I'm used to my tree."

"Don't you ever get dizzy?"

"No, I never get dizzy, Ben, that's one thing about me. I'm real healthy, I never been sick a day in my life."

"You never—I mean, in the night or something, you never fall out?"

"Oh, sure," Joe said, a little embarrassed to be talking so much about himself. "I fall out of bed all the time. I twitch around a lot when I sleep, that's because I got what they call a nervous disposition, I guess. Then sometimes I fall out, you know, that's only natural, because it's so narrow. There ain't too much room."

I stopped dead in the trail, staring at him. "And it don't *bother* you? You don't break anything, bones or anything?" I couldn't believe it.

"Well, it wakes me up," Joe admitted. "But I ain't *broke* anything yet."

I shook my head and started walking again. "Joe," I said, "you're a strange one, now. I couldn't *stand* that."

"Don't that ever happen to you, Ben?"

"Well, sure," I laughed. "But I expect it's a bit different when a man lives in a tree."

"Oh, sure. It's different all right, there's no doubt about that. But you know, Ben, a man gets used to about anything."

If he could take a fall like that—it somehow convinced me absolutely that he hung from his knees and looked around. I don't know why, but I was dead certain. Maybe not all the time, but once in a while. By god, I'd ask him to *do* it for me.

We switched off on a tiny, faintly marked trail about then, and I saw where I'd gone wrong before. It is amazing how small a trail a man needs when he travels alone. I began to scan the lower branches all around, trying not to be too obvious. I didn't think he would be too high, particularly when he fell out all the time. Ten feet, twenty feet maximum was what I figured, if the ground was soft.

"Well, here we are," Joe said cheerfully.

I stopped and looked all around. I couldn't see anything. I looked back down at Joe. Suddenly the realization piled up in my throat. I have never in my life been so close to tears out of sheer mean disappointment.

Joe's tree was not a tree at all. It was a stump. It was the biggest cedar stump I had ever seen, almost nine feet across. The entire inside was hollowed out, probably burned out years ago by lightning. It made an almost perfect circular little room, with a tiny narrow cot and even a little table by the head of it. It stood maybe seven or eight feet tall, and over the top was a sort of roof of overlapping planks that would send the rain shooting down over the back. The quarter of the trunk facing us was broken out, making a perfect door, and there was even a blanket hooked at the top to use when the wind was blowing. Just in front of the door was a rock fire-pit and a couple of little racks.

Joe had gone in, and was poking around under the cot. It was a nice normal cot, with a straw mattress and everything. "I don't have a hell of a lot," he said, his voice muffled. "Like I told you, Ben."

He finally had to get down on his belly, and came out with a pair of pants and a shirt. "This here's about all I'll need," he said apologetically. "You got cooking gear at your place, haven't—Ben, what's the matter?"

"Nothing," I said. "Nothing." I couldn't move. I stared at the snug little house and thought I was going to cry.

"Ben, you don't look so good. Are you going to throw up or anything?" Joe came and took hold of my arm, looking very concerned. "Listen, Ben, you better come in and sit a bit. You look awful pale."

"No, no, I'm all right," I said. He gently guided me inside, and I sat on the edge of the bed, looking out the door at the forest, where all the rest of the trees stretched up a hundred feet or more. At that moment I believe I was the most terribly disillusioned man the world had ever seen, since the Beginning. The one thing I really wanted out of life had been . . . I couldn't bear to think about it.

"Honest to god, Ben, you don't look good," Joe said worriedly. "Are you dizzy? Or what?"

It infuriated me that he should be so concerned about me. After all, it was his fault. After what he had done to me, the idiot insisted on babbling and being friendly.

"It's all right, it's all right, just never mind, Joe," I said, trying not to sound enraged in my voice. There was an injustice about it all that hurt me deep, like a gut wound. "I guess—I guess I just had it in my mind wrong."

"Yeah," Joe said. "It's funny the way that happens, ain't it. *What*'d you have in your mind wrong, Ben?"

"Never mind. Just never mind. I can't explain it."

"I get things wrong in *my* mind, too," he said sympathetically. "Lots of times I do that."

I finally began to gather my feelings up, like poking through the wreckage of an explosion. I looked around at the roof, and the table, and the cot. It was as good as a cabin. And when he fell out of bed, he had about a foot and a half to drop, just like everybody else.

Joe laughed, self-consciously. "Tell you what, Ben," he said. "I'll carry the pants, and you can carry the shirt if you want to."

I said nothing.

"I mean, that ain't *fixed* or nothing," he said anxiously. "You could carry the pants if you wanted to. Ben?"

3

I remember that evening at Joe Champion's tree very clearly. It was probably one of the major events of my life, but possibly it is also because it is one of the last things I remember clearly of that summer. The next month, the next two months, are like a fevered dream in my mind. The forms shift when I try to think about them, everything merges and swirls and drifts crazily. Days slid into nights and then it was day again. Full moons came and miraculously thinned down into blackness and time darted by like fish rushing upstream. Each day was a sharp and flashing splinter, glimpsed briefly, dazzling, and then gone.

The fever, the burning, closed around us like a fist. We worked until we could not stand, and then found something to do sitting down. Sam had already warned us that after the framing it would slow down. But even warned, I was not prepared. It seemed to go so slowly that it was almost unbearable. A day flickered past, and she looked the same as she had looked the night before. It tore the guts out of us all to have given everything we had, and to see no change for it, no result.

But the rail stringers went up, and the rail, and the rider keelson was bolted down on top of the keelson. The deck knees were fixed to the clamps—somehow—I don't even remember it—and then, miraculously, the first deck beams stretched across the space that had seemed normal before, but now seemed terribly empty.

The whipsaw rasped in our ears, and our hearts pounded to the slow swinging rhythm of the adze and the ax. We reached the ultimate, final limit of our strength every day. We reached the point we *could* not drive any more; forced beyond ourselves and drove again. Each night it was clear to me that I was finished, I could not possibly work again. I had to rest. And each morning I was drawn back to her, relentlessly, hopelessly. Time itself became something meaningless, there was no sense of its passing. There was only urgency, drive, work.

When a man could not take it any more, it seemed perfectly normal that he should drop where he stood and sleep for an hour in the hold, or by the whipsaw, or in the shadow of the hull. If he was in the way the others simply carried him off where he would not be stepped on. In an hour, or two hours, he would be back on the job. How he felt was his own business, and nobody asked him. As long as he worked everything was right.

In all this time we did not permanently lose one man, and there were no serious accidents and no serious mistakes. Tired as we were, we did not make errors. We even found that the terrible blinding fatigue was useful; we had skills we had never before realized. We were able to do things because we were too tired to realize we *couldn't* do them. We were not responsible, since we were far beyond the point of safety or accuracy, but we no longer seemed subject to human feebleness. The image herself was more real, more strong, more important than our weaknesses; she compensated for our mortality. She had taken us fully now, she had set us afire to get herself built, and she saw to it that things went right. We did not think about it, any more than a saw thinks about cutting. We were the tools; we worked.

Peter Morgan set up a rope machine a hundred yards from the ways. He had worked in a rope factory in his native country, and knew the business. It was a great help to us, but no one thought to thank him. After all, had he not known, we would have found some way to do it. We found some way to do anything that needed doing. Three of us worked the rope machine for three days, winding the heart yarns of the cordage we had salvaged from the Netarts Bay wreck. The hearts were not too badly rotted, and from them we wove the long coils of line, seemingly endless, that we would need.

Peter had originally set up the rope walk pointing inland, and we spent the first day working in that direction. That night, talking around the fire, we discovered that for some reason it made us all nervous to have the rope walk running off in that direction. It had to be changed. We didn't know why, but it had to be changed, and it was. I later figured out the reason: the rope walk was pointing away from Her, and none of us could stand it. We had to work too far away. It was insane, but it was normal and right.

In these days I tasted for the first time the deepest pride a man can feel: the knowledge that he will endure. He will survive, he will endure, and no matter what demands are made on his body and mind, he can meet them. At base all life is a question of endurance, and all work. Beyond a certain point work becomes a question of surviving, of enduring what the work requires. Those who burn hottest are those who are most certain of their ability to endure, who can afford to spend their energy wildly, knowing they will endure. They are, I suppose, madmen. They are the men who drive themselves beyond all reason. So be it; they are the madmen, but they get the work done.

The first two weeks after the raid by the Klickitats, we did not sleep by the Ship. Reluctantly we wandered off at nightfall to Vaughn's, which was nearest, or to my place, stacking ourselves on cabin floors wherever we could find space, and often enough where there was no space. But now we had night work as well, and it was unpleasant inside.

We were picking oakum at night, and the smell of tar was viciously strong in the little rooms. We took vast lengths of the tarred rope we had salvaged, and cut it into six-inch lengths. It was stiff as rock, but we soaked it all in boiling water, until it was soft enough to pick. Then we went at it until our fingers were raw and hurting from the heat and tar, picking the fibers into tiny shreds for caulking the seams. Even with the door open, the smell of salt and tar was so oppressive we had to go out for air from time to time.

After two weeks, the urgency in our minds about the attacks had diminished. I decided to go back to sleeping by the Ship, and to set up a tar-softening kettle down there. Eb Thomas was with me, but I had the idea. He was too butt-headed to admit I was braver than he was, so he came along. I had no idea of bravery; I was just tired. Too tired to walk all that way home at night, wasting valuable energy, too tired to sit in a tar-smelly room and pick oakum with a bunch of skeletons no more alive than I was. If I had to pick oakum—and I had to—I was going to do it outside, and be in sight of the Ship, at least.

Being outside again, we could hear the occasional rifle shots that echoed over the Bay in the middle of the night. We heard from time to time that such and such a bunch had gotten hold of some alcohol, gotten excited, and come in to get us. The guards always seemed to catch them. At least they never got to us. After Eb and I went down all the regulars started sleeping by her again, the only difference being that we had our own guns with us now. They were never used. It was probably useless, anyway. We were so exhausted and hurting when we finally got to sleep that they could have had our heads with never a protest from anybody. The only thing that could make us move was the invitation to work. Being killed didn't even seem very serious, except that it would have a very bad effect on your work.

But I will admit that, at this time, I considered myself immortal, genuinely immortal. At least temporarily. I had a conviction I never admitted to anyone. I was absolutely certain nothing could happen to me while I was working on Her. I was convinced She was protecting me. She needed me. She needed me to build Her, and I didn't think She would let anything happen. And She didn't. At least, not to us.

To us, the gunshots in the night were only a kind of whiplash. They didn't happen every night; perhaps every other, even every third. There was no pattern. But they always seemed to come when we needed them for a spur. Just when we were lowest, just when we had finally drained the last of our energy, just when we could see no possible way to face the morning—there would be a raid. And the first clatter of rifle fire would pierce our dulled minds like a knife. The sense of urgency would be back again, as strong as ever. There was no reasonable explanation for this—no connection between the sound of rifles in the night and the building. But we were far beyond the point of reason, and the firing said, *Hurry, hurry, there is not much time.*

To others, those sharp explosions that ripped the silence of the night meant other things. Two Killamooks were shot one night, two of the guards. The raids had been going on so long that we had ceased to think of them as danger. But that night two guards scuffled with a group of Yaquina come up from the south, and they were killed. Then there was wailing in the nights, and the women sang at the village.

The worst news was brought to us by Indian Jim one night. A bunch of us were sitting around the nauseous steaming kettle, picking oakum. I suppose from a distance it would have looked like a feast, the cheery fire, the kettle, the little group of men. None of us felt feast-like, we ached too much.

Indian Jim came silently around the hull. We looked up as he came near. It occurred to me later that nobody had even thought of reaching for a gun. If it had been a pack from Outside we would all have been dead. But the guards were so effective we didn't even think about it any more. And, for me at least, the protection of the goddess was absolute.

"*Klahowya*, Jim," I said. "No *muckamuck*, no food. Just oakum."

"You come," Jim said to me.

I walked over to him, standing a few yards away, just at the edge of the fire circle. "What is it, Jim?"

"Kilchis *chako kokshut*," he said.

"Hurt! How hurt?"

"*Sukwalal kokshut. Mika mitlite Boston metsin?*"

"What is it, Ben?" Eb Thomas called.

"He says Kilchis is hurt. He wants to know if we've got white man's medicine."

"How'd he get hurt?" Thomas said.

"Jim says he's gun-hurt. Figure it out for yourself." I turn back to Jim. "No, Jim," I told him. "We don't have a damn thing."

He looked at the ground, and I couldn't read his expression. Finally, without saying another word, he turned and went off, disappearing silently into the darkness that was all around. I went back to the fire, worried.

"How bad is he hurt, Ben?" Thomas said.

"I don't know. He didn't say."

"Maybe somebody ought to go find out."

"Yes," I said, trying to think. "Yes, I'll go in the morning."

Jim's words echoed in my dreams the rest of the night, the guttural rhythms of the Jargon making me twist in my sleep. *Sukwalal kokshut sukwalal*. Gun-hurt, shot.

Chapter Eleven

I genuinely intended to go see the old *tyee* in the morning, but the work stacked up so that it was impossible. Thomas and Vaughn had to leave, which we had not expected. The one thing we had been unable to improvise was the running gear. We had not been able to salvage enough from the wrecks to do the job. We also needed fresh tar for the caulking, when the time came. All this material had to be bought in Astoria, and Vaughn and Thomas took the horses all the way up and back. They were gone nearly a week, leaving us two men short. To make up for their absence, the rest of us had to work so much the harder.

As always, when we needed a fresh spur to drive us on, we got it. Every time we entered a new phase, the enthusiasm piled up in us as strong as it had been on the first day. And every time the new phase seemed the most important of all; *this* was great, all the rest was merely leading up to this superb, fine moment. How had we been able to get so excited about framing, when it was obviously planking that was the best part of shipbuilding?

And I noticed another thing about this time, which I have never been able to explain to my own satisfaction. At least ten million times since the first day—a hundred thousand the first day itself—we had been hammered down with the undeniable realization that we knew nothing. We were blocks of wood, we were stones, we were cows and fish and clouds and trees. We were anything, except shipwrights. But in spite of it all, by christ, we *felt* like shipwrights. We had the image of ourselves as shipwrights, and no matter how many times it was proved differently, it did not deeply affect us. Throughout the entire process, we never understood how pitifully *little* we understood. I suppose this deliberate ignoring of our ignorance was necessary; in some sort a measure of survival. Had we known how stupid we were, we would have died. Or worse, been afraid to build her.

I remember this very clearly on the first day of planking. As always, there was a sort of conference before the day's work, in which Sam explained what had to be done, and what the rules were, and how to do it. I will admit now that after the first forty-five minutes of explanation, I had still not caught the subject. I got more nervous, more and more embarrassed as Sam went on and on with terms I had never heard and operations I didn't believe possible to materials that didn't exist. After the framing I felt pretty cocky and shipwrighty. I was surprised and, I suppose, a little bit wounded in my pride that I couldn't even figure out what he was talking about. It was, in fact, this way each time the activity changed, but each time I forgot about it and approached the next step in the full confidence that I would understand it all immediately. I felt a little better when I observed the hazy, distant looks of the others.

One of the problems that morning was that for the first forty-five minutes, Sam did not once use the word plank, which I was sort of waiting for as a clue. He went on and on about something he called "strakes" and "wales," and how it would go when a fellow started messing around with strakes and wales. He even got off a couple of jokes, I think, but it is difficult to fully appreciate humor when you don't speak the language. We smiled, however.

It was finally Peter Morgan, god bless his unembarrassed soul, who asked the question that seemed essential to the problem:

"Sam, what's a strake?"

Sam was at that moment squatted on the sand by the ways, his ever-present calipers serving as a drawing instrument. He looked up at Peter Morgan, then he looked at all of us, finding, I believe, the same incomprehension and hopefulness on every face. Perhaps even Sam had momentarily forgotten the exact content of our tiny skulls.

"A strake?" he repeated. "What do you think I been talkin' about for an hour?"

"Strakes," Peter admitted freely. "But what are they?"

Sam looked back down at the sand for a moment. "That's what you call a plank when it's on a ship's hull," he said in a low, depressed voice. Finally he sighed, and discouragedly rubbed out the drawing he'd been making. "All right," he said patiently. "We'll start again. The first to go on are the wale strakes. They got to be . . ."

They had to be thicker than the rest, for one thing. The first few planks down from the deck formed the wale, and were of heavier timber to give protection and add vertical stability to her. Sam told us that in the big men o' war there were several belts of wales at different levels on the hull, where reinforcing was needed. Upper chain wale, lower chain wale, upper wale, lower wale. Sometimes a wale at the waterline a foot thick, for protection against enemy balls. Since this seemed one of our lesser worries, only the first few strakes from the deck would be wale strakes.

I suppose I had the idea that planking consisted of taking a plank— a strake—and fastening it to the side of the Ship, then taking another one and doing the same. I was quickly disabused.

For one thing we ran into another question of beauty, and Sam initiated us into the 5-4-3 rule. For a ship to be beautiful the planks have to follow certain lines with respect to the deck and the shape of the hull. These lines are determined by the 5-4-3 rule, which told us that the width of a plank amidships is 5/5, the width forward is 4/5, the width aft is 3/5. The planking is thus not exactly parallel, but tapers both fore and aft. This gives you a beautiful line. As far as I was ever able to determine, this is the sole reason for the 5-4-3 rule.

Sam admitted a little hesitantly that the 5-4-3 was one of the *un*written rules of shipbuilding. An informal agreement with the goddess. There seemed to be two unwritten rules for every written one, and the distinction was perfectly useless. We had to follow the unwritten ones as faithfully as anything else. And in any case we would never have known the difference, as everything *we* had for rules came out of Sam's head.

The shape of a hull is breathtaking in its beauty, but it is bitchily agonizing to try and cover that complex curve evenly with flat lumber. We found that each strake had to be individually shaped to fit the curve of the hull, the curve of the strake above, and the 5-4-3 rule. The edge of each also had to be beveled for the caulking seam, and there were half a dozen other rules for each piece of lumber, which I'd had in my mind as more or less rectangular. Fortunately, this calculation was such that Sam couldn't trust it to any of us, and he did it all.

With his calipers he measured down from the deck at about every other frame, marking off the points on a long vertical batten he called a spiling staff. These points were then transferred to the rough plank, and all of them connected by a fair curve. This gave the top profile of the first wale strake, and she would fit snugly up at the deck. The bottom profile was determined by the 5-4-3 rule. When these curves had been carefully shaped out, the plank was a funny-looking beast, a sort of sway-backed shape that looked as if it had been impossibly warped. But when it was lifted up into place and bent around the frames—she was perfect. The shape itself meant nothing, except as it became part of the curve of the hull.

Before each strake could be mounted, it had to be lined off, which was not so difficult. Even I could do it, and it restored my shaky shipwright's confidence. While Sam was laying out the profile of the strake on the raw lumber I was lining out her planking, simply by stretching a chalk line along the face of the frames the strake would cover. This rapidly showed up any high ones, bulges or irregularities. These were dubbed off with the adze until the line sighted in a fair, smooth curve, and I knew the plank would fit down snug against the frame and bear evenly.

The butt joints, where the ends of the planks came together, were also subject to their own rigid rules. These were not complicated, however, and Sam spelled it all out on a piece of wood, which we consulted religiously every three minutes to be sure it hadn't changed. It was a sort of drawing of the side of the hull, with the butt-joint pattern:

```
 NO butts closer than three frames to each other
 ←(3 fr)→         unless there is
 A FULL STRAKE BETWEEN
                 ←2fr→ then you can Use a Distance of two Frames
 Don't NEVER put two butts on the Same Frame unless there is
                                              1 ↑
         THREE                                2
                                              3 ↓
 FULL STRAKES IN BETWEEN. COUNT THEM!
```

Single fastenings on planks 8" wide and under, double-and-single on planks between 8" and 11", full double on planks above 11". DON'T FORGET!

It seemed like planking wasn't going to be so simple as it looked. Once again I ended the first day of a new phase thinking that when you got right down to it, a man had a hell of a lot to learn in this world.

But we did learn it, and perhaps in the end that was the greatest miracle of all. We either learned everything we had to know, or did it right without knowing how. She was getting herself built and she knew what she wanted. She wouldn't let us go too far wrong. There is a wonderful confidence in knowing you are necessary to a goddess.

About halfway through the planking it began to go smoothly and regularly, just as if we knew what we were doing; there was no longer the necessity of the constant meticulous explanations of what She wanted. We were able to take a few of the men off and put them to work on the spars. I was one of them. And again—I might be one of the world's greatest experts on framing and planking, but it turned out that spar making was a bit different.

The mainmast, for example. I didn't mind the calculation of the length so much, because it seemed so logical. I couldn't *follow* the logic exactly, but it was based on the Ship herself, and anything that was based on the Ship herself was bound to seem logical. You added together the distance along the deck from stem to sternpost, and the widest beam, which you measured *outside* the wales. Half the sum of length and beam was the total length of the mainmast, and there was such an intimate relation between it and the other parts of the Ship that it seemed inevitable it should be exactly that length.

But when we got to *tapering* the spars, logic disappeared and we followed the ritual because we were told to, without making any effort to understand it. We measured up from the foot of the mast to the exact height at which the deck would come. The diameter there was simple: 7/8" for each 3 feet of total length. But then the rest of the mast had to be tapered off and shaped up to the head, which, needless to say, was not just *any* old taper. The length from deck to head was divided into quarters, and each quarter had its proper proportions. Sam, with his merciless calipers, allowed no margin for high spirits or fanciful invention. On scrap lumber he wrote out the proportion of diameter at each quarter mark, and this for every mast, yard, boom and gaff in her. We had a separate measuring board for each piece. I still have the board for the lower mainmast, mounted over my fireplace.

Starting with the diameter at deck level, the mast was tapered and shaped to these proportions, according to my board:

First quarter: 60/61   Second quarter: 14/15   Third quarter: 6/7
Head, lower part: 5/8   Upper part: 3/4   Heel: 6/7

Thinking back about that measuring board—and all the others—it is clearly impossible that we did it. But somehow, facing little bits of the impossible every morning, with your tools in your hands, it manages to get done one way or another.

The last stage was the most infuriating: the caulking. Of all the waiting, that was the worst. It was painful, slow and tedious and unbearable. Only Sam knew anything about it, of course, and he patiently explained how to tamp the oakum down just right in the seams, so the men following behind with the tar would have a good base. Neither too loose nor too tight. The edge of each strake was beveled slightly to take the caulking, the rule being 1/16" of taper for each inch of plank thickness. Sam showed us that by taking a folded two-foot rule and opening the legs 5/8", you automatically had the angle of taper. It was a trifle under the 1/16 rule, actually, and he debated it in his mind for some time before showing us. But it was standard building practice, and he finally accepted it as close enough. If it was close enough for him, it was close enough for us.

When the caulking crew had finished, Sam went over her inch by inch. When he finally stood back to look at her, we all held our breath.

"Well," he said reluctantly. "I guess she'll do."

The cheer that went up then must have been heard all the way to Oregon City. Sam turned and scowled at us. "Don't holler afore you're bit," he said ' "You ain't got the wood in her yet."

"Well, let's *get* it in, then!"

Sam looked dubiously at the sky. "Ain't sure we got time today."

"Sam!"

"What?"

"Sam, *please*. We got the steps in, all we got to do is raise the mast. We *got* to do it."

"Foot of a mast makes a lot of pressure," Sam mumbled. "Got to be right. Got to be strong, your step, got to *hold*."

"Sam, it's right, you know it is. You checked it all a dozen times. Come on, let's put the mast in, Sam."

The rest pleaded with him, too. It suddenly seemed terribly important to get the mainmast stepped today. After the long and tedious agony of the caulk-and-tar, we couldn't wait. We were worse than young men in love, we couldn't sit still.

Nothing would do but Sam had to climb down into the hold all over again and inspect the solidity of the step and peer at the rider keelson where the foot of the mast would sit.

He finally climbed out again and stood on the deck, looking down at the ring of anxious faces that stared up at him, half open-mouthed. We were so tense that Joe Champion didn't even put his hands on his head.

"Who's got some money?" Sam said.

We looked at each other, and there was some fumbling in pockets. Nobody had any money.

"Sam, it's all gone. We put up every cent of cash money for the running gear," Vaughn said. "What do you need money for?"

"Are you crazy?" Sam said in a tone of disbelief. "We can't step that there wood without a *coin* under her. Why she wouldn't float a week!"

"Well, *somebody's* got a coin," Vaughn said, turning to scan the crew impatiently.

"*I* ain't got a half-dime to my name," Thomas said. "I ain't had for a month or better."

"Me neither," somebody else muttered.

"Well, *get* some," Vaughn said, panicky. "We can't hold up for a thing like *that*, for god's sake."

"Listen," I said. "Somebody run down to the village and borrow something from the Indians."

"That's it, that's it!" Thomas hollered. "I'll do it."

He was already off, running and hopping over the scrap lumber and junk around the ways like a scared deer. The rest of us fidgeted nervously. I started around the Ship, checking the caulking because there wasn't anything else to do. Somebody came behind me, and then *everybody* decided to inspect. In a few minutes the whole crew was trooping mechanically around the ship like a school of fish in a pool, staring at the hull without really seeing it. Sam stayed on deck, saying nothing while we circled around and around.

After what seemed an eternity Thomas came storming back, out of breath and red in the face.

"What the hell took so long?" Vaughn demanded.

"I had—I had trouble," Thomas panted.

"Just did you *get* it, is all."

Thomas dug in his jeans and came up with a couple of small white shells.

"Thomas, my god, you idiot! We send you after money and you bring back *seashells*? What's wrong with your *mind*, boy?"

"It's money, it's money," Thomas said. "They didn't have no white money, but they gave me this."

"He's right," I said. "That's *haikwa*, that's what they use for money. It just looks different than ours. Sam? Can we use the *haikwa?*"

Sam frowned. "Well, I don't know, I never heard of—"

"Sam, it's just money that's different, that's all. In England they use English money, don't they?"

"Yus, but—"

"And back east they use American money, don't they? It's just the same idea."

"I don't know," Sam said dubiously.

"Sam, we're in Indian country, she's an Indian ship, we *got* to use Indian money, don't you see?" I was really desperate.

"The mast foot'll smash that damn little shell to powder," Vaughn said to me, but not loud enough for Sam to hear.

"But it'll *be* there. That's what's important, ain't it? It'll *be* there."

Sam looked around him at the Bay. Off the bar the breakers rumbled softly, lit in red streaks by the late sun. The lumpy peaks of the coast range were glowing warm. Sam looked at it all, letting his eyes caress it almost as they caressed the Ship. The forest that stretched endlessly up into the ridges, range after range of rollers coming massively in from infinity to explode themselves at our feet. For a long time he let his eyes rest in the direction of the village itself, out of sight behind the small hill. It was our country, the Bay. Our country and our Ship and our Indians and our water and trees and ferns and grass and deer and seabirds calling like the distant high wail of souls tormented.

"All right," Sam said. "Let me have it."

The mast went down and crushed the shell and was tied into the step. It was pure joy. She stood a thousand feet tall, spearing up into the sky like a fire. She seemed to fly, she seemed to shiver and want to spiral off like a hawk riding the wind. The life ran through her and made her so beautiful it gave me a kind of joy I'd never known. The sun made her gold and orange and warm and you could hardly bear to look at her.

Eb Thomas, old butt-head Eb Thomas with his nature's wonders, sat down on the ground and began to cry.

It was the 29th of September, 1854. We had done it in 103 days. One hundred and three days that were worth a lifetime. Nothing would ever be the same again, not for any of us. We knew what a man could do, now.

2

The launching itself was delayed for two days. It clouded over during the night, and by morning the sky was infinite Oregon gray, and a steady drizzle enveloped all the Bay. It looked as it had looked the first day I saw it, shifting behind a moving curtain of rain and mist. The rains had held off until we got the mast in her, but now they were impatient to soak the land, and we would have them for seven or eight months.

Even the coming of the rains seemed good to us. The summer had been long and fair, one stretch of sixty-seven days without rain. The world had conspired this year to let us work and we could only be grateful for as much as we had had.

There were small things to do yet, trimming up, finishing off, and we hoped at first that the weather would break, so we could launch under clear skies, as we had built. But after the second day, we were back in the familiar pattern of rain, our winter-thinking. In Oregon after two days of rain it seems as though it has been raining since the world began, and you cannot remember the last time you saw sun. We decided to go ahead anyway, or we would likely have to wait until next spring.

There was a good deal of argument about the launching. Sam said we had to grease the ways; it was absolutely essential, or she wouldn't go down. But since we had no grease, it was obviously *not* essential. We would have to find some other way.

"Somebody's got to render out a cow, that's all there is to it," Sam said.

We were sitting in Vaughn's cabin the evening of the second day of rain. Sam, Vaughn, Thomas, myself, and a couple of others.

"Well, Eb," I said. "You got the most cattle of anybody in the Bay. Looks like it's up to you."

"Listen, I didn't bring my animals in here to grease *ways* with," Eb muttered.

"Sam," Vaughn said. "You just got it in your mind it has to be done *one* way, is all." It had been so long since any of us dared argue with Little Sam that I think Vaughn was enjoying the sensation of disagreeing for its own sake.

Sam clasped his hands between his knees and looked worriedly at the floor. "Well," he said finally, "you just show me how to do it *without* grease."

"Listen," Vaughn said. "I got a plan."

"I don't want nothin' to do with it," Eb Thomas said suddenly, sitting up straight. "Somebody'll get hurt."

"Listen," Vaughn said in a hurt tone. "Has anybody *ever* got hurt by one of my plans?"

"No, but Eb's right," I said. "People come awful close. Trouble with your plans, Vaughn, they go so smooth in your head and they never seem to work outside of it. And one of these days . . ."

"Well, hell, then," Vaughn said, settling back sullenly. "Figure it out your ownselves, then, if you don't want to hear my plan."

We all thought about it silently, and it was obvious nobody had any ideas. Finally Eb, who could clearly see one of his cows being butchered, said discouragedly, "All right, what is it?"

Vaughn leaned forward, coming to life again, with an excitement in his voice. "Listen. What's slipperier than mud? Nothin'. And particular the mud from the Bay bottom. We'll grease the ways with mud from the Bay. It's sort of—fitting, anyway."

"Won't work," Sam said softly.

"You know, Vaughn," I said, "I think the best thing about the Ship is that you didn't have any plans in your head for months. Sam had all the plans. But they come out of *his* head, and they *worked*. That's the whole difference right there."

"I never *knew* such a bunch of—I don't know whats," Vaughn said impatiently. "Look. We plaster the bottom with good gooey mud, all right? Then we plaster the ways, too. That makes two coats of the slipperiest, greasiest, slidiest stuff in the world. You'll hardly be able to hold her with the chocks. Then Sam gets up with a bottle of wine, and he busts it over her bow. Even that bottle of wine makes her slide a little bit, because that mud's so terribly slippery. She wants to *go!* Everybody's there, the guys are down by the chocks with sledges, and the crowd gives a cheer. A *real* cheer, I mean. When they hear that cheer the boys give one good swing with their sledges at the chocks and—BANG!"

He slammed his hand down on the table. We jumped, startled, and the Ship began to move. Slowly at first, then picking up a little speed on that greasy, slippery, slidy mud. The stern plowed into the water, throwing a great wave to either side, she rolled a bit and settled square, riding like a duck. The wash moved slowly out away from the hull, and the crowd gave another hearty holler.

"Won't work," Sam said again.

"Listen," Vaughn said. "Suppose I *prove* it to you? Suppose I prove it to you with a demonstration that it'll work. How about that?"

"Well, hell, it's worth a try," Thomas said.

"You're just worried about one o' your cows," I said.

"Listen, Ben Thaler," Thomas said. "Don't you worry about what *I'm* worried about. I don't have to have a butt-head like you tell me what—"

"All right, come *on*, you guys," Vaughn said. "You ain't argued for weeks. All right, listen, it's all settled. You come down to the ways in the morning, I'll prove my plan'll work, and we'll launch in the afternoon. All right?"

"Don't see how you can prove what ain't true," Sam said.

"I'll *show* you how, Sam, I'll give you a *demonstration!* What more can you ask than that?" Vaughn stood up at the table. He was so anxious to finish the conversation right there I thought he was going to walk out of his own house.

"All right, there's nothin' to lose, anyway. If it don't work, Eb can—"

"Let's see what Vaughn's got in his mind afore you start figurin' what I can do, Ben Thaler," Eb said.

So that was the way it was. We gathered down by the ways in the morning. Vaughn was standing there like a stage magician waiting for the hall to fill. He had a good audience. The fever was running high ever since the stepping of the mast, and there were a dozen Indians always hanging around in the drizzle, caught up by the excitement, but not knowing exactly what to expect.

I couldn't take my eyes off Her. We had moved from one impossible beauty to the next, each more intense than the one before. Now She was finished and it was almost unbearable to look at Her. You thought you'd be blinded, you thought you'd explode, you forgot to breathe. As far as Vaughn was concerned, my preoccupation just annoyed him.

"Listen, you got to pay attention to the demonstration," he said severely. "If you think she's pretty now, just wait until she's launched. Imagine what she'll look like riding out on the Bay under full canvas. Just imagine her comin' in from Astoria, ridin' across the bar with the sunset behind her, shinin' through the sails like fire . . ."

I imagined. Jesus.

"But we got to get her off the ways, first," Vaughn said conclusively. "Now pay attention to this here demonstration and I'm going to show you how we do it."

He had brought up a bucket of bottom mud from the Bay, and had it beside him. He took two scrap planks, about two feet long and a foot wide.

"This here's the Ship," he said. "And this here is the ways, all right?"

Two of the Indians came over to look more closely at the boards. Vaughn turned them over for inspection, showing there was no trickery, I suppose. One of the Indians said something to the other in Salishan, the second just shrugged.

"Now, just stand clear, boys," Vaughn said. He propped the end of one board up on a log, so it slanted down. "This is the ways," he muttered, almost to himself. "Now we plaster the ways with mud, like so . . ." He scooped up great gobbets of mud from the bucket and plastered the whole upper surface of the board an inch thick, like a woman frosting a cake. There was no doubt it was gooey, we could see that all right. It began to slide a little, he plastered it so thick.

"Then we give a little dollop to the hull . . ." He scooped and smoothed mud on the other plank. Then, very carefully, he lowered the second plank on the first, muddy side down, so he had a sort of mud sandwich with one end propped up on the log. Little rivulets of water oozed out from the crack.

"And she's ready," Vaughn said triumphantly.

"So? She ain't movin'."

"Then you knock the chocks out," Vaughn said. With terrifying suddenness he leaped up in the air and landed on the planks with both feet. The top one scooted out from under him like a greased pig. A flat spray of mud squirted from between the planks. Vaughn was thrown over backwards when the top plank slid, and he almost seemed to hang suspended in the air for a brief moment before he descended like a falling tree, landing flat on his back.

It knocked the breath clean out of him and he lay there flat, making awful gasping noises. We were all horrified by the abruptness of it, and stared down at him for a minute without doing anything. He was suffering trying to catch his breath, making grunting frog-like sounds in his throat and jerking around a little.

The Indians looked at each other, then back at Vaughn. One of them rattled off something, and another contradicted him. They began a lively argument, pointing at Vaughn, at the boards, at the mud bucket and even out across the Bay, explaining it to each other. They began to get angry.

"Vaughn, are you all right?" I said.

"Guh—guh," he gasped. Finally he turned over on his side. Thomas squatted down beside him and began to pound him on the back.

"Come on, come on, you just got the wind knocked out of you."

One of the Indians shoved the other one.

Vaughn finally got his breath back and stood up victoriously. He walked over where the top board had flown and picked it up. He waved it in the air, splattering droplets of mud all around. "All right," he said proudly. "Will it work or won't it? Is that a demonstration or is that a demonstration?"

The other Indian shoved back, and they were separated by friends.

"By god," Eb Thomas said. "She really flew all right, I'll say that. "

Sam stared glumly down at the planks. He knew it wouldn't work, but he also knew that nothing he could say would have one-tenth the dramatic force of Vaughn's demonstration.

A third Indian came over and picked up the other board and showed it to the two who had been arguing. He chattered away in a confident tone, pointing at the board, the mud, then turning to point at Vaughn and the mud bucket and all the rest of us. The two original belligerents listened quietly for a few seconds, then their faces hardened menacingly. They both began to talk at once, impatient with the third man's stupidity. It was clear that if their own theories might be dubious, *his* was perfectly imbecilic.

"Well, I think she'll work," Eb Thomas said. "I say go ahead."

"How about it?" Vaughn said. "Is that a demonstration or is that a demonstration?"

"Well," I said, "it was *impressive*, but . . ."

The Indians had either settled their argument or abandoned it. The whole crowd pushed forward in a line and solemnly shook hands with Vaughn, one by one. Then they filed off home, thoughtful.

"All right, hell," I said. "Let's try it."

Chapter Twelve

It may seem difficult to get excited over a bucket of mud, but we were like a bunch of young men going courting. Bucket after bucket of the gooey stuff we hauled out of the Bay bottom in the shallows. Vaughn had recently become an authority on the sliding qualities of mud, and he supervised with his customary capability. I think we all became fairly expert, sliding it between our fingers and considering it gravely. This was necessary because of the quantity needed; we had to shift our 'mine' from time to time as we got through the top layer of silt and discovered that beneath was sand, which would not work at all. And when we moved over even a few feet we found that the character of the mud, viewed with a practiced and critical eye, was entirely different. There were ten thousand different kinds of mud on the Bay bottom, of which most were unacceptable by reason of grit or particles of shell or waterlogged sticks or simply wrong consistency. Ours had to be rich and butter-creamy, like the demonstration mud.

The amount required was really remarkable; you have no idea how much mud it takes to cover the entire bottom of a ship with a thick and heavy coat, not to mention the ways. We stood in lines out into the water, hip-deep in the waves, scooping and passing. As a bucket chain it was inefficient because every man in the chain felt called upon to examine the consistency and give his opinion of the mud and the gatherer at the end. After a few repetitions of this the end man tended to get annoyed and there were arguments until we simply started rotating the scoopers and putting them back at the dry end of the chain.

"Dry" is perhaps not the word, as the rain continued to drift down all day, and those who were spreading by the Ship were nearly as wet as those out in the Bay itself. The drizzle got heavier and heavier all afternoon until about four o'clock. Vaughn cheerfully suggested it was an advantage, as otherwise we would have the problem of the mud drying out.

But about four o'clock the rain itself stopped, and the sky began to lighten in the west.

"Look at that," Vaughn said, craning his neck. "It's going to clear."

"Hell it is," Thomas muttered. He was already in his winter mood.

"No, look over there," Vaughn said, pointing. "There's blue sky."

And it was. A tiny patch, but it was growing.

"It's going to clear for us to put her in the water!" Vaughn said, jubilant. "It's a *omen!*"

Nobody agreed with him out loud, but nobody disagreed either. We all wanted to believe it. As the clear patch spread across the western horizon Vaughn became more and more exhilarated, as though he were sweeping away the overcast with simple enthusiasm.

By five o'clock, practically the whole western sky was clear of cloud. You could see the horizon itself, a clean, flat line of joining between sea and sky. You had to admit it looked very auspicious.

The Indians who had watched Vaughn's demonstration in the morning had apparently spread the word in the village. Small groups drifted around to watch us haul mud all afternoon. Obviously they had never before realized plain mud could be so interesting and useful. And when they saw the bucket after bucket loads we were bringing up, their attention was solidly fixed. After all, with one single bucket of mud Vaughn had provided the most amazing performance of the year for them; what would we not do with two hundred, or three hundred. The possibilities were endless, and by six o'clock, when the ways and Ship were thoroughly plastered, practically the entire village was there.

I looked for Kilchis, and suddenly remembered he was hurt. I had figured it was nothing serious, or we certainly would have heard about it in the weeks since it had happened. The Ship was the biggest thing that had ever happened in the Bay, and it seemed fitting that he should watch her launched. But perhaps he was not interested. He had never understood exactly what it was about.

"Where's Sam? He's got to bust the bottle, he's got to christen her."

"He's around someplace. Hey, Sam!"

Sam scurried around from the other side of the hull, looking worried.

"Sam, you ready for her?"

"Yus, yus," he nodded quickly. We knew he had the name all picked out, but he had refused to tell anybody what it was. No amount of cajoling would get it out of him; he'd just shake his head and say, "I ain't telling. You'd just argue with me and it ain't to be argued about. It's right. I tell you that, it's right, it's the only name she *can* have." So we had to let it go at that.

There was a lot of speculation going around, of course, ranging from *Oregon's Glory* to *The Seven Winds* and passing by the *Samuel Howard*. I didn't engage in the argument because I had confidence in Sam. The name had to *mean* something, it had to express—somehow—everything that had gone into her, it had to sum up the whole process, the agony, the dreaming, the driving of the goddess when She got hold of us and threw us into the work. Sam *knew*; he knew what She was. It would be Right.

"Holy god," Vaughn said suddenly. "I forgot the champagne!" He took off fast for his cabin, and in a few minutes reappeared at the door with a bottle in his hand. It was only about a quarter full, the clear white diluted alcohol Means used to sell. Hastily Vaughn uncorked it and dipped it into the Bay, keeping the neck upright so the water could run in without the whisky running out. When it was full he swished it around and studied it with satisfaction before recorking it. There was only a little sediment, smokily floating.

"Champagne's weaker'n whisky, anyway," he said, winking at me conspiratorially. "And I b'lieve we're going to need about all the whisky we got for the party."

It was all right with me. As far as I was concerned pure Bay water would have been the best thing in the world to launch her with.

There was a kitchen chair up at the bow for Sam to stand on when he broke the bottle on her. Sam was waiting beside it, wringing his hands nervously and casting apprehensive glances at the crowd. By this time every white man in the Bay was there and a good nine-tenths of the Indians. Never had so many people been collected in one spot in all the history of the Bay.

Vaughn handed the bottle to Sam. Sam smiled a little and started to get up on the chair. Vaughn put his hand on the little man's shoulder and drew him back. Smiling genially at the poor bewildered Sam, Vaughn himself climbed up on the chair. He stood with his back to the Ship, holding both hands up in the air for silence. "Ladies and gentlemen," he said officially. "Ladies and *gentle*men!"

Gradually everybody quieted down. Eb Thomas sidled over to me and said, "I never heard nothin' about Vaughn givin' a *speech.*"

"It has fallen to my lot to memorialize this vessel," Vaughn said.

"That's sure god what he's going to do, though," I told Eb. "Listen, he's been practicin', you can tell."

"This moment marks a historic—ah, moment, in the history of this Bay," Vaughn said. "As this vessel takes the water, so our community takes wing."

Little Sam was still standing beside him, looking alternately at the bottle he held in his hand and Vaughn. Finally he quit looking at Vaughn and stared intently into the bottle, turning it around and around in his hands with a worried expression.

"She is our lifeline, our tie to the Outside, and prosperity rides in her hold!" Vaughn declaimed.

He got applause from time to time as he went on. The Indians didn't understand any of it, but figured he had the right. When the whites applauded, so did they. In the end, I expect the Indians were better suited to listen to Vaughn than we, as they were accustomed to the interminable and often incomprehensible tribal speeches. When I thought it over *I* didn't even mind. It would have been kind of empty just to have Sam get up and bust the bottle on her. Vaughn's speech gave you a chance to work up some tension of anticipation, perhaps even more than was strictly necessary.

Considering the temptation his speech was very moderate, not lasting over five minutes or so. Though I personally believed this was because he had not had time to memorize more than five minutes' worth of mumble. Finally he paused, his hands upraised in a last gesture of pride and general noble feeling.

"And to the man who is responsible has fallen the lot of christening this vessel. Without him, without his wisdom and skill, it would never have been possible. *Good old Sam Howard!* Come on up here, Sam."

There was a great cheer from the crew, and people reached forward to pat Sam on the back. He didn't see any of them. He was looking at Her, the last time he would see Her before She took to the water. The curving, pregnant hull, the masts with their canvas tightly furled. He got up on the chair, blinking, paying no attention to anyone but Her. He was silent for a long time up there, simply running his eyes over Her. Then he mumbled, "I christen thee—"

"Speak up, Sam, *louder!*" Vaughn said.

Sam didn't even glance at him. His voice was as firm as I had ever heard it when he started again. I suddenly realized I was holding my breath. It had to be right, it just had to be.

"I christen thee—*Morning Star of Tillamook.*"

He swung the bottle and it shattered across her bow. The crowd roared, and I heard the solid "thunk" as the sledge smashed away the chocks. I watched Sam. He stared off beyond Her at the sea and his eyes were shining.

She shivered once, and there was another heavy, dull sound, like the sound of the sledges magnified. Mud squirted out of the ways as she settled off the chocks, drenching the sledge-men from the waist down with a tidal wave of thick, gooey slime. The enormous weight of her hull squeezed water out of the muck remaining and trickles of almost clear liquid ran down the wood and into the bay. There was a moment's shocked silence as we watched her settle firmly, immovably on the ways.

Then Vaughn said, "Let's give her three times three anyway, boys!"

"HIP HIP HOORAW!"

"HIP HIP HOORAW!"

"HIP HIP HOORAW!"

Even the Indians joined in, sensing the importance of the moment, howling and singing their own songs. Some of them looked disappointed, particularly those who had watched Vaughn's undeniably more interesting demonstration.

Sam got down off the chair silently and started to walk away. Vaughn wouldn't let him go. He jumped up on the chair again and started a rousing good version of "For He's a Jolly Good Fellow" in honor of Sam and everybody joined in, good-naturedly slapping Sam on the back and joshing him. He stood in the middle of the crowd, looking at the ground. After a few more songs and choruses Vaughn leaped energetically off the chair and hollered, "All right, everybody up to my place!"

"Hooraw for Sam, hooraw for Vaughn!"

"HOORAW FOR US ALL, YOU SILLY BASTARD!"

The crew moved off in a bunch, sweeping Sam along irresistibly. As Vaughn passed us he said, "Say, Eb, tomorrow would you—"

"Yeah," Eb said discouragedly. "Tomorrow I'll butcher a cow."

"How's *that* for a omen, Vaughn?" I asked him.

"Hell, who believes in *omens?*" he said. "Listen, Ben, don't be superstitious, it brings bad luck."

I didn't say anything more, but I wasn't feeling lucky.

"Don't be *down* about it," Vaughn said, clapping us both on the back. "She's official now, getting her in the water's just a formality. She's as good as launched."

"In your head, maybe."

"Listen, Eb," Vaughn said seriously. "Maybe the way you think about a thing is just as important as what is."

"Yeah, you can think up your little dreams all day," Eb said bitterly. "Me, I got to butcher a cow."

But Vaughn refused to be distracted by Eb's pessimism. "Well, Ben," he said, "what do you think of her? Where'd Sam get that name, anyway? She's real pretty, *Morning Star of Tillamook*."

I stopped short. "You don't—you don't remember the wom—" I shivered involuntarily, and without my wishing it there came into my mind not the woman—I could not even remember what she looked like—but the sharp, clear image of Cockshaten writhing half-strangled on the ground in his own blood and vomit, and Sam's fever-eaten eyes as he lay rigid below the slowly swinging corpse.

"Remember what?" Vaughn said curiously.

"Nothing. Nothing. I guess he—made it up, or something. He must have made it up."

"Well, it's real pretty anyway," Vaughn said admiringly. "Sort of—I don't know, sort of expresses her character, like. *Morning Star.*"

"Yes," I said after a minute. "Yes, I guess maybe it does."

"You look glum, Ben," Vaughn said. "By god, what you need's a party, and that's *just* what we've got."

2

And that was *just* what we had. Vaughn produced four bottles of Means' watered whisky and set them triumphantly in the middle of the table. It doesn't seem much for fifteen men, but I discovered that night how little difference the quantity makes; it's the mood that counts.

How he did it I still don't know. Vaughn was on fire with his delight, and by the time we were packed into his cabin each of us was as thoroughly convinced as he that She had been launched—it was all over—it was finished. We had done it. We were already drunk on Her blood.

"There she is, boys," he said, thumping the bottles down. "Your reward's in heaven, but have a little sip now."

The corks came out like magic, and the first swallow almost did the job. The bottles whizzed through the crowd like deer through brush and were two-thirds empty by the time they got back to the table.

"Don't worry about a thing, boys, there's more where that came from!" It was a damned lie, but we *didn't* worry; we couldn't.

When we were all in the cabin there scarcely seemed room enough to move. But there was movement enough for any fifty cabins, a restless milling and pushing and turmoil. What space was not filled solidly with men was filled with tension. I have never known, before or since, an atmosphere like that. I saw men sick on one swallow of whisky, I saw men crying on two and passed out on three. We had burned and burned, and now it was all over. All the energy that was left in us would go up in one huge explosion.

Vaughn got a fiddle from someplace in back, and he started to play. He didn't fiddle very well, but he did it loud, and that's what we needed.

"Hooraw, Vaughn! Go it, boys! Where the hell's Sam? Get Sam up here, it's his shoutin' day!"

Three or four of them dragged Sam mercilessly over from the corner where he was trying to hide, and hoisted him up on their shoulders. He hung on to a couple of handfuls of hair and looked scared as they paraded him around the room three times. It was like moving through water; there was no space ahead of the triumphal procession and none behind. Still they moved, and the gap of their passing was quickly filled by the milling pack, boiling and surging like a wake behind them, reaching up to touch Sam or pat him on the back.

After the third circuit they put him up on the table. He stood there looking around at the solid mass of humanity, blinking nervously, his shoulders low, saying nothing.

"God *damn*, Vaughn! I can't *hear* you!"

Vaughn scraped away at the fiddle, he raked the bow doggedly across the strings and they suffered from it, squeaking and wailing through the cabin with the nerve-shattering sound of breaking glass.

There was a sharp and agonizing emptiness in us all, a hunger, a thirst, a loneliness we did not know how to appease. We tried to fill it with the noise and the music and the whisky and the shouting. But there is no filling the hot and anguished void that opens in a man's belly when the work is through. She had come to life and we were dying of Her beauty. We had burned for Her and we burned still and we would always burn, but the work was through, the work was gone. She betrayed us like a woman and left us burning wildly in the night. She became the living goddess and we died, becoming men again. The terrible emptiness of being merely human spun in our bellies like a firewheel.

Only Sam did not seem tormented. He stood still and let the boiling ocean surge around him, seeming elsewhere. In time they let him down, forced a bottle in his hand, and he slipped off like a shrew, darting for the safety and obscurity of a corner.

Somebody had the wonderful idea of having a traveling orchestra so *everybody* could hear. Two guys got behind Vaughn's chair and pushed him around the room, the chair legs screeching terribly on the plank floor. This was a lot of work, shoving him through the crowd, and they soon had to have a relief crew. Vaughn paid little attention, he didn't care if he traveled or not. He fiddled beatifically, smiling and scraping, smiling and scraping. They finally shoved him back into another corner and everybody clapped like the devil and Vaughn stood up and bowed deep, but he never stopped fiddling. He had found a way to fill his own emptiness and nobody was going to stop him.

Eb Thomas had been glum through the first part, thinking about the cow, I suppose. I remember seeing him sitting by the fireplace with men shoving back and forth in front of him in a blur. When I could catch a glimpse of Eb himself, he was staring down at the floor, sucking absently on a bottle when it came around to him.

Suddenly, without any warning, he leaped up like a madman and howled at the ceiling. Then he began to dance. It wasn't too much of a dance, and after a while he got tired of making up new figures. So he stood in one place and stomped with his boots, jumping and thundering and trying his damnedest to break through the floor.

He climbed up on the table and began to jump with both feet at the same time, turning in circles and bellowing incomprehensibly. The noise was tremendous, like being inside a bass drum with a maniac pounding it. Or two maniacs. Then he stomped with alternate feet, lifting his knees high in the air and bringing the massive boots down with the force to crush rock. From time to time he threw his head back and gave a high, wild wail like a wolf, screaming out his loneliness to the ceiling. Then he got down on his knees and pounded on the table with his fists. The veins stood out on his forehead and his face was running with sweat. Somebody reached up and grabbed him by the shirtsleeve. He yanked away and the sleeve tore off at the shoulder.

"HOORAW FOR EB!"

A bunch began to drum with their feet on the floor just to keep him going, see how long he would last.

Vaughn's fiddle got faster and faster. His face too was swollen and drenched with sweat. In the corner he played and played and his eyes bugged out and his hair fell down over his face.

"Come on, Vaughn! Let's *play* that thing!"

Vaughn's face was maniacal, obsessed, and the fiddle screeched like a dying bird. Thomas' feet pounded and roared on the table, shaking the whole cabin with thunder. I thought my ears would never hear anything but that steady roar of boots and the shrill crying of the fiddle.

Peter Morgan jumped up on the bench and reached for Eb. "Get down out a there, Eb," he said fuzzily.

Eb swung around at that moment, just as Peter reached for him, his arms whirling wildly. He caught Peter across the chest, knocking him clean back off the table. There were so many men around there was no question of him hitting the floor; he just knocked down a pile.

"EB'S THE CHAMPION! EB'S THE CHAMPION!"

"HOORAW! LET'S KNOCK DOWN EB!"

Two or three grabbed for him at the same time, but it was like reaching for a rock in an avalanche, they couldn't get hold of him. They got his shirt, though, and it came tearing off in shreds. He was left with just the collar, attached around his neck like a necklace. Long threads and one tiny strip of cloth hung down, glued to his back with sweat.

He pounded his feet and whirled around with his fists out like hammers. "HOORAW FOR EB THOMAS!" he shouted. "HOORAW FOR ME!"

Peter Morgan struggled to his feet, stepping on the men he had knocked down. "Hooraw for me, too," he said, insulted.

Then everybody started hollering hooraw for themselves. We were so damned gigantic nothing would do but we let our names be known. We would bring down the sky, just by telling it who we were. We were Her men.

Then, almost suddenly, it was dark, without anybody having seen the night sneaking up on us.

"God damn, I've gone blind from this rotten whisky!" somebody complained.

"Listen, you guys," Vaughn said. But the roaring continued.

"LISTEN! I'll get some lamps, but you got to promise not to bust them up or anything."

Peter Morgan lurched through the pack and put his arm affectionately around Vaughn's shoulder. "Vaughn, hell," he said, with tears in his eyes. "We wouldn't bust your lamps, Vaughn. Would we bust your goddam lamps?" Peter was really hurt by Vaughn's lack of confidence.

"You got—LISTEN, YOU GOT TO PROMISE!"

"Hell," Peter said. "You're my pal, Vaughn. We built her, din' we? I'll promise anything. You jus' tell me what to promise and I'll promise her all right."

"You got to promise not to bust my lamps."

"I promise," Peter said. He smiled winningly at Vaughn and passed out, sliding down to the floor along Vaughn's body like a tree scraping another. Somebody grabbed his legs and dragged him quickly under the table where he wouldn't be trampled to death.

"LOCOMOTIVE LOCOMOTIVE!" Eb Thomas hollered.

I looked around, but I didn't see any locomotive. "What does that *mean*, locomotive?" Vaughn said.

"Mean? Mean?" Thomas said, bewildered that anybody should ask him. "*I'm* a locomotive," he decided finally. "Get the hell out o' my way! HOOOO-OO-OO-OO!" He began to charge around the room with his head down, butting anybody that got in his way and hooting. It was very realistic, all that butting and hooting.

"You think he's a locomotive?" somebody asked me seriously.

"I don't know," I said.

"Well, *I* don't," the other confided. "I think he's a buffalo. What do you think?"

Vaughn went and got a couple of camphine lamps and stood looking for some safe place to put them. The tide surged relentlessly around him as he studied strategic locations. It was hopeless. He finally stuck one of them above the fireplace and another on the window ledge, then went around making everybody promise individually not to break them. The one on the fireplace fell off by itself, I guess, or maybe from vibration.

It was a very funny moment when that lamp fell off and the blue and yellow flames from the spilled camphine twisted around like snakes on the floor. Somebody poured the rest of the alcohol on it to put it out. The flames got paler, but I think they lasted longer. We finally threw a blanket over it and everybody took turns stomping it to death under the blanket. Vaughn swept the broken glass into the fireplace.

While this was going on I saw William Hendrickson across the room, who'd been on the whipsaw from beginning to end. His eyes were wide and excited and he was waving at me with both arms, flailing desperately in the air to get my attention. He couldn't stand up.

I shoved my way over to him, and it was like plunging into the breakers. The turmoil kept shoving me off balance, but there was no room to fall down. I careened from one bunch to another, hearing scattered snatches of conversation.

"I'm going to throw somebody in the water," came an enthusiastic voice.

"Who?"

"I don't know, but I'm going to do it. I just thought about it." He looked around gleefully, picking his victim.

By this time the fire was out and Eb Thomas fell down. He wasn't unconscious, he just fell down.

"EB'S PASSED OUT! OL' EB!"

"No I ain't," Eb said. His voice was barely audible, raucous and hoarse from all the hollering he'd been doing. He had a little trouble getting up.

"Yes, you are passed out. PUT EB UNDER THE TABLE!"

So they put him under the table with Peter Morgan and wouldn't let him out. The whole bunch gathered around the table and wouldn't let him out. Eb started pounding around on all fours like a wild animal in a cage, snarling and snapping at the forest of legs that barred his passage.

"Don't let him bite you," somebody hollered. "That's a mad dog under there!" It was a mistake, because it gave Eb the idea.

He did bite somebody in the calf and almost lost his teeth when the other kicked at him instinctively. The bitten howled with rage and tried to get at him under the table. Eb hunched himself up small and laughed and laughed. He was sitting on Peter Morgan, but Peter didn't mind.

I finally made it across the room to Hendrickson. His face was agonized and he grabbed my trouser leg, looking up at me, panicky. "Ben," he said desperately. "Ben, listen."

"All right, all right. What's the matter?"

"Ben, we did it, didn't we? We built her? We did it?"

"Sure, Bill, sure we did. We all did it."

He let go my trouser leg and stared up at me with that wild, panicky look for another second. Then he put his head back against the wall, turning sideways. "We did it," he mumbled "God, we did it." He began to vomit, falling over on his side on the floor.

The guy Eb had bitten was still furiously trying to get at him under the table. The heavy legs scraped across the floor as he shoved at it, and finally the whole massive thing fell over with an enormous crash that shook the cabin. It was so funny to see Eb, sitting hunched up on top of Peter Morgan that the attacker forgot what he was doing and doubled over with laughter. Eb grinned at him.

After getting the fire out Vaughn had gone back to his corner with his fiddle and was still scraping away. He looked dead, but he didn't look so crazy any more. He had a sort of peaceful smile on his face. The music wasn't so loud now because he had broken a string. He pushed and pulled at the bow, listening to it carefully, smiling and content in some other world I couldn't reach. As I moved away from Hendrickson a gleeful face pushed itself up to me and the same guy let me in on his secret. "Ben, I'm going to throw somebody in the water. By *god*, I am."

"Good for you," I said. "Not me."

"Oh," he said disappointed. "Oh." He turned away from me and looked at everybody, and gradually the inhuman joy of his idea transformed his face into radiance again as he contemplated a whole room packed solid to the rafters with victims.

I had gradually been buffeted around after leaving Hendrickson; every time I stopped, to look at Vaughn or talk to the drowner, I got shoved a few steps by the bodies that seemed to be hurtling faster and faster. I felt something pluck at my shirtsleeve and turned around.

It was Sam, still in the same corner to which he had sneaked in the beginning. I grinned at him. "Well, Sam. Real celebration, ain't it?"

He smiled at me, very friendly, and looked square in my eyes. "Where is she, Ben?" he said, in a low and normal voice.

It chilled me, the way he was so calm and smiling.

"She's right down to the ways," I said. "We'll get her launched—"

He took hold of my shirt front. The smile was still on his face, but had disappeared from his eyes. They began to swim with the same wildness that had so frightened me before.

"Where is she, Ben? Where is she?"

"Sam, don't—" I tried to make him loosen his grip.

"Where is she, Ben?" He smiled.

"She's gone," I said. "She's gone."

He let go my shirt then. His face was pale and lifeless. Suddenly he dropped to his knees in the corner and began to weep. His shoulders shook and throbbed, but I could hear no sound.

The remaining camphine lamp flickered as the door blew open. I stumbled away from Sam, desperately glad of the excuse. I bounced back and forth through the crowd, making for the door, muttering "I'll get it, I'll get it."

I got to the doorway and reached out into the darkness for the edge, when I saw that it had not blown open at all. A figure stood there, waiting quietly, almost invisible in the drizzling rain that had started again. It was Indian Jim.

"*Jim!* By god, come on in."

"*Mika chako,*" Jim said. I could barely hear him for the roaring and shaking inside the cabin. They were dragging the overturned table all around the room, sweeping Eb and Peter Morgan with it.

"I can't come now, Jim," I said reasonably. "There's a kind of a party, *hyas sundy*, big party—"

"*Kilchis memaloose,*" Jim said.

I was suddenly sober. The noise behind me faded to a rumble like the steady sound of the breakers and my ears were ringing. I remember sticking my hand out to support myself on the door frame and feeling the cool wetness of it. I felt dizzy, and didn't know if it was the alcohol or not.

"*Kilchis memaloose,*" Jim said again. "You come." He turned and disappeared into the gray and black of the dripping night. I closed the door from the outside and followed him into the darkness. The rain was chill after the overheated room. I couldn't know exactly what Jim meant; the Jargon has no tenses. But *memaloose* is death. Past, present, or future; time is a detail.

3

It sometimes happens that a dream becomes nightmare, almost without transition. The scene does not change, but it is suddenly invested with a new and terrible significance. It was like that when I stooped through the skin flap and entered Kilchis' lodge.

There was the same rhythmic thump, thump, thump of Thomas' boots—but it was not a dancing man. The same rasping shriek of Vaughn's untuned fiddle—but it was the scream of a woman. The same half-lit faces, twisted with tension and agony and wildness in the flickering light of the fire, the same bodies moving with a terrible, ungrasped significance.

All along the length of the lodge stretched a line of seated, naked men, their faces and bodies painted in patterns I had never seen, great black slashes of soot across the brown skin. Before each of them was a long pole, attached to the ridge beam by a leather loop. Steadily and relentlessly the poles rose and fell, thumping on blocks of wood set in the sand floor. Facing them was another line of Indians, neither naked nor painted; just the people who had come to sing their *tyee* into death. They were mostly old, but there were half a dozen of the young men. From time to time one of the old people would stand and make a song in the space between the two lines, or a dance. When I came in an emaciated old man was dancing a figure that looked like the movements of the beach birds, sharp, nervous, jerky.

The poles of the professional death-singers rang like heartbeats through the lodge. Sometimes a woman's voice would be raised in the death song, sometimes simply in a wailing cry that rustled in my brain like a shifting fire.

I walked the length of the lodge behind the poles. No one paid any attention to me. On the sleeping platform at the far end was the huge form of the *tyee*, wrapped in blankets and robes until only his head was showing. He was on his back, looking at the ridgepole above him through half-lidded eyes. He was so motionless I did not know if he were still alive or not. Indian Jim motioned me to stand by him. I waited there while the pulsing roar of the poles caught my heart up and forced it into the same anguished, throbbing rhythm.

In a moment the great black face turned slightly toward me. The firelight molded it in red and black planes, like the glow of dying coals, and his features seemed to shift as the light of coals shifts in a soft breeze. He looked the same, the great, rough-hewn visage seeming to be a single massive carving, hard and immobile, not composed of parts but a simple whole.

Finally his lips moved slowly, and I bent over to him. I was abruptly struck by a nauseous odor, like rotten meat, and involuntarily flinched away from it.

"Kilchis—" I said.

"You must stay," he said painfully. "There is no one else."

"Kilchis, what is it? I heard you were hurt, but—I thought—"

"It was—nothing," he said. "The ball—it was nothing. It hurt my side. But the *puli*, the rottenness. All hurts are the same size when the *puli* is in them."

He closed his eyes for a moment, and his face turned back up toward the roof. When he spoke again his voice was low and even. The poles thundered behind me and a woman's shriek made me shiver. Kilchis did not hear them.

"Vaughn sees only what is in his mind," Kilchis said. "Tenas Sam is *sullics*. You must keep peace with my people. There is no one among the Boston to keep the peace when I am gone."

He breathed slowly and long. There was a long pause between phrases, while he gained enough strength for the next.

"The other Boston *tyee*, he with the beard that came before to the Bay. He understood. We could keep the peace between us, it was agreed. But he did not come back. Why did he not come back when he said he was coming? I do not know. Others came, but there was no agreement and now some of my people have died. I should not have let them stay." He closed his eyes again.

Indian Jim was standing beside me, and I turned to him. "How'd he get hurt, who was it?"

"A band of the Yaquina young men from the south."

"Why did he have to go out there? The guards were enough, he didn't have to go out there." I suppose I was talking more to myself than to Jim.

"He is the *tyee*," Jim said simply.

Kilchis spoke again. "If the other Boston *tyee* does not come back, you must keep peace among the Bostons. You understand what I say?"

"Yes, Kilchis. I'll try. I'm not—I'm not a *tyee*, Kilchis."

"No," Kilchis said softly. "No, you are a small man. But there is no one else. My people suffer now. I must trust a man who is not strong to keep the peace. That is bad, it is hard for a man who is not strong."

He turned again and looked at me for a long time; then turned back and spoke to the ridge above. "I do not understand the Boston. You live on the same land with my people. The same Bay, the same trees, the same rivers. But your world is not the world of our people. In your minds you are different from us. You live with a world you make in your minds, and not the world that is real. I do not understand this. I see it, but I do not understand how it can be. It is a terrible world you live in, there in your minds. It is dangerous for my people. They must be protected."

"I'll do everything I can, Kilchis," I said. "You're going to get well—"

"All that is over now," he said, almost impatiently. "I die now, like all before me and all after me. Can you not see even death clearly? The people must be protected. I want peace."

"Kilchis—"

He turned his head toward me again, fixing me with his eyes. "This is what I have to tell you. I want peace in my Bay." Then he turned his face to the wall.

Indian Jim took me by the shoulders. "You go now," he said.

"No, wait—" There were ten thousand things I wanted to say, questions to ask. Jim forced me around, away from the still form of the *tyee.*

"He isn't—"

"It comes now. He is finished with you."

Blindly I let him pull me past the line of poles. My heart followed their pulse, my throat was caught up and tight with the keening note of the death-singing women. I pushed through the skin flap and was suddenly outside again.

"Jim, listen to me. I want—I want to do something—"

"You have done something," Jim said. "Estacuga, Cockshaten, Kilchis. The Boston have done something in this Bay, yes." He spoke without anger, without blame. It was simply a fact. He blamed us no more than he would blame a falling tree in the forest. He accepted the world as it was.

"You go now," he repeated. He turned back inside, letting the flap fall behind him.

I stood for a moment outside, listening with half my mind to the muted thumping of the poles and the voices of anguish, cut off from me by the plank walls. The air was cold, the first sharp cold of fall. The rain drifted down and wet my face and collected in droplets in my hair that streamed down my temples and neck. The wind blew chillingly, lightly, brushing the treetops one against the other. I was alone.

I found myself down by the beach, without remembrance of going there. My shirt was soaked and cold rivulets of rain ran down my back and collected around my belt. I turned my collar up, and it did no good. The mist was thick, I could see only a few yards into the swirling grayness. By the time I reached Her I had almost lost the sensation of a real world.

There was only the faint light from the moon, hidden deep in some vast reach beyond the overcast. A luminous stain above me from which the light seemed to seep, as the water seeped from the sky. The masts were black against the gray of the mist, and disappeared in swirling clouds. I could not see their tops. The hull itself swelled out toward me, silent and massive in the night. It stretched in a swooping curve to either side of me and was lost in the shifting rain as though She swam deep in some murky sea.

I put my hand on the hull, feeling the smoothness of the plank and the roughness of the tarred seam. I walked around toward the bow, running my hand along the planking. When I reached the other side I could faintly see the light of the camphine lamp in Vaughn's window, glowing helplessly in the endless infinity of mist.

Even that tiny light made a reflected gleam on the hull, almost as faint as the reflection of a star. I touched the glow with my fingertips and it vanished. Droplets ran down from my touch, trailing streaks through the velvety covering of mist. I rested the side of my face against the hull and closed my eyes. The cold wetness was real. She was real.

I do not know how long I was there. The rain misted down and drowned the land. It soaked the Ship and ran in icy rivulets from her spars and rails and planks, washing her beauty, immersing her in the clean and neutral waters of this world. The mist dissolved the substance of reality and merged all things, what had existed, what would exist. And what, in the end, could a man point to as reality?

Estacuga, Cockshaten, Kilchis. Or the passion of the goddess, the beauty like fire, the blinding hot image of love. I did not know which was real, for they were not of the same world. But I had known the love of goddesses and there was nothing of it I would change. Nothing.

She took her place in the world, She was a part of it now. She lived and was bathed in the rain and the moon and the Bay and the clouds and streams. She needed me no longer; new lovers touched her body with their hands of mist.

The brief spark flickered up the slope ahead, almost drowned in fog. A world of sorts was there, where Thomas thundered with his boots a song he could not sing, where Sam sat weeping in a shadowed corner for a love he'd never known. Gray enough, sad enough. But I had nowhere else to go.

I started up the rise, back into the realms of faint reality. Semblance of life; a world I did not want. The night was dark and silent and the cold rain chilled my skin.